AMERICAN MAGNIFICAT

To Dan Groody, CSC

4/16/2010

Colleague & Friend, with all

best wishes?

American Magnificat

Protestants on Mary of Guadalupe

Edited by Maxwell E. Johnson

Foreword by Timothy Matovina

Concluding Reflection by Virgil Elizondo

LITURGICAL PRESS
Collegeville, Minnesota

www.litpress.org

Cover design by Ann Blattner. Illustration: *Under the Rainbow: The Virgin of Guadalupe embraces Martin Luther and Frederick Douglass*. Mural painted by Flavio Pellegrino at Trinity Lutheran Church of Manhattan / La Iglesia Luterana Trinidad. Used by generous permission of Trinity Lutheran Church of Manhattan, the Rev. Heidi Neumark, pastor.

Excerpts from documents of the Second Vatican Council are from *Vatican Council II: Volume 1, The Conciliar and Post Conciliar Documents*, by Austin Flannery, OP © 1996 (Costello Publishing Company, Inc.). Used with permission.

Scripture texts in this work are taken from the *New Revised Standard Version Bible* © 1989, Division of Christian Education of the National Council of the Churches of Christ in the United States of America. Used by permission. All rights reserved.

1   2   3   4   5   6   7   8

Library of Congress Cataloging-in-Publication Data

American Magnificat : Protestants on Mary of Guadalupe / edited by Maxwell E. Johnson ; foreword by Timothy Matovina ; concluding reflection by Virgil Elizondo.
    p.   cm.
  ISBN 978-0-8146-3259-8
  1. Guadalupe, Our Lady of. 2. Protestant churches—Doctrines.
I. Johnson, Maxwell E., 1952–

BT660.G82A48 2010
232.91'7097253—dc22   2009035531

Contents

Foreword

Devotion to Our Lady of Guadalupe has evolved for nearly five centuries into a deeply rooted, multifaceted tradition. The Guadalupe basilica in Mexico City is the most visited pilgrimage site on the American continent. After Jesus of Nazareth, her image is the most reproduced sacred icon in the Western Hemisphere. Theological analyses of Guadalupe have shaped and been shaped by every epoch of Mexican history since the seventeenth century. She continues to appear in the lives of her faithful in Mexico and beyond: on home altars, T-shirts, tattoos, murals, parish churches, medals, refrigerator magnets, wall hangings, and in countless conversations and daily prayers.

Long acclaimed as the national symbol of Mexico, at the unanimous request of the Roman Catholic bishops of the hemisphere, in the 1999 apostolic exhortation *Ecclesia in America* Pope John Paul II acclaimed her the "mother and evangelizer of America," from Tierra del Fuego to the northernmost reaches of Canada, and decreed that her feast "be celebrated throughout the continent" (11). Today Guadalupe appears among an increasingly diverse array of peoples, places, and religious groups in North America and beyond. Shrines dedicated to her exist as far north as Johnstown, Cape Breton, Nova Scotia. Bishop Fred Henry of Calgary, Alberta, has advocated making Guadalupe's feast a holy day of obligation—a day of required attendance at Mass— for all Canadian Catholics. Her numerous devotees encompass a Mexican artist who is a self-proclaimed "Guadalupan Jew." Her image adorns a Sikh temple near Española, New Mexico, as well as the shrine room at the Kagyu Shenpen Kunchab, a Tibetan Buddhist center in Santa Fe.

American Magnificat: Protestants on Mary of Guadalupe accentuates yet another element of the expanding Guadalupe phenomenon: the growing Protestant engagement of Guadalupe. A number of Protestant congregations now celebrate the December 12 Guadalupe feast. In his groundbreaking work *The Virgin of Guadalupe: Theological Reflections of an Anglo-Lutheran Liturgist* (2002), the editor of this current volume, Maxwell E. Johnson, acclaims Guadalupe as a source of "hope and strength to a people wandering in despair." He also notes that "Guadalupe permeates Hispanic-Latino culture in the Americas" and thus "not to pay wider and close theological attention to the image, narrative, and cult of the Virgin of Guadalupe would be a serious error" for those who minister among Latino peoples. Johnson's enlistment of the collaboration of Episcopalian, Lutheran, Methodist, and Presbyterian authors in this volume further enhances his leading contribution to the Protestant engagement of Guadalupe. Collectively the essays in this volume illuminate new vistas in theologies of Guadalupe through their emphasis on the interrelations between developments in the scriptural and theological understanding of Mary with Protestant reception and thought about Guadalupe.

An ecumenically diverse range of views on Mary of Guadalupe should come as no surprise. The canonical gospels themselves present various early Christian memories and portraits of the mother of Jesus, each evangelist emphasizing different aspects of Mary's life and faith. In what could be construed as a more Protestant understanding of Mary, Mark presents her as a concerned mother whose life hinges more on her faith than on her motherhood. From the perspective of many Marian devotees, Mark 3:20-35 is the most shocking text on Mary in the New Testament. Jesus' family arrives in Capernaum "to take charge of him, saying, 'He is out of his mind'" (NJB). Mark implies that Mary was one of these family members, stating further on in the passage that "his mother and his brothers arrived, and as they stood outside they sent word to him to come out." Jesus does not go out to greet them, but instead replies: "Who are my mother and my brothers?" Then he sets his gaze on the disciples seated around him and declares, "These are my mother and my brothers. Whoever does the will of God is brother and sister and mother to me." This statement does not exclude Mary from being part of Jesus' "true" family, but it does relate that, even for Jesus' own mother, faith and the following of God's will were what mattered. St. Augustine summarized this meaning of the text succinctly: "It means more for her, an altogether greater blessing, to have been Christ's disciple than to have been Christ's mother."

Luke/Acts has the most extensive treatment of Mary and thus it is not surprising that Roman Catholics tend to gravitate more toward Luke's rendering of Mary, not just as a woman called to discipleship, but as a model disciple to be emulated. The infancy narrative passages in Luke 1–2 are some of the most commonly known biblical texts in which Mary is a central figure as they encompass the joyful mysteries of the rosary: the annunciation, the visitation with the *Magnificat*, the birth of Jesus with the visit of the shepherds, the presentation, and the finding in the temple. From the outset Luke reveals that Mary is both family member *and* believer. He presents Mary as one blessed not just because she is called to be Jesus' mother but even more because of the faith with which she courageously accepts God's will and calling in her life. Luke highlights Mary's example of faith throughout his infancy narrative, in four passages about Jesus' public ministry in which she is mentioned, and as one of those who gathered in faith and prayer on the day of Pentecost.

Theologies of Our Lady of Guadalupe continue in the same vein as the gospel writers. Guadalupe is arguably the most ecumenical Marian apparition tradition in the history of Christianity in that Guadalupan theological writings tend to focus on issues and concerns that resonate across denominations. Indeed, from the first published theological work on Guadalupe—Miguel Sánchez's influential 1648 book *Imagen de la Virgen María*—down to the present, those who have explored the theological meaning of Guadalupe have given scant attention to frequently neurologic ecumenical questions about Mary, such as belief in her perpetual virginity, immaculate conception, and assumption. Rather, theologians have examined the Guadalupe image, apparitions account, and its historical context as a means to explore the collision of civilizations between the Old and New Worlds and the ongoing implications of this clash for Christianity in the Americas and beyond. Today Guadalupe is most frequently associated with both the struggle to overcome the negative effects of the conquest of the Americas and the hope for a new future of greater justice, faith, conversion, harmony, and evangelization. Theologies of Guadalupe are thus an ongoing effort to articulate a Christian response to one of the most momentous events of Christianity's second millennium: the conquest, evangelization, and struggles for life, dignity, and self-determination of the peoples of the Americas. On these vital questions there are certainly great possibilities for ecumenical convergence.

Published theological works on Guadalupe have increased remarkably in recent decades. The trend in theological discourse that has most influenced these analyses is the attempt to more systematically articulate the context out of which a particular theology arises, especially the efforts to develop theologies from the perspectives of marginalized peoples. Latina and Latino theologians in the United States, for example, have articulated claims like Guadalupe's significance as the premier evangelizer of Mexicans and Mexican Americans, a source of empowerment for women, a symbol of hope and liberation, a sign of ecclesial unity, an inculturated expression of the Christian tradition, and a paradigm of authentic human freedom and relationships, among various other themes.

I am honored to welcome readers to this volume whose range of contributors further enhances theological analyses of Guadalupe through a Protestant engagement of the Guadalupe tradition. A number of these essays are especially insightful in their integration of Guadalupe with liturgy, devotion, and scriptural and theological themes that are at the core of Christian faith. Several essays examine the *Magnificat* and amplify the chorus of that liberating hymn as a font of new life in the Americas. Together the essays further the evangelical urgency proclaimed in the Guadalupe tradition: building an evangelizing church and a just social order in the Americas. To these and the other inspirations that await you, I welcome you as reader to journey with these authors into the fascinating faith phenomenon of Mary of Guadalupe.

Timothy Matovina
University of Notre Dame

1

Introduction:
Can Protestants Celebrate the Virgin of Guadalupe?*

Maxwell E. Johnson

 The event and image of the Virgin of Guadalupe, *La Virgencita* ("the dear Virgin"), or *La Morena* or *La Morenita* ("the dark one"), are so obviously Roman Catholic and clearly part of the self-understanding of Mexican and Mexican American Roman Catholics. Why, then, would Protestants of any stripe, whether Anglo or Hispanic-Latino, want to celebrate or pay any attention whatsoever to her and her story? That is the question I sought to address in my study, *The Virgin of Guadalupe: Theological Reflections of an Anglo-Lutheran Liturgist*,[1] and this is the question, I am pleased to note, other theologians from differing Protestant traditions join me in pursuing

---

* A major portion of this essay was originally given as a public lecture, "Santa María de Guadalupe y la Teología Luterana," at the Benedictine Abbey of Tepeyac, Cuautitlán, Mexico, October 21, 2005. An abridged version appears as "Why Would Lutherans Celebrate the Virgin of Guadalupe? A Theological Meditation," in Virgilio Elizondo, Allan Figueroa Deck, and Timothy Matovina, eds., *The Treasure of Guadalupe*, Celebrating Faith: Explorations in Latino Spirituality and Theology (Lanham, MD: Rowman & Littlefield, 2006), 87–94.

[1] Maxwell E. Johnson, *The Virgin of Guadalupe: Theological Reflections of an Anglo-Lutheran Liturgist*, Celebrating Faith: Explorations in Latino Spirituality and Theology (Lanham, MD: Rowman & Littlefield, 2002).

in this volume. For, as United States Roman Catholicism and Protestantism alike become intentionally more multicultural as we all seek to be open to the experiences and gifts of the other at our doors and at our borders, and as Hispanic-Latino people come in increasing numbers to all of our churches, is it not necessary for us to listen to their stories and to embrace their images and symbols? And, clearly, one of those central stories, images, and symbols is the Virgin of Guadalupe.

It is often said, with some exaggeration, of course, that "not all Mexicans are Roman Catholics but all are Guadalupanos." Hence, as our Christian identities become increasingly "Latinized" in this country, the story and image of Guadalupe might well seek and find a place among us as "Protestant Christians," even among us Anglos, as some of the essays in this collection certainly suggest. Note, please, I did not say that we Protestants should "use" the Virgin of Guadalupe in order to attract Roman Catholic Hispanic-Latinos to our churches or to try to make "converts" out of Hispanic-Latino Catholics, something that has certainly been alleged by Roman Catholics from time to time.[2] Such deceptive use of the cherished religious symbols of others has no place among us! But Mary of Guadalupe may well find her own home among us as she comes along with others into our midst and into our congregations. In fact, there are signs throughout our country that she is already here, with one of the newest Evangelical Lutheran Church in America (ELCA) parishes in Irving, Texas, bearing the name of La Iglesia Luterana Santa María de Guadalupe; with the last official act of Archbishop George Carey, former Archbishop of Canterbury, being the consecration of Our Lady of Guadalupe Episcopal Church in Waukegan, Illinois; and with several parishes of diverse denominations now finding room for her image and celebrating her December 12 feast. Indeed, the Virgin of Guadalupe is appearing everywhere, it seems, as tattoos, jewelry, fine art, folk art, home altars, yard shrines, rugs, ornaments and decorations for cars, baseball caps, T-shirts, *paños* (pieces of cloth or handkerchiefs painted by prison inmates), computer mouse pads, murals on the sides of buildings and homes, or *veladoras* (devotional candles) in grocery stores. And now, increasingly, she is to be seen even in Protestant churches and contexts, such as, for example, in Flavio Pellegrino's lovely mural from Trinity Lutheran Church, Manhattan, on the cover of this book, in which she embraces Martin Luther and Frederick Douglass.

---

[2] See the essay by Edgardo A. Colón-Emeric, below, pp. 107ff.

Ever since I spent time in Mexico and first visited her basilica in Mexico City over thirty years ago, images of the Virgin of Guadalupe have been a presence in my life. During Advent in the days prior to December 12, in fact, my family and I often hang a tapestry of her facing out on the inside of our front door which is then illuminated by the lights inside our house. A few years ago on December 12, having ordered a pizza from Bruno's Pizza—*the* place for pizza in South Bend, Indiana—a young man, who was Hispanic-Latino, came to deliver it. Pointing to the tapestry, he said to me, "It is beautiful." And, in response, I said something like, "Oh yes, today is her feast. Happy feast!" And he said, simply, "She's my Mom." Not in a formal sense of "She's my *Mother*," but with the simple and beautiful language of intimacy and relationship, "She's my *Mom*." Now, I don't know if this person was Roman Catholic, had any real religious background whatsoever, or was a member of one of the numerous fundamentalist communities that seem to be attracting large numbers of young Hispanic-Latinos. But I began to ask myself from that moment on, "If this person were to come into a Lutheran congregation, would we tell him that *he* is welcome but his 'Mom' is not, even though his 'Mom' is also the Mother of Jesus, our Brother, in her Mexican appearance?" I think not! I believe, however, that there are other reasons beyond hospitality, openness to the other, and cultural sensitivity that might provide reasons as to why we, as Protestant Christians, as Hispanic-Latino Protestants, and others, might want to celebrate the Virgin Mary of Guadalupe.

Protestants Can Celebrate Mary of Guadalupe because She Proclaims the Gospel

First, I believe that we Protestants can celebrate Mary of Guadalupe because, like Mary herself in her great New Testament hymn of God's praise, the *Magnificat*, she proclaims to us the Gospel, the good news of our salvation in Christ, the good news of God who scatters the proud, exalts the lowly, fills the hungry with good things, and remembers his promises to Abraham and his children forever. The great New Testament scholar, the late Raymond Brown, once wrote regarding Guadalupan devotion:

> [F]or a people downtrodden and oppressed, the devotion made it possible to see the significance that the Christian Gospel was meant to have. In the Indian tradition, when Mary appears in the ancient garb of the mother of the Indian gods, she promises to show forth love and compassion, defense and help to all the inhabitants of the land. Ten

years before, the whole Indian nation, their gods and their tradition had been torn down. She hears their lamentations and remedies their miseries, their pains and their sufferings. In the devotion to the Lady, the Christian Gospel proclaims hope for the oppressed. When one looks at the first chapter of Luke one realizes how authentic a Gospel hope that is. . . . For Mary, the news about Jesus means that God has put down the mighty, and He has exalted the lowly. . . . The Gospel of God's Son means salvation for those who have nothing. That is the way Jesus translates it, and that is the way Mary translates it. . . . Luke presents Mary as a disciple not only because she said, "Be it done unto me according to your word," but because she understood what the word meant in terms of the life of the poor and the slaves of whom she is the representative. I think that is exactly what happened in the case of Our Lady of Guadalupe. She gave the hope of the Gospel to a whole people who had no other reason to see good news in what came from Spain. In their lives the devotion to Our Lady constituted an authentic development of the Gospel of discipleship.[3]

And in her essay below in this volume, the Rev. Bonnie Jensen, former executive director of the Women of the ELCA, has also drawn attention to Mary of Guadalupe in the following manner:

I was struck by how lowly, insignificant people have to beg the church to regard them with the esteem with which God regards them. We are not sure whether Mary appeared in a vision to this poor man. Perhaps we have our Protestant doubts. Yet even if we question the vision, the tragic truth remains: the poor and lowly often have to beg the church to proclaim and live out its message of a merciful, compassionate God![4]

So also United Methodist Church historian Justo L. González narrates the following event from his own experience:

When I was growing up, I was taught to think of such things as the Virgin of Guadalupe as pure superstition. Therefore, I remember how surprised I was at the reaction of a Mexican professor in seminary when one of my classmates made some disparaging remarks about Guadalupe. The professor, who was as Protestant as they come and who often stooped because he was then elderly, drew himself up, looked at my

[3] Raymond E. Brown, "Mary in the New Testament and in Catholic Life," *America* (May 15, 1982): 378–79.

[4] Bonnie Jensen, "We Sing Mary's Song," p. 168 below.

friend in the eye, and said: "Young man, in this class you are free to say anything you please. You may say anything about me. You certainly are welcome to say anything you wish about the pope and the priests. *But don't you touch my little Virgin!*" At that time, I took this to be an atavism of an old man who had been fed superstition in his mother's milk. But now I know better. What he was saying was that . . . there was in there a kernel of truth that was very dear to his heart—and all the dearer, since so much of the religiosity that he knew, both Catholic and Protestant, denied it. For generation upon generation of oppressed Indian people, told by word and deed that they were inferior, the Virgin has·been a reminder that there is vindication for the Juan Diegos. And that is indeed part of the gospel message, even if it has not always been part of our own message.[5]

The problem, as González notes further, is precisely the relationship of religious faith and culture. Does one need to deny one's very culture in becoming or being Protestant, especially when that culture has been shaped to a large extent by Roman Catholicism itself? He writes elsewhere that

there is in much of Latino Protestantism a sense of cultural alienation that is very similar to that produced by the much earlier Spanish colonization of the Americas. Just as Spanish Roman Catholicism told our native ancestors that their religion, and therefore much of their culture, was the work of the devil, so has Anglo Protestantism told us that the Catholic religion of our more immediate ancestors, and therefore much of our culture, must be rejected. . . . In many ways, just as for many natives in the sixteenth century it was necessary to abandon much of their cultural traditions in the process of becoming Catholic, so are many Latinas and Latinos forced away from their cultural roots as they become Protestant. And in both cases, this cultural alienation is depicted as good news![6]

Consequently, he continues: "Caridad, Guadalupe, and novenas are not

[5] Justo L. González, *Mañana: Christian Theology from a Hispanic Perspective* (Nashville, TN: Abingdon, 1990), 61; emphasis added.

[6] Justo L. González, "Reinventing Dogmatics: A Footnote From a Reinvented Protestant," in *From the Heart of Our People: Latino/a Explorations in Catholic Systematic Theology*, ed. Orlando O. Espín and Miguel H. Díaz (Maryknoll, NY: Orbis, 1999), 225. On the "Catholic" roots of Hispanic-Latino culture see also Roberto S. Goizueta, *Caminemos con Jesús: Toward a Hispanic/Latino Theology of Accompaniment* (Maryknoll, NY: Orbis, 1995), 8ff.

part of my more immediate tradition. Yet they are part of my culture. Does that mean that, like my native ancestors five centuries ago when faced by the initial Catholic 'evangelization,' I must renounce my cultural heritage in order to affirm my Christianity? I do not believe so."[7]

We can celebrate the Virgin of Mary of Guadalupe, then, because she proclaims to us the Gospel and because the message of Mary of Guadalupe is the same as that of Mary's own *Magnificat* of praise in the Gospel of Luke. Indeed, in so many ways, the Virgin of Guadalupe is simply the Mary of the Bible!

We Can Celebrate Mary of Guadalupe because She Embodies for Us God's Unmerited Grace

A second reason we might celebrate Mary of Guadalupe as Protestants is that she embodies for us in a special way God's gracious act of salvation, God's own unmerited and free grace. How quickly even Lutherans seem to have forgotten Martin Luther's own high regard, esteem, and praise for the Blessed Virgin Mary in his life and writings, even long after the Reformation had begun. Contemporary Luther scholar Eric Gritsch summarizes Luther's views, noting that for him:

> Mary is the prototype of how God is to be "magnified." He is not to be "magnified" or praised for his distant, unchangeable majesty, but for his unconditional, graceful, and ever-present pursuit of his creatures. Thus Mary magnifies God for what he does rather than magnifying herself for what was done to her. . . . "Being regarded by God" is the truly blessed state of Mary. *She is the embodiment of God's grace*, by which others can see what kind of God the Father of Jesus Christ is. . . . Mary sees wisdom, might, and riches on one side and kindness, justice, and righteousness on the other. The former reflect human works, the latter the works of God. God uses his works to put down the works of [people], who are always tempted to deify themselves. God's works are "mercy" (Luke 1:50), "breaking spiritual pride" (v. 51), "putting down the mighty" (v. 52), "exalting the lowly" (v. 53), "filling the hungry with good things," and "sending the rich away empty" (v. 53). . . . [And] Mary is the "Mother of God" who experienced his unmerited grace. Her personal experience of this grace is an example for all humankind that the mighty God cares

[7] González, "Reinventing Dogmatics," 228.

for the lowly just as he cares for the exalted. . . . Thus she incites the
faithful to trust in God's grace when they call on her.[8]

It is precisely the language of God's free grace that several contemporary Catholic authors use to speak about the Virgin of Guadalupe today.
That is, according to them, the God proclaimed in the Guadalupan story
is none other than "the God-who-is-for-us,"[9] characterized by "a maternal
presence, consoling, nurturing, offering unconditional love, comforting,"
and "brimming over with gentleness, loving kindness, and forgiveness" as
"an unconditional and grace-filled gift to the people."[10] And, if so, then
the story of Mary of Guadalupe is precisely a proclamation of the God
who justifies "by grace alone." And that this gift is received "through faith"
is surely exemplified in the response of Juan Diego, who, like Abraham
and countless prophets in the Hebrew Bible before him, interprets this
encounter as a call to his own prophetic ministry both to his own people
and to the governing (ecclesiastical) authorities to whom he was sent. It
must be recalled here that in distinction from several other visions of Mary
throughout history, especially the more modern ones, Mary of Guadalupe asks for *nothing* to be done other than the building of what she calls
a "temple." And this temple is itself to be nothing other than a place or
"home" where all peoples might encounter divine love, compassion, help,
and protection, and where their laments would be heard and all their
miseries, misfortunes, and sorrows would find remedy and cure. In other
words, this temple, this "Beth-El" (House of God) of the Americas was (and
is) to be a place where the God of unconditional love, mercy, compassion,
grace, and forgiveness is proclaimed and encountered.

Even the implications and call for justice and liberation so often associated in a particular way with the Virgin of Guadalupe are also consistent
with a Protestant understanding of justification by grace through faith.
From within his Reformed theological perspective Daniel L. Migliore

[8] Eric Gritsch, "The Views of Luther and Lutheranism on the Veneration
of Mary," in *The One Mediator, The Saints, and Mary*, ed. H. George Anderson,
J. Francis Stafford, Joseph A. Burgess, Lutherans and Catholics in Dialogue 8 (Minneapolis, MN: Augsburg Fortress, 1992), 236–37; emphasis added.

[9] Orlando Espín, "An Exploration into the Theology of Grace and Sin," in Espín
and Díaz, eds., *From the Heart of Our People*, 139.

[10] Jeannette Rodríguez, "Guadalupe: The Feminine Face of God," in *Goddess
of the Americas, La Diosa de las Américas: Writings on the Virgin of Guadalupe*, ed.
Ana Castillo (New York: Riverhead Books, 1996), 25–31.

writes of the relationship between the sovereignty of grace and the pursuit of justice exemplified in Mary's *Magnificat*, saying:

> Neither the biblical portrayal of Mary's passion for justice expressed in the Magnificat nor the classical Reformed emphasis on the sovereignty of grace lead to passivity or complacency. On the contrary, acknowledgment of salvation by grace alone goes hand in hand with a passionate cry for justice and a transformed world. This passion for justice remains anchored in God; trust is not transferred to revolutionary ideologies. Nevertheless, zeal for God's honor and the manifestation of God's justice in all creation ignites a real rebellion and a spirit of resistance against all forces of injustice and all the powers and principalities that oppose God's redemptive purposes.[11]

If Migliore himself is not concerned specifically with Mary of Guadalupe in this context, the parallels are obvious. As in the *Magnificat*, so in Guadalupe is manifested Mary's own "zeal for God's honor," which, perhaps today more than ever, has led to a "real rebellion and a spirit of resistance" against racial, social, and economic injustice in the world. At times, that rebellion and resistance may indeed be transferred more to revolutionary ideologies than to the biblical *God* of justice and/or righteousness. But the persistent presence of the Guadalupan image often associated with movements of rebellion and resistance nonetheless keeps open the possibility of hearing what Migliore calls "*God's* righteous concern for the poor" and its implications expressed so powerfully in Mary's own *biblical* proclamation, her *Magnificat*. To be justified by grace alone sets one free in the name of God to risk oneself and one's identity in the pursuit of God's own justice and righteousness for the world.

I would like to suggest that we might best appropriate the story and image of the Virgin of Guadalupe under the category of parable, that is, "the Virgin of Guadalupe as parable of justification," or, "Mary of Guadalupe as parable of the reign of God." By the use of the word "parable," I mean to draw attention to how the Guadalupan story actually functions. That is, as modern New Testament scholarship on the parables of Jesus has come to emphasize, parables function as "stories that defy religious conventions, overturn tradi-

---

[11] Daniel L. Migliore, "Mary: A Reformed Theological Perspective," *Theology Today* 56, no. 3 (October 1999): 354.

tion, and subvert the hearer's expectations"[12] about how God is *supposed* to act in the world and, in so doing, "make room" for the inbreaking of God's reign. If contemporary biblical scholarship is correct, the parables of Jesus, as reversals that make room for the advent of the reign of God as surprising gift and invite the action of response to that reign, point unmistakably to Jesus as the Great Parable of God himself. Indeed, it is precisely the Crucified One who functions as the ultimate parable of divine reversal and salvation, especially as this is proclaimed by St. Paul in 1 Corinthians 1:27-31:

> God chose what is foolish in the world to shame the wise; God chose what is weak in the world to shame the strong; God chose what is low and despised in the world, things that are not, to reduce to nothing things that are, so that no one might boast in the presence of God. He is the source of your life in Christ Jesus, who became for us wisdom from God, and righteousness and sanctification and redemption, in order that, as it is written, "Let the one who boasts, boast in the Lord."

The narrative and the widespread presence of the image of Mary of Guadalupe can certainly be interpreted then as functioning parabolically in the same sense as the biblical parables themselves. For the Guadalupan story is precisely a parable of the great "reversals" of God, the subversion of both indigenous and Spanish cultural-religious worldviews and assumptions, standing them on their heads, in order to "make room" for something new. Juan Diego is none other than precisely one of the "low and despised in the world," who, in this encounter, becomes himself the prophet or messenger of the reign of God even to the ecclesiastical authorities, and, as an indigenous *layperson*, subverts even the heavily clerical leadership structure of Spanish colonial church life. It is no wonder that, increasingly, Juan Diego is becoming today the model for the ministry of the laity, the concrete example of the priestly ministry of the baptized—the "priesthood of all believers" in our traditional terminology—especially within Mexican and Mexican American contexts.[13]

Nor is it any wonder why early ecclesiastical responses to the Guadalupe event would have been so strongly negative. Then, as now, Guadalupe challenges the wise, the powerful, the noble, and the strong to a new

[12] Nathan Mitchell, *Real Presence: The Work of Eucharist* (Chicago, IL: Liturgy Training Publications, 1998), 48.

[13] See Roberto Piña, "The Laity in the Hispanic Church," in *The New Catholic World* (New York: Paulist Press, 1980), 168–71.

conversion to the presence of the reign of God as located precisely in the weak, the lowly, the despised, and the rejected. This is nothing other than what Lutherans like to call a *theologia crucis*, a "theology of the cross." For, like the parables of Jesus, the Virgin of Guadalupe, as parable of the reign of God, or parable of justification, is connected to the great biblical stories of reversal, which point, ultimately, to the great reversal of the cross. As such, the narrative and image of Guadalupe belong, most appropriately, in close association with images of the Crucified One himself. For it is only in light of the image of Christ crucified, in the image of the cross, where the meaning of Mary—of Guadalupe—as "the embodiment of God's grace" is best revealed and appropriated.

In this light, perhaps, Protestants can come to appreciate the following insight offered by Virgil Elizondo in his *Guadalupe: Mother of the New Creation*:

> What most people who have not experienced the Guadalupe tradition cannot understand is that to be a Guadalupano/a (one in whose heart Our Lady of Guadalupe reigns) is to be *an evangelical Christian*. It is to say that the Word became flesh in Euro-Native America and began its unifying task—"that all may be one." In Our Lady of Guadalupe, Christ became American. Yet because the gospel through Guadalupe was such a powerful force in the creation and formulation of the national conscious-ness and identity of the people as expressed, understood, and celebrated through their art, music, poetry, religious expression, preaching, political discourse, and cultural-religious expressions, its original meaning—that is, the original gospel of Jesus expressed in and through native Mexican terms—has become eclipsed. This has led some modern-day Christians—especially those whose Christianity is expressed through U.S. cultural terms—to see Guadalupe as pagan or as something opposed to the gospel. It is certainly true that just as the gospel was co-opted and domesticated by Constantine and subsequent "Christian" powers, so has Guadalupe been co-opted and domesticated by the powerful of Mexico, including the church. Yet neither the initial gospel nor the gospel expressed through Guadalupe has lost its original intent or force, a force that is being re-discovered as the poor, the marginalized, and the rejected reclaim these foundational gospels as their chief weapons of liberation and as sources of lifestyles that are different from those engendered by ecclesial and social structures that have marginalized, oppressed, and dehumanized them.[14]

---

[14] Virgilio Elizondo, *Guadalupe: Mother of the New Creation* (Maryknoll, NY: Orbis, 1997), 113–14; emphasis added.

And, as former Lutheran campus pastor Richard Q. Elvee at Gustavus Adolphus College, St. Peter, Minnesota, has written:

> The power of the pregnant Virgin asking Native Americans in a native tongue to become bearers of the Good News of Jesus Christ to the Americas was a powerful experience. Native peoples, who were being exterminated by foreign disease and decimated by oppression and war, became the bearers of the news that Jesus Christ was waiting to be born in the Americas. The oppression of the conquistadors would not destroy the people. God's messenger, the mother of Jesus, came to give hope and strength to a people wandering in despair. These conquered people were to teach their European conquerors the meaning of God's call of faith. These seemingly hopeless people were to become the hope of a hemisphere. With Jesus waiting to be born in the Americas, the Mexican people were to give him a home.[15]

What could be more "evangelical" than that?

Protestants Can Celebrate Mary of Guadalupe because She Is a Type and Model of What the Church Is to Be in the World

It is not only that the Guadalupan story proclaims the unconditionally gracious, loving, merciful, and compassionate God who justifies the Juan Diegos of the world by grace alone through faith. In addition, the very image of Mary of Guadalupe is revelatory of the multiracial, multiethnic, multicultural, *mestiza* (mixed) church that came to be incarnated as the result of the sixteenth-century cultural confrontation between Spain and Mexico and still struggles to be born in our own day. Both the person and the image of Mary of Guadalupe, we might say, function as a *typus ecclesiae*, a "type," or "image," or "model" of the church. As Eric Gritsch has noted with regard to Luther's Marian theology: "to Luther Mary was the prime example of the faithful—a *typus ecclesiae* embodying unmerited grace. Mary is a paradigm for the indefectibility of the church."[16]

The third reason, then, Protestants can celebrate the Virgin of Guadalupe is that she is a type and model of what the church is to be in the

[15] Ibid., 1.
[16] Gritsch, "The Views of Luther," 241.

world. That is, if the narrative of Mary of Guadalupe can be interpreted correctly as being about justification by grace alone through faith, then the image—which depicts the *typus ecclesiae* herself as pregnant with the Incarnate Word—can surely be seen as, like a mirror's reflection, what the church itself, thanks also to God's unmerited grace, is and is called to be as similarly "pregnant" with the same Incarnate Word for the life and salvation of the world. Indeed, for those who might object that it is precisely *Christ* who appears to be absent from this narrative and image of justification, the words of Virgil Elizondo need to be heard: "The innermost core of the apparition . . . is what she carries within her womb: the new source and center of the new humanity that is about to be born. And that source and center is Christ as the light and life of the world."[17] And in this sense, then, Mary of Guadalupe is truly "of the gospel" because the narrative and image of Guadalupe is, ultimately, about *Christ*!

Indeed, the interpretation of the image of the Virgin of Guadalupe as an image and model of the church itself may be one of the most profound Guadalupan gifts that Mexican and Mexican American spirituality can make to the whole church catholic in our day. For the church being called into existence is, more than ever before, one called to be clearly multicultural and *mestiza* in form, and such a church of the future appears to be already present proleptically in Mary of Guadalupe's *mestiza* face. To gaze contemplatively upon her image, then, is to gaze at the future church in the making, and to gaze at what we hope, by God's grace and Spirit, the church of Jesus Christ, racially, culturally, and even ecumenically, will become.

There may be yet, however, another and very simple reason why Protestants might want to celebrate the Virgin of Guadalupe. In one of his Christmas Eve sermons Martin Luther once said:

> This is the great joy, of which the angel speaks, this is the consolation and the superabundant goodness of God, that man (if he has this faith) may boast of such treasure as that Mary is his real mother, Christ his brother, and God his father. . . . See to it that you make [Christ's] birth your own, and that you make an exchange with him, so that you rid yourself of your birth and receive instead, his. This happens if you have this faith. By this token you sit assuredly in the Virgin Mary's lap and are her dear child.[18]

[17] Elizondo, *Guadalupe*, 128–29.
[18] Martin Luther, "The Gospel for Christmas Eve, Luke 2[:1-14]," in *Sermons II*, vol. 52 of *Luther's Works* (Philadelphia, PA: Fortress Press, 1974), 15–16.

Perhaps, then, in the words of both my pizza delivery person and Martin Luther himself, Protestants can celebrate Mary of Guadalupe, porque "Ella es nuestra mamá, ella es nuestra mamita"; because, finally, in faith, she is also *our* Mom!

The essays in this volume, whether directly or indirectly, deal positively with various facets of the Guadalupan phenomenon from diverse Protestant perspectives. In "The Virgin of Guadalupe: History, Myth, and Spirituality,"[19] Alberto Pereyra (Lutheran) argues for a theological approach based on an indigenous or native spirituality encouraging us "to be flexible and walk to the Tepeyac of our own spiritual experience."[20] Cody C. Unterseher (Episcopalian) provides an excellent overview of modern Protestant thinking on Mariology in "Mary in Contemporary Protestant Theological Discourse,"[21] with special attention given to the recent ecumenical dialogue document produced by the Anglican-Roman Catholic International Commission (ARCIC II) in February 2004, *Mary: Grace and Hope in Christ*. Reminding us that "the Cold War between Protestants and Roman Catholics over Mary has ended,"[22] Unterseher underscores that in the context of immigration issues in the United States,

> Christians of all church bodies are rapidly having to find ways of embracing Latino/a cultural expressions. Anglo-European Christian communities in the United States will soon have no choice but to confront (or to be confronted by) the dark-skinned, pregnant Mary dressed in red and veiled in blue-green, who herself was an alien—both in Egypt and in the Americas.[23]

Carl C. Trovall (Lutheran), in "Juan Diego: A Psychohistory of a Regenerative Man," looks not so much at the Virgin of Guadalupe herself but at intriguing parallels between Martin Luther and Juan Diego as historical figures within a sixteenth-century context who in their differing ways facilitated a "reformation" in faith, life, and culture. Using the categories de-

[19] This essay originally appeared in *Currents in Theology and Mission* 24, no. 4 (August 1997): 348–54.

[20] See p. 28 below.

[21] An earlier version of this essay appeared in *Worship* 81, no. 3 (May 2007): 194–211.

[22] Scot McKnight, *The Real Mary: Why Evangelical Christians Can Embrace the Mother of Jesus* (Brewster, MA: Paraclete Press, 2007), 5.

[23] See p. 46 below.

veloped by Erik Erikson in his work on figures such as Gandhi and Luther, Trovall presents Juan Diego as a great *homo religiosus* and "'generative man' for a whole generation of Mexican people as well as their descendants."[24] "Beyond Word and Sacrament: A Reformed Protestant Engagement of Guadalupan Devotion,"[25] by Rubén Rosario Rodríguez (Presbyterian), provides a strong Christocentric interpretation of the Virgin of Guadalupe's narrative and image, a surprising and even radical approach given the historical iconoclasm of classical Calvinism. Ecumenically sensitive, and rooted in a classic Protestant theology of creation, Rodríguez suggests that, "while not every Christian community need embrace the Guadalupan devotion, every Christian community can broaden its understanding of God by listening to what Guadalupe teaches us about creation and liberation."[26]

On December 12, 2004, the *Chicago Tribune* reported a story about a controversy surrounding a small local Hispanic-Latino United Methodist Church, Amor De Dios, where an image of the Virgin of Guadalupe had been enshrined by the pastor and neighborhood processions and rosaries in her honor had been held.[27] Roman Catholics and Methodists alike (especially Methodists who had left that congregation as a result, as well as other Methodist pastors) were both highly critical of this parish and its new practices.[28] How fortunate, then, to have Edgardo A. Colón-Emeric's essay, "Wesleyans and Guadalupans: A Theological Reflection" as part of this volume. Colón-Emeric argues, in particular, that "a serious engagement with the sources of Wesleyan theology prepares the way for a Methodist reception of Guadalupe, a Wesleyan Guadalupanismo."[29]

Along somewhat similar lines, José David Rodríguez (Lutheran), in "The Virgin of Guadalupe from a Latino/a Protestant Perspective: A Dangerous Narrative to Counter Colonial and Imperialistic Power," reminds us that

---

[24] See p. 53 below.

[25] Another version of this essay appears in *Journal of Ecumenical Studies* 42, no. 2 (2007): 173–95.

[26] See pp. 100–101 below.

[27] This is available at http://www.religionnewsblog.com/9726.

[28] I have since learned from a colleague who at the time was teaching at McCormick Theological Seminary in Chicago that the pastor of this parish had been reading my *The Virgin of Guadalupe: Reflections of an Anglo-Lutheran Liturgist*.

[29] See p. 109 below.

the Virgin of Guadalupe confronts us with a powerful and important challenge for the mission and ministry of the church. This story constitutes an important link in a provocative memory of an ancient biblical tradition that even today witnesses to the power of God that emerges from weakness. For Martin Luther and Christian believers of all times, this type of power was made evident in Mary's song of the *Magnificat*. Contemporary theologians find in Mary's witness the continuation of a narrative of faith empowering the liberation struggles of oppressed and excluded sectors of society. For an increasing number of believers who claim our heritage of faith and cultural identity from the sixteenth century in these lands called the Americas, this divine power was also reflected in the story of the Virgin of Guadalupe. This popular expression of Mary's witness dating from the sixteenth century in Mexico constitutes an important symbol of our tradition of faith to resist the forces that throughout time and space, intend to oppress our people and tear down our human dignity.[30]

The next four essays all deal with issues related either to celebrating the feast of the Virgin of Guadalupe or to various devotional elements and practices. My own contribution, "The Development of the Liturgical Feast of the Virgin of Guadalupe and Its Celebration in the Season of Advent,"[31] provides an overview of the historical development of the December 12 feast itself from the sixteenth century to the present. In addition, I argue that for both Protestants and Catholics the feast of the Virgin of Guadalupe can be viewed as a *major* feast of the Advent season uniting both the eschatological and incarnational orientations of that liturgical season.

Formed initially by Methodist, Congregationalist, and Presbyterian Christianity, author and poet Kathleen Norris in "Virgin Mary, Mother of God,"[32] offers a very personal account of how her encounters with Benedictine monasticism on the plains of North Dakota and elsewhere brought her face-to-face with the black Madonnas, especially with Our Lady of Einsiedeln and the Virgin of Guadalupe. With specific regard to the Guadalupe narrative, she writes, "As a Protestant I'll say it all sounds suspiciously

[30] See p. 128 below.

[31] An earlier version of this appeared in Maxwell E. Johnson, *Worship: Rites, Feasts, and Reflections* (Portland, OR: Pastoral Press, 2004), 243–64.

[32] This essay appeared originally in Kathleen Norris, *Amazing Grace* (New York: Riverhead Books, 1998), 13–25.

biblical to me, recalling the scandal of the incarnation itself, the mixing together of human and divine in a young, unmarried woman."[33]

Bonnie Jensen (Lutheran), in what was originally a homily, "We Sing Mary's Song,"[34] given at a Consultation on Justice and Justification held in Mexico City December 7–14, 1985, by the then American Lutheran Church (now part of the ELCA), directs our attention to the fact that

> behind the vision's gilded cactus leaves, miraculous roses, and imprinted cloak is the longing for a God who comes, not in the might of military conquest, nor in the ecclesiastical forms and evangelism plans of a mighty church, but in simple, compassionate respect and regard for the lowly, the hungry, the women, the poor, the children.[35]

Even if many Protestants can come to agree on some kind of overall positive theological approach to the narrative, feast, and image of the Virgin of Guadalupe, can they move another step toward some kind of devotion and prayer? In his *The Thousand Faces of the Blessed Virgin Mary*, George H. Tavard asked appropriately: "is it not possible on the basis of justification by faith and on the strength of Luther's example to count as a permissible *adiaphoron* a contemplative attitude before the mother of Christ, made of gratitude, admiration, and love?"[36] And in my own study of Guadalupe I agreed with Tavard and suggested that within Lutheranism at least something like the "Hail Mary" ending at "Blessed is the fruit of your womb, Jesus," might be highly appropriate. But I stopped short of advocating or defending a more direct invocation of Mary or the saints (i.e., "pray for us"). Robert Jenson (Lutheran), however, has taken that next step in "A Space for God,"[37] wherein he argues strongly, and convincingly, in my opinion, the following:

> Interestingly, Luther and Melanchthon were happy to say that the saints as a company pray for us, that the church in heaven prays for the church on earth. To invoke Mary's prayer as the prayer of the *mater dei*, the

---

[33] See p. 162 below.

[34] This essay appeared originally in *Word and World* 7, no. 1 (1987): 1–3.

[35] See p. 168 below.

[36] George H. Tavard, *A Thousand Faces of the Blessed Virgin Mary* (Collegeville, MN: Liturgical Press, 1996), 117.

[37] This essay originally appeared in Carl Braaten and Robert Jenson, eds., *Mary, Mother of God* (Grand Rapids, MI: Eerdmans, 2004), 49–57.

prayer of the Container of the Uncontainable, is to invoke precisely this prayer. Perhaps, indeed, Mary's prayer, as the prayer of the whole company of heaven, is the one saint's prayer that even those should utter who otherwise accept Melanchthon's argument against invoking saints.[38]

If Jenson is not directly concerned in this essay with the Virgin of Guadalupe per se, the implications of his approach for Guadalupan devotion could not be clearer since it is precisely Marian devotion that is the issue.

The first word and last word in this collection belong to two of my Notre Dame Roman Catholic colleagues, who are themselves both first-rate Guadalupan scholars, Timothy Matovina, who writes the foreword, and Virgil Elizondo, who writes a concluding reflection in response to the other essays included herein. Matovina has written extensively on Guadalupan topics related to faith and culture in the Southwestern United States, especially Texas,[39] as well as with regard to the 1648 Spanish, rather than the Náhuatl, version of the Guadalupe narrative, namely, the *Imagen de la Virgen María, Madre de Dios de Guadalupe*, composed by Miguel Sánchez,[40] a diocesan priest from Mexico City.[41] And, since so many of the authors in this book depend on Elizondo's compelling methodological and hermeneutical approach to the Virgin of Guadalupe, as exemplified in his many books and articles,[42] it is highly fitting that he have the opportunity to respond to this honor and offer his own insights. To both of

[38] See p. 178 below.

[39] Timothy Matovina, *Guadalupe and Her Faithful: Latino Catholics in San Antonio from Colonial Origins to the Present* (Baltimore, MD: Johns Hopkins University Press, 2005). See also his essay, "Theologies of Guadalupe: From the Spanish Colonial Era to John Paul II," *Theological Studies* 70 (March 2009): 61–91.

[40] For the text see Miguel Sánchez, *Imagen de la Virgen María, Madre de Dios de Guadalupe: Milagrosamente aparecida en la Ciudad de México, celebrada en su historia, con la profecía del capítulo doze del Apocalipsis* (Mexico City: Imp. Vidua de Bernardo Calderón, 1648; reprinted by Cuernavaca, Morelos, 1952).

[41] Timothy Matovina, "Guadalupe at Calgary: Patristic Theology in Miguel Sánchez's *Imagen de la Virgen María* (1648)," *Theological Studies* 64 (December 2003): 795–811.

[42] See especially his *Guadalupe: Mother of the New Creation* and *La Morenita: Evangelizer of the Americas* (San Antonio, TX: Mexican American Cultural Center Press, 1980).

these colleagues, and to all of the authors participating in this collection, I am most grateful.

Special thanks also go to my former graduate assistant Annie Vorhes McGowan, a doctoral candidate in liturgical studies at the University of Notre Dame. Her research and editorial assistance have been invaluable to me. Special thanks also go to my current graduate assistant, Nathaniel Marx, a doctoral student in liturgical studies at Notre Dame, for his excellent assistance in proofreading. And my thanks go as well to both Peter Dwyer and Hans Christoffersen for their willingness to take on this project and see it to completion under the imprint of Liturgical Press.

Finally, because the narrative of the apparitions of the Virgin of Guadalupe to Juan Diego may not be familiar to all readers of this collection, I provide by way of an appendix, an English translation of the popular Náhuatl version, the *Nican Mopohua*, traditionally attributed to Antonio Valeriano (1520–1605), but now commonly agreed to have been composed from various sources by Luis Laso de la Vega, the vicar of Guadalupe in 1649.[43] The particular translation used here, by kind permission of Orbis Books, is that of Virgil Elizondo from his study, *Guadalupe: Mother of the New Creation*.[44]

Maxwell E. Johnson
March 25, 2009
The Annunciation of Our Lord

[43] See Lisa Sousa, Stafford Poole, and James Lockhart, eds., *The Story of Guadalupe: Luis Laso de la Vega's Huei tlamahuiçoltica of 1649*, UCLA Latin American Studies, vol. 84 (Stanford, CA: Stanford University Press, 1998).

[44] Elizondo, *Guadalupe*, 5–22.

2

The Virgin of Guadalupe: History, Myth, and Spirituality

Alberto Pereyra

 The Virgin of Guadalupe is the greatest spiritual symbol in Central America, Mexico, and the Southwest of the United States of America. Also she is the most powerful female icon for millions of people who have followed her spiritual influence for centuries. Her place among the many divinities of Mexico and Central America is very well-known for religious leaders of those areas. Many people go to Mexico yearly to pay spiritual tribute, respect, and honor to her.

Her followers did not frequently ask about her historicity or her apparition to the Indian people in Tepeyac.[1] The history of Guadalupe's origin was never a question for those who believed in the real presence of Jesus' Mother in Tepeyac. Questions about her authenticity and her connection with Tonantzin, an Aztec goddess, came from scholars or non-Catholic people.

The sixteenth century was crucial for Spain's conquest and implementation of its policy of domination of the New World. It was a time of resistance by the Indians who did not want to surrender themselves, their

---

[1] [Tepeyac is] a place close to Mexico City, where, traditionally, people believe that Guadalupe appeared to Juan Diego.

culture, religion, and economy to the invaders. It was at this time that one could see mysterious apparitions of virgins in the New World. Those apparitions were symbols of acculturation through which Spain wanted to impose its culture and religion. The Náhuatl spirituality was not excluded from that process, which concerned those in Spain in charge of evangelism and acculturation of the new lands.

The Indian cosmogony was a configuration of the earth, its divinities, the people, and their history. Indians' divinities were dual, female and male. The female aspect of God was never a second category of importance in God's substance. In this duality one can find different names for these female and divine expressions. *Tonan* means the mother of the earth, *Coatlique* means the earthly mother, and *Cihuacoatl* means a woman serpent or mother of wisdom. They understood *Toci* as God's mother and the heart of the earth and *Tonantzin* as our venerated mother. Tonantzin had her sanctuary in Tepeyac.[2]

The Legend

For the first quarter of the sixteenth century, the relationship between the conquerors and Indians was tense. Exploitation and slavery of Indians made communication impossible. For Indians everything from Spain was hostile, even Christianity. Communications between civil authorities and missionaries were very difficult too. At this time legend says that on December 9, 1531, Guadalupe appeared to Juan Diego, a humble Christianized Náhuatl Indian, when he was on his way to Tlatelolco to hear Mass. He heard music and a voice that pronounced his name. Juan Diego walked in the direction of the voice and suddenly saw a beautiful woman, radiant and light, who introduced herself as the Mother of the True God from whom everything lives, the Creator of heaven and earth. She wanted a temple to be built at that site and wanted to live among the Indian people to serve them in their needs and painful lives. The Lady asked Juan Diego to talk with the bishop in his palace. The bishop received Juan Diego but did not believe the story. Juan Diego returned to his people and on the way, the Virgin appeared to him again inquiring about her message. Juan Diego was sad about the answer of the bishop. He asked the Virgin to send a messenger more important than himself, since he was only a poor,

[2] See Virgilio Elizondo, *La Morenita: Evangelizer of the Americas* (San Antonio, TX: Mexican American Cultural Center Press, 1980), 24.

noneducated Indian. The Lady asked Juan Diego to return to the bishop's palace and give him a sign. On December 12, Juan Diego had another encounter with the Lady of Tepeyac who at this time asked Juan Diego to take some beautiful roses from the mountain to the bishop as proof of her petition. Juan Diego took the roses to the bishop. When Juan Diego opened his *tilma* (Indian cloak like a poncho), the roses fell from it. On top of the *tilma* was the figure of Our Lady of Guadalupe. The bishop and his servant saw this and fell on their knees before such a miracle.[3]

The Doubt

Not everybody agrees with this legend. Historians' critical eyes see other dimensions of the narrative. In 1970, Xavier Campos Ponce, a Mexican historian, used the historical-critical method to research the legend of Tepeyac.[4] His conclusions denied the authenticity of the legend because it did not have enough basis in the events of early postconquest Mexico. Many of the apparition materials came from the people's piety and popular religiosity.[5] Campos Ponce also quotes the prestigious Mexican historian

[3] Elizondo, *La Morenita*, 77ff.

[4] Xavier Campos Ponce, *La Virgen de Guadalupe y la Diosa Tonantzin* (Mexico, D.F., 1970).

[5] See also Louise M. Burkhart, "The Cult of the Virgin of Guadalupe in Mexico," in *South and Meso-American Native Spirituality: From the Cult of the Feathered Serpent to the Theology of Liberation*, ed. Gary H. Gossen, vol. 4 (New York: Crossroad, 1993), 188ff. Burkhart also quotes James Lockhart, *The Nahuas after the Conquest: A Social and Cultural History of the Indians of Central Mexico, Sixteenth through Eighteenth Centuries* (Stanford, CA: Stanford University Press, 1992); and William B. Taylor, "The Virgin of Guadalupe in New Spain: An Inquiry into the Social History of Marian Devotion," in *American Ethnologist* 14, no. 1 (1987): 9–33.

Editor's note: To this list of critical studies today must be added the following: Stafford Poole, *Our Lady of Guadalupe: The Origins and Sources of a Mexican National Symbol, 1531–1797* (Tucson: University of Arizona Press, 1995); Richard Nebel, *Santa María Tonantzin, Virgen de Guadalupe: Religiöse Kontinuität und Transformation in Mexiko* (Immensee, Switzerland: Neue Zeitschrift für Missionswissenschaft, 1992), (published in Spanish as *Santa María Tonantzin, Virgen de Guadalupe: Continuidad y transformación religiosa en México* [Mexico City: Fondo de Cultura Económica, 1995]); and D. A. Brading, *Mexican Phoenix: Our Lady of Guadalupe: Image and Tradition across Five Centuries* (Cambridge: Cambridge University Press, 2001).

and bibliographer, Joaquín García Icazbalceta, the first historian to apply a historical-critical approach to the Guadalupan records, who developed similar conclusions about the documents of the legend. Campos Ponce also brings an original contribution about the testimony of the bishop of Tamaulipas, Mexico, Don Eduardo Sánchez Camacho, who in 1910 wrote a document declaring the apparition of Guadalupe in the Tepeyac to be false.[6] The document resulted in Sánchez Camacho's persecution by the Roman Catholic Church in Mexico and President Porfirio Díaz, leading to exile in the United States. Later Sánchez Camacho returned to Mexico and died in isolation at his ranch El Olvido.

The Myth

Carlos Fuentes, Mexican writer, describes the presence of the Lady of Tepeyac as one of the masterpieces of Indian spirituality and syncretism.[7] Fuentes sees the creation of this new myth in the sixteenth century providing a new spiritual dimension for Indians. The question is this: was Tonantzin, the Aztec goddess, erased from the soul of Indians or do they worship still the mother of the gods in Tepeyac? Fuentes praises not the Spaniards in creatively giving new directions for worshiping in the New World but Indians in accepting the new symbol, which embraces their devotion to Tonantzin. A risky answer says that Tonantzin will be forever in Tepeyac under the names of Virgin of Guadalupe, Mother of God, Jesus' Mother, or Mother of the Creator. People can see in Tepeyac the feminist worship of the universal goddess whether she is Tonantzin or Guadalupe. The myth goes beyond the semantic of names. In the New World, Tonantzin was not the first and only goddess who suffered a metamorphosis from goddess to saint. The Indians knew about those transformations as symbols of submission. Guadalupe in Mexico has her spiritual counterparts in La Caridad de Cobre in Cuba, the Virgin of Coromoto in Venezuela, the Virgin of Alta Gracia in the Dominican Republic, and the Virgin del Valle in Argentina. The Indians accepted those symbols to protect their own spirituality. The goddess is still alive!

Aztecs did not have Christ in their theology and never accepted totally the Second Person of the Trinity. In their theology they had the god

---

[6] Campos Ponce, *La Virgen*, 147.

[7] Carlos Fuentes, *The Buried Mirror: Reflections on Spain and the New World* (Boston: Houghton Mifflin Company, 1992), 146.

Quetzalcoatl, the Plumed Serpent who died and promised to return. Aztecs believed that Hernán Cortés was Quetzalcoatl and asked him to wear Quetzalcoatl's mask. The Christ figures in Mexico are all baroque and defeated, dead, prostrate, bleeding, whether they are on the cross or laid out in a glass bier. By contrast, the Virgin of Guadalupe is still the Lady of Tepeyac with roses and perfume. One can walk into a church in Mexico and see this difference, a glorious presence of the Mother rather than a triumphant Christology.[8] People can see two different altars in the same church, one dedicated to a defeated Christ and the other to the glorious transformation of Tonantzin, full of flowers and lights. Fuentes adds that after the transformation of Quetzalcoatl into Christ, it has been impossible to know who is worshiped at the baroque altars of Puebla, Oaxaca, and Tlaxcala.[9] The same applies to Mary and Tonantzin.

Our Lady of Guadalupe's story brings to us the heart of popular religion in the Southwest. Alex García-Rivera analyzes stories, which he divides into the "little story" and the core of the story, the semiotic or interpretation of the symbols of the story.[10] García-Rivera uses Virgil Elizondo's method of analysis to reflect on the semiotic of the Virgin of Guadalupe's story.[11] Elizondo points out the message of the symbols of the "little story." He states that at the time of the apparition, the Spanish were building churches over the ruins of the Aztec temples. The tearing down and the building up was symbolic of the deeper struggle to destroy a people, even if the intention was to rebuild it. Juan Diego dared to go

---

[8] *Editor's note*: For a view opposing this common approach to Hispanic-Latino Christology see Justo L. González, *Mañana: Christian Theology from a Hispanic Perspective* (Nashville, TN: Abingdon, 1990), 148–49, who argues that, far from being a denial of a triumphant Christ, the "baroque and defeated, dead, prostrate, bleeding" images of Christ are actually to be seen from within a context of human suffering *and* a very high Chalcedonian Christology. That is, these images are of the *God*, who suffers for and with his people, just as they are images of the truly *human* Christ who is able to suffer. See also my study, *The Virgin of Guadalupe: Theological Reflections of an Anglo-Lutheran Liturgist*, Celebrating Faith: Explorations in Latino Spirituality and Theology (Lanham, MD: Rowman & Littlefield, 2002), 145ff.

[9] Fuentes, *The Buried Mirror*, 146.

[10] Alex García-Rivera, *St. Martín de Porres: The "Little Stories" and the Semiotics of Culture* (Maryknoll, NY: Orbis, 1995), 29.

[11] Virgilio Elizondo, "Our Lady of Guadalupe as a Cultural Symbol," in *Liturgy and Cultural Traditions*, ed. Herman Schmidt and David Power (New York: Seabury Press, 1977), 130–31. Quoted in ibid.

to the city of power. He demanded that the powerful change their plans and build a temple, not according to the plans of Spain, but within the *barriada* of Tepeyac, in the native land.[12] The center of Guadalupe's attention was not the splendor of the Spanish plans but the poverty and misery of those who lived on the periphery of society.[13]

The methodological reading of the semiotic leads us to penetrate the "mystery" of the "little stories" to the core of the story. Many times people were put down because of their illiteracy. Even today the message of our Western culture is codified in volumes that few people can read. Many times people cannot read insurance papers or contracts, medical terminology in hospitals, specialized magazines, and so on. Similarly, we can read the "little story" but not the core. Missionaries to other lands treated people as pagan because they could not read the symbols of their spirituality. Many people died in the sixteenth century or in times of the conquista because they did not know the semiotic of those who worshiped God under different symbols. The conquerors read only one side of the story, the myth without the semiotic, and they blamed and killed the victim of the imposing dominant culture. The key or truth of the semiotic was at the side of Juan Diego, and the bishop, as a dominant authority, could not understand it.

The Myth as Spirituality

The rereading of the event of Tepeyac opened a new dimension for Latino spirituality in the New World. The vision in Tepeyac has a parallel with Exodus and the call of Moses. It is a messianic mission for a people who were enslaved and exploited under the power of a modern pharaoh. The issue was not the temple but the freedom of the people who inherited the land from their ancestors and then had to work in that land as slaves under their invaders. December 12 and the Tepeyac became a historic sign of liberation. The time and the geographic place played an important role for the memory of a people who had no memories. Tepeyac was the central point for the New World, equidistant from the North and the South extremities. There was no United States or Argentina at that time. The mountain of the revelation became the center of the message of liberation for a continent in submission to the invaders. North and

[12] Ibid.
[13] Ibid.

South had a new promise, not a "promised land" but the recovery of their dignity as human beings and children of God. More and more studies on the semiotics of the culture related to the Lady of Guadalupe bring more light to the symbols of Juan Diego's vision. Juan Diego heard a peaceful music coming from the mountain followed by the voice of the Lady who spoke to him in Náhuatl, the language of the Indian, not in Spanish, the language of the oppressors. The voice expressed the intention of the Lady to communicate with the Indian people and her willingness to be with them, to live among them, to heal their pain, and to bring hope. The roses of the message to the bishop grew in the mountain where only desert plants grew.[14] Voice, flowers, and music were the components of the first revelation of the Lady to the Indian and to the bishop, who represented the dominant culture. The miracle of the flowers happened when Juan Diego was looking for help for his *tío* (uncle) who was sick. The Lady told Juan Diego not to worry about him because she would cure him, which did happen. The semiotic of this miracle refers to the people, because in Spanish *tío* means people as well as uncle.[15] The promise of healing was for the whole people, not just for a particular ill.

Roberto S. Goizueta sees in the event of the Tepeyac an interrelation of human action or "praxis."[16] This interaction is rooted in human action or in the life of the community.[17] The dialogue between Juan Diego and the Lady is not precisely an individualist Western-oriented conversation but a communal dialogue between two persons who represent two dimensions of life and promise. The dialogue includes precious elements for the Latino people such as talking face-to-face, touching, flowers, music, and walking the way. The Lady makes clear to Juan Diego and in the message to the bishop that she is not a goddess—she is the Mother of the True God. Thus, the encounter is not a dialogue with merely one of the representatives of the gods or goddesses. This is a communal praxis in which the Lady is interested in the pains and suffering of a people whom she wants to serve. She is not interested in their liberation from the military and economic power of the invaders but in their conversion to a new people and a new

---

[14] Virgilio Elizondo, *Galilean Journey: The Mexican-American Promise* (Maryknoll, NY: Orbis, 1983), 10.

[15] People can say *tío* for a person, without having blood relation, or one can say *tíos*, plural, for people—*esos tíos*.

[16] Roberto S. Goizueta, *Caminemos con Jesús: Toward a Hispanic/Latino Theology of Accompaniment* (Maryknoll, NY: Orbis Books, 1995), 77.

[17] Ibid.

world. There was no time frame or dateline but rather a promise and concern of being with those *tíos* who suffered and needed healing.

Virgil Elizondo introduces another dimension of the encounter in Tepeyac. The semiotic again gives us symbols of interaction. Elizondo sees in the encounter a process that started in April 1519, when Hernán Cortés arrived in Mexico.[18] It was a process of an encounter between two races, two worlds, and two cultures. Twelve years later in the process the Lady becomes the Mother of *raza mestiza* (mixed clan, family, race, or blood). The time, which started with *La Malinche*, an Indian Princess who became Cortés's wife and his language interpreter, came to its climax when the Lady talked to Juan Diego. The sacralization of the Indians and *mestizos* as human beings was declared in the encounter of the Tepeyac. The proclamation of the *mestizaje* as creation of God destroyed the violent imposition exercised by missionaries on the soul of Indians, the only place they could not conquer with the sword. The years of imposition of the Spanish culture, in spite of becoming free and independent from Spain later on, destroyed the way to return to preconquest patterns. Elizondo adds that "The cultural clash of sixteenth-century Spain and Mexico was resolved and reconciled in the brown Lady of Guadalupe. In her the new *mestizo* people finds its meaning in its uniqueness, its unity."[19] Another symbol of identification with the *mestizo* people was the color of her skin. She was brown, the color of Indian skin. That is why people call her even today *La Morenita*, the brown Lady. Today one can walk inside churches and hear people say "She is like me, *morena*." People make a clear distinction between the Northern European imported saints and *La Morenita*. In the radiant clothes, as Juan Diego saw the Lady, and in the *tilma* presented to the bishop, one can see a black belt or waistband, the symbol of a pregnant woman. The pregnant woman is a symbol of the *mestizaje* inside the Lady, and the delivery will be the freedom of those in slavery, Indians and *mestizos*, the birth of a new day, an eschatological dimension of the new race.

It is impossible to separate the issue of the historical proofs in the Tepeyac without considering the impact on the Latino people. Whether we have or do not have clear proof of the apparition in the Tepeyac, it will not destroy Our Lady of Guadalupe's influence on Latino spirituality. People can destroy all arguments about the historical presence of the Lady

[18] Elizondo, *Galilean Journey*, 10.
[19] Ibid., 12.

in the Tepeyac, but they cannot destroy the symbol, the devotion to her. This would repeat the actions of the conquerors, destroying their political, educational, and spiritual systems, yet they could not destroy their souls. Latino spirituality is not limited to the Juan Diego experience but is a communal spirituality, which comes down through the centuries. It is not an individual experience such as the formula, "receive Jesus Christ as your personal Savior." This spirituality is preserved in the core of the community and its religious celebrations and experiences.

Latino spirituality opens new fields for doing theology different from the traditional North Atlantic theology. The Lady of Guadalupe is an inspiration and a *locus theologicus* from the feminine point of view. C. Gilbert Romero talks about the Latino devotional as a symbol of pilgrimage.[20] This symbol belongs to the people and is present in celebrations in homes. People pray the rosary together with the whole family, every day, once a week, once a month. They pray in front of the home altar where there are many symbols of the family's pilgrimage: photographs, stones, statues of saints, rosaries, crucifixes, candles, books of prayers. Not everyone can understand those symbols because they belong to a particular praying community. Only those who know the semiotic symbols will have the key for understanding such spirituality.

In daily life no one can go all over the city and attend religious services from different confessions and be at home with all of them. Many times those symbols belong to the popular religion. They are not part of a system, which the structure supports, such as the bishop who received the news about Guadalupe. His first reaction was to reject the message because he believed that it was from "other indigenous gods." It was something pagan and sinful to deal with that did not deserve his precious time. The semiotic reveals to us something we cannot see at first. It is like water we drink, but we do not know if it is good until the laboratory tells us whether it is pure.

Rosa María Icaza sees Latino spirituality as a unity of faith and life. She says it would be irrelevant to preach a sermon among Latinos that does not continue their lives beyond the liturgical ceremony.[21] Inside the liturgical

---

[20] C. Gilbert Romero, *Hispanic Devotional Piety: Tracing the Biblical Roots* (Maryknoll, NY: Orbis, 1991), 50.

[21] Rosa María Icaza, "Prayer, Worship, and Liturgy in the United States Hispanic Key," in *Frontiers of Hispanic Theology in the United States*, ed. Allan Figueroa Deck (Maryknoll, NY: Orbis, 1992), 135.

process or home devotions is "the sacredness of ancestral traditions."[22] These traditions do not belong to a liturgical book but to the community, which worships in different places and times. The paradigm of the Virgin of Guadalupe runs through many of those traditions. Components of the Latino spiritual traditions are varied. Each region and country of Latin America can create its own symbols, celebrate its own saints, regional festivals, and celebrations. We can share an endless list of celebrations such as Posadas, Día de los Muertos, baptisms, quinceañeras, confirmations, weddings, rosaries, novenarios, azahares (orange blossoms), Holy Week, Easter, and so on. All these areas open new possibilities for doing theology from a particular locus. For example, Our Lady of Guadalupe inspires a variety of topics regarding feminist theology.[23]

How do Lutherans feel when people start talking about a mission among Latinos in our neighborhood? First, people are concerned about the translation of our Lutheran confessions from German. Second, they wonder if "those people" know English as the official language of communication. Third, if "they" come to our church, where can we put them? In a room isolated from the sanctuary, they will have their own "community" and can talk their language. Many questions like that emerge in a planning committee on evangelism, which is why it is very difficult for Lutherans to attract people from other cultures to our churches. We need to be flexible and walk to the Tepeyac of our own spiritual experience. We cannot see the world merely from our own windows or preach the Gospel through videos, tapes, or correspondence. The cultural drama is always there. Latinos or other people from different cultures are not a hard disk on our computers where we can erase from their souls all their spirituality and insert a new program. The Roman Catholic Church tried for five hundred years and came to the conclusion that it is impossible to change Indian spirituality. The challenge to welcome, learn from, and incorporate Indian spirituality is still before us.

---

[22] Ibid.

[23] There are a number of good books in this area. The author recommends at least two important books: Jeanette Rodríguez, *Our Lady of Guadalupe: Faith and Empowerment among Mexican-American Women* (Austin: University of Texas Press, 1994); and Ada María Isasi-Díaz, *En la Lucha, In the Struggle: Elaborating a Mujerista Theology* (Minneapolis, MN: Fortress Press, 1993).

3

Mary in Contemporary Protestant Theological Discourse

Cody C. Unterseher

 In spite of her own evangelical claim that "all generations will call me blessed" (Luke 1:48b), the Blessed Virgin Mary has not held a particularly prominent place in the devotional life or theological imagination of Protestant Christians. "[T]he connection between Protestantism and Mariology has long seemed to many to be such an obvious contradiction in terms that anything resembling an attempt at a 'Protestant' or 'ecumenical' Mariology might be readily dismissed by some beforehand as an oxymoron."[1] On the popular level, many Protestants have considered Mary with some affection as the mother of Jesus—such sentiments often arising in the liturgical seasons of Advent and Christmastide. Anglicans and Lutherans of a particularly "high church" persuasion have in some places maintained devotions including the recitation of the rosary, the *Angelus*, and the "Little Office."[2] All too often, however, Marian piety and theological reflection

[1] Maxwell E. Johnson, *The Virgin of Guadalupe: Theological Reflections of an Anglo-Lutheran Liturgist*, Celebrating Faith: Explorations in Latino Spirituality and Theology (Lanham, MD: Rowman & Littlefield, 2002), 1.

[2] The "Little Office of the Blessed Virgin Mary" is a form of the Liturgy of the Hours or Divine Office said devotionally by certain Roman Catholic confraternities and religious communities. Early evidence for its development dates from the eighth century.

have been dismissed by Protestants as part of the medieval patrimony of Roman Catholicism jettisoned during the sixteenth-century reforms. At worst, Mary has been one among many theological and ideological victims of anti-Catholic polemics. As Lutheran pastor Charles Dickson explains,

> Luther referred to Mary as "God's workshop" and went on to say, "As the Mother of God, she is raised above the whole of humankind" and "has no equal." Contrast this with the modern Protestant attitude that criticizes Marian devotion in the belief that it detracts from the central and unique place Christ occupies in human salvation and you begin to get a picture of the current crisis of division.[3]

Yet, because Mary does hold a significant place in the gospel narratives, Protestants have had to wrestle with fundamental issues in Mariology. Generally speaking, Protestant beliefs about Mary center on her receptive cooperation in the annunciation and her maternity. Thus, most Protestants would be willing to affirm the virginal conception of Jesus, but they would deny the perpetual virginity of Mary because it lacks clear scriptural warrant. Likewise, they would affirm with the Council of Ephesus (431 CE) that Mary is the Mother of God, but they would be reticent to ascribe to her the title "Mother of the church." And but for a few noteworthy exceptions, there is little or no reflection on the conception of Mary or the end of her life—much less dogmatization around these events.

Such a matter-of-fact approach to the Marian data of Scripture and the early church has characterized much of Protestant history. Yet the last half century has seen something of a revival in interest among some Protestants in things Marian. "Renewed interest in a theology of Mary [among Protestants] was sparked in modern times by the Second Vatican Council and the ensuing ecumenical dialogues."[4] This essay will survey three particular aspects deriving from that renewed attention, attending first to the dominant theological images or categories that are being retrieved, appropriated, and employed by individual Protestant theologians for understanding

---

[3] Charles Dickson, *A Protestant Pastor Looks at Mary* (Huntington, IN: Our Sunday Visitor, 1996), 109.

[4] Carl E. Braaten and Robert W. Jenson, eds., *Mary, Mother of God* (Grand Rapids, MI: Eerdmans, 2004), viii. Other obvious factors would include the sharing of resources and scholarship resulting from the liturgical movement and its posterity, and the rise of feminism as a major cultural force both within and beyond explicitly religious settings.

Mary. It will then summarize the key points and principal conclusions of the 2004 Anglican–Roman Catholic International Commission statement *Mary: Grace and Hope in Christ* as one example of fruitful ecumenical dialogue. Finally, it will consider Protestant appraisals of, and interest in, the Virgin of Guadalupe as one example of Marian appropriation in relation to inculturation. In all of this, the fact that Protestants can sustain biblically faithful, spiritually fruitful mariological reflection in their own right—as well as in dialogue with Christians in Catholic (and Orthodox) traditions—becomes clear.

Models of Mary in Protestant Thought

Mary as Exemplar or Model Disciple

The most amenable model for understanding Mary within Protestant circles is perhaps that of exemplar, or "model disciple." Deeply embedded in the evangelists' accounts, this model is evident throughout Mary's recorded life. Indeed, from beginning to end, Mary in a sense embodies the patterns of Christian spiritual development, from proclamation through conversion to abiding fidelity even in the face of hopelessness.

In the Lukan annunciation account, the virgin declares: "Here am I, the servant of the Lord; let it be with me according to your word" (Luke 1:38). Mary submits before the word of God at this most pivotal moment of salvation history, cooperating fully with God's plan. Mary is the "one who hears and reflects on the divine word and . . . embraces it positively."[5] Indeed, as Baptist theologian Timothy George notes, "Mary was a disciple before she was a mother, for had she not believed she would not have conceived."[6] After the nativity of Jesus, and again after finding him in the temple at age twelve, Mary "pondered" and "treasured all these things in her heart" (Luke 2:19, 51b); that is, she took her lived experience—as must every Christian—into the encounter of prayer.

---

[5] Joel B. Green, "Blessed Is She Who Believed: Mary, Curious Exemplar in Luke's Narrative," in *Blessed One: Protestant Perspectives on Mary*, ed. Beverly Roberts Gaventa and Cynthia L. Rigby (Louisville, KY: Westminster John Knox, 2002), 11.

[6] Timothy George, "The Blessed Virgin Mary in Evangelical Perspective," in Braaten and Jenson, *Mary, Mother of God*, 115–16.

Her experience as mother of a lost child (Luke 2:41-51) and the re-definition of familial relationships in Jesus' proclamation of the reign of God (Mark 3:31-35),[7] posit a crisis of faith for Mary. Both of these scenes are illustrative of Jesus' expansive understanding of "family" in light of the reign of God. At the same time, they strike an emotional blow to the rela-tionship between mother and son. Yet, as Daniel L. Migliore comments,

> These stories do not constitute a put-down of Mary. Rather they are a reminder to us all of the confusion and temptation that are a part of the life of faith. They remind us that the church and individual Christians must live a life of continuous repentance. . . . *Mary exemplifies the reality of Christian discipleship that all followers of Jesus and the church as a whole must be* "semper reformanda": *always being reformed by the Word of God.*[8]

In constructing a discipleship model of Mary, Protestant authors fre-quently turn to the episode recorded in John 19:25-27. At the foot of the cross and in the face of defeat, Mary remains loyal to her son; at the same time she remains mother. The inner thoughts of this woman of faith at the cross are not recorded, but it seems quite safe to assume that Mary experienced the full range of human emotions in the face of such a tragedy. "It was at Calvary that Mary's discipleship was reaching its apex, and she was learning in the core of her being that God's ways were not hers."[9]

Finally, attention is increasingly being paid to the place of Mary in the first Christian community at Jerusalem.[10] Although Acts 1:14 yields no more than a passing mention of her presence in the pre-Pentecost

---

[7] The redefinition recorded in Mark's narrative, "whoever does the will of God is my brother and sister and mother" (3:35), corresponds with the scene in Luke's account where a woman in a crowd praises Jesus' mother (11:27). In response, Jesus states, "Blessed rather are those who hear the word of God and obey it!" (28). Both cases represent a renovated definition of the family within the eschatological reign in Jesus' proclamation.

[8] Daniel L. Migliore, "Woman of Faith: Toward a Reformed Understanding of Mary," in Gaventa and Rigby, *Blessed One*, 127; emphasis original.

[9] Penelope Duckworth, *Mary: The Imagination of Her Heart* (Cambridge, MA: Cowley, 2004), 91.

[10] Roman Catholic scholar Elizabeth A. Johnson provides a particularly strong and provocative theological assessment of Mary at the Pentecost event and in the life of the Jerusalem church; see *Truly Our Sister: A Theology of Mary in the Communion of Saints* (New York: Continuum, 2003), 297–304.

assembly, evangelical author Scot McKnight sees this as "an indicator of her importance to that first gathering of the followers of Jesus." Luke's annunciation account depicts Mary as experiencing a radical outpouring of the Holy Spirit in the conception of Jesus; Pentecost parallels that event in its location near the beginning of Acts. Following Luke's logic, Mary would have been present in the Jerusalem community as something of a forerunner or prototype for the Pentecost experience. "We never hear about her again in the pages of the New Testament, but we can be sure that she continued to be the woman she had been: courageous, dangerous, faithful, assertive, and hopeful for the kingdom of God," an example of what the nascent church was being called to become.[11]

The exemplar or disciple model exhibits the highest level of theological development among Protestant scholars, no doubt due to its multiple biblical foundations. It also seems to provide an accurate outline of the lived Christian experience, making it an accessible point of connection for people of faith. Undoubtedly, Mary was a disciple—one who learns—in the deepest sense, and her fidelity is worth emulation.

> Mary seems readily to embrace the patterns and rhythms of God's kingdom, irrespective of their alien quality. This does not mean that discipleship comes easily for Mary, or naturally. She exhibits the need to ponder events infused with the presence of God. . . . [Mary is] an exemplar . . . one whose life is in sync with God's saving plan.[12]

This model fails, however, precisely on the foundation that it is built: Mary's character in the Scriptures is not portrayed as that of a disciple. She is above all the *mother* of Jesus. This is not to suggest that as mother Mary was not or could not have been in some sense also a follower, a disciple; nor does it mean that her discipleship as such was not exemplary, not worthy of imitation. Yet, when Mary is understood as exemplar, it must always be borne in mind that her discipleship developed organically within parental and familial bonds. This raises a question that may be particularly uncomfortable for some Protestants: who is Mary, as disciple, *pro me?* Does taking Mary as model disciple not put the individual Christian in a relationship with her? Or does she remain simply the heroine of biblical narrative to be disinterestedly emulated? Furthermore, "identifying Mary

---

[11] Scot McKnight, *The Real Mary: Why Evangelical Christians Can Embrace the Mother of Jesus* (Brewster, MA: Paraclete Press, 2007), 108.

[12] Green, "Blessed Is She," in Gaventa and Rigby, *Blessed One,* 17–18.

as an example lends itself too readily to the sort of Protestant moralizing that reduces biblical texts to their outcomes in human conduct. . . . Mary becomes a tonic to render readers into better people."[13] The model remains commendable in its strengths, but Protestant sensibilities (particularly those that tend toward the evangelical) may inhibit its full potential for appropriation.

Mary as Prophet

Both in the annunciation and at the foot of the cross, Mary is confronted with apparently "impossible" situations; yet she also remains the perennial recipient of God's promise, articulated in the angel Gabriel's message: "nothing will be impossible with God" (Luke 1:37). Beverly Roberts Gaventa thus sees Mary placed in the long line of Old Testament prophets, whose faith in God was against the odds.[14] Indeed, the evangelist Luke models the entire annunciation episode on the pattern of prophetic callings in the Old Testament.[15] Furthermore, Mary's canticle, the *Magnificat*, places her squarely within the prophetic tradition of Israel. "Its imagery of God's exalting of the lowly and humbling the mighty recalls prophetic themes and anticipates the presence of those same themes in Jesus' sermon at Nazareth" (see Luke 4:16-21).[16] As with the prophets, Mary announces God's umbrage against the unjust wedding of religion and politics that enables the systematic marginalization of the poor, the diseased and the vulnerable.

> In her soaring song of praise to God, Mary bears witness to the justice and mercy of God. Her humility before God is coupled with courage to declare God's judgment on injustice and oppression and to announce the coming of God's justice and mercy that turns the order of this world upside down. . . . Her song is indeed a song of the dawn of a revolution . . . spiritual as well as political. It comes not from us but from God.[17]

[13] Beverly Roberts Gaventa, "'Nothing Will Be Impossible with God': Mary as the Mother of Believers," in Braaten and Jenson, *Mary, Mother of God*, 33.

[14] Ibid., 28–29.

[15] For a full elucidation of Luke's modeling of the annunciation on the paradigm of prophetic callings in the Old Testament, see E. Johnson, *Truly Our Sister*, 248–51.

[16] Gaventa, "Nothing Will Be Impossible," 23.

[17] Migliore, "Woman of Faith," 124–25.

Robert W. Jenson sees a more archetypal connection between Mary and the prophetic tradition of Israel. Noting that a prophet is not only one who speaks forth God's word, but also one who, like the temple, becomes a *place* where God is addressed, Jenson states: "In a way, a prophet was a sort of historically functioning, mobile Temple; the building in Jerusalem could not go with the people into exile, but prophets could."[18] From this spatial image of the prophet, Jenson draws an analogy to the person of Mary: "When God's creating Word came into its own singular identity into the world, Mary brought him forth as though she were all the prophets put together—indeed, 'as though' is not a strong enough way to put it."[19] Not only proclaiming God's word, but embodying it in her own person, Mary is the archetype of the entire prophetic tradition.

"It is significant," Episcopal priest Penelope Duckworth notes, "that while Christianity has been reluctant to name Mary as a prophet, Islam places her close to that calling."[20] Although it is the case that nowhere in Scripture is Mary named a prophet, this model seems to present fewer theological difficulties than Mary as disciple. While Jenson's approach leaves itself vulnerable to being labeled as allegorical (along the lines of medieval interpretations of the Song of Songs), the *Magnificat* itself attains the heights of classical prophecy, declaring God's favor for the marginalized and dispossessed while pronouncing woes on the powerful of the world.[21] For those Protestants whose liturgical and devotional sensibilities include praying the *Magnificat* each evening, Mary's prophetic voice becomes an ongoing challenge to engage in social action. "Although the Magnificat has been beautifully arranged for choral voices and sung repeatedly in daily offices, it remains a stark challenge to inequity and a call to faith for the dispossessed."[22]

Mary as Mother of the Church

Of all the possible models theologians could employ in retrieving Marian tradition for Protestants, certainly the most problematic is that of

---

[18] Robert W. Jenson, "A Space for God," in Braaten and Jenson, *Mary, Mother of God*, 54–55. See also chap. 11 below.

[19] Jenson, "A Space for God," 56.

[20] Duckworth, *Mary*, 20.

[21] A comparison of the Lukan *Magnificat* (1:46-56) to its Old Testament parallels (1 Sam 2:1-10, Ps 113, and Isa 61:10a) seems to warrant this estimation; also see E. Johnson, *Truly Our Sister*, 263–71.

[22] Duckworth, *Mary*, 19.

Mary as Mother of the church. The history of this model includes the unfortunate casting of Mary in a mediatorial role vis-à-vis God the Father, as described by Elizabeth Johnson:

> One of the key roles of the mother in a patriarchal family, where she is supposedly the "heart," is to intercede on behalf of her children with the rather more distant father, who is supposedly the "head." Her merciful influence can soften punishment and obtain benefits that would otherwise not be forthcoming. Reinscribing this human institution into heaven makes Mary the merciful mother who intercedes for her wayward children before a basically loving but definitely just, perhaps testy, sometimes even angry God the Father. The whole theology of her maternal mediation derives from this scenario.[23]

It is a history of devotion to such maternal intervention that stood behind the rejection of much (in some cases, all) of the Marian tradition during the sixteenth-century Protestant reforms.

The narrative of Mary and the beloved disciple at the foot of the cross (John 19:25-27) is often cited in Catholic and Orthodox traditions as the scriptural warrant for understanding Mary's motherhood in the church. But Lutheran pastor and theologian David Yeago suggests a different basis: "Mary is irreducibly presenting the relationship of the church and of the believer to *the Christ who is attested in Holy Scripture*."[24] This is to say that the entire mystery of Christ as recorded in the New Testament becomes the scriptural framework for understanding the church's relationship to him. Yeago goes on to ask:

> Is Mary in any sense a "presence" within the redemptive relationship of the church and of the believer to Christ? If we are clear in our minds that Christ the savior is the *scriptural* Christ, that the redemptive relationship of the church and of the believer [is] to this Christ . . . then the answer to this question is obviously "Yes." *Mary is present within the redemptive relationship of the church and of the believer to Christ by virtue of her presence in the scriptural testimony to Christ.*[25]

Mary is the mother of him who is the "the firstborn within a large family"

---

[23] E. Johnson, *Truly Our Sister*, 33.

[24] David S. Yeago, "The Presence of Mary in the Mystery of the Church," in Braaten and Jenson, *Mary, Mother of God*, 59–60; emphasis original.

[25] Ibid., 33; emphasis original.

(Rom 8:29). Thus, for Yeago, the overarching question is not whether Mary is the mother of the church; rather, the question is how the church is configured in relationship to Christ, the son of Mary. Only when that configuration is properly articulated can Mary be located in relationship to the church.

Christian Methodist Episcopal minister and womanist theologian Cheryl A. Kirk-Duggan views this motherhood in terms of human solidarity and companionship. Drawing an image from popular music, she styles "Proud Mary" as one who

> is the fierce Pietà, the protective Madonna, the committed virgin, the welcoming Sponsa; at once fragile and sturdy. She is simultaneously flawed and perfect, sensual and sexual, a public yet quite private person. *Proud Mary knows the character of herself and especially of her children.* She is a trustworthy leader and helpful companion. She is an independent spirit with a big heart. Proud Mary knows she is on a journey, crossing portals of the known and the unknown. And *she is there to journey with others*, out of the hell of addiction, through labor pains, through graduations and weddings, at the dawn of birth and the sunset of death.[26]

The "Proud Mary" that Kirk-Duggan presents is one who knows and takes care of her children, and on her own motherly initiative. Yet, is not such care and presence a form of intervention—even when it is not formally sought? Is this Mary then not only mother but also intercessor?[27]

It seems, in fact, that the model of Mary as Mother of the church cannot be separated from an ascription to her of the role of intercessor. Yeago has identified a broad scriptural warrant for this model; nevertheless, many Protestants—as heirs to a tradition that has historically eschewed invocation of the saints—will be left uneasy. Penelope Duckworth suggests a careful distinction that may be of some aid in this context. "While invocation means calling upon a higher power, advocation means calling

---

[26] Cheryl A. Kirk-Duggan, "Proud Mary: Contextual Constructions of a Divine Diva," in Gaventa and Rigby, *Blessed One*, 82; emphasis added.

[27] Kirk-Duggan's presentation of "Proud Mary" has the strength and energy that characterizes much of womanist and feminist theology. Yet, it is ironic that many feminist theologians—notably Elizabeth A. Johnson—have moved decidedly away from maternal and intercessory images for Mary, asserting that much of the content for these images has in fact been illegitimately expropriated by tradition from pneumatology; see E. Johnson, *Truly Our Sister*, 71–92.

for the prayerful assistance of others. . . . [W]e are asking others to pray
to God on our behalf, and we recognize that God alone has the power to
answer or respond to those prayers."[28] The assistance, the presence and
the solidarity sought in calling on Mary as Mother of the church derives
solely from her configuration to Christ, and comes ultimately from God
alone. With such a view—repugnant to neither traditional Protestant nor
"Catholic" sensibilities—invocation of Mary, precisely as Mother of the
church, seems to be at least theologically plausible for the Protestant
imagination.

Mary in Ecumenical Dialogue: A Recent Example

Following the Second Vatican Council (1962–1965), Roman Catholic
and Protestant theologians engaged in a number of ecumenical dialogues,
official and unofficial, on topics relating to church structure and authority,
ministry, sacramental theology, and other various elements of Christian
life. Regarding Mariology, the Anglican-Roman Catholic International
Commission (ARCIC) is the most recent official ecumenical dialogue to
produce a report.[29]

ARCIC began its work in 1969 and has advanced in two stages (1969–
1981 and 1982–2004). The first stage (ARCIC I) resulted in the publication of the document *Authority in the Church II*. In the course of that
dialogue, participants discerned a number of points of mariological agreement, including that "she was prepared by divine grace to be the mother
of our Redeemer, by whom she herself was redeemed and received into
glory." At the same time, the statement noted that "[t]he dogmas of the
Immaculate Conception and the Assumption raise a special problem for
those Anglicans who do not consider that the precise definitions given by

[28] Duckworth, *Mary*, 115. For an alternative view, see Jenson, "A Space for
God," 56.

[29] The results of the Evangelical Lutheran–Roman Catholic Dialogue in the
United States and the work of the French and Swiss Dombes Group are also of
exceptional note. See H. George Anderson, J. Francis Stafford, and Joseph A.
Burgess, eds., *The One Mediator, the Saints, and Mary*, Lutherans and Catholics in
Dialogue 8 (Minneapolis, MN: Augsburg Fortress, 1992); Alain Blancy, Maurice
Jourjon, and the Dombes Group, *Mary in the Plan of God and in the Communion
of Saints: Toward a Common Christian Understanding*, trans. Matthew J. O'Connell
(Mahwah, NJ: Paulist Press, 2002).

these dogmas are sufficiently supported by Scripture."[30] From these points, both of convergence and difference, the second stage of dialogue (ARCIC II) began its work. The resulting agreed statement, *Mary: Grace and Hope in Christ*, was released in February 2004.

The statement of ARCIC II unfolds in four sections:

Mary According to the Scriptures

Mary in the Christian Tradition

Mary Within the Pattern of Grace and Hope

Mary in the Life of the Church

The first section comprises a thorough examination of the scriptural pericopes that speak of the Virgin Mary, including the Old Testament prophesies and psalms that—among Roman Catholics, at least—have been understood as alluding to her. Also considered is the vision of the woman "clothed with the sun" recorded in Revelation 12.

The second section traces the history of Marian thought and devotion from its earliest developments through the Reformation to twentieth-century renewals in Marian liturgical piety and teaching in both churches. This section concludes with a revealing summary of the points about which Anglicans and Roman Catholics are in substantial agreement:

> Our two communions are both heirs to a rich tradition which recognizes Mary as ever virgin, and sees her as the new Eve and as a type of the Church. We join in praying and praising with Mary whom all genera-tions have called blessed, in observing her festivals and according her honour in the communion of the saints, and are agreed that Mary and the saints pray for the whole Church. . . . In all of this, we see Mary as inseparably linked with Christ and the Church. [31]

The third section addresses the economy of salvation as articulated in both Scripture and the earliest Christian tradition. Adopting an ap-parently eschatological understanding of the unfolding of God's plan for human fulfillment in Christ, the document asserts: "We thus view the economy of grace from its fulfillment in Christ 'back' into history, rather

---

[30] ARCIC I, *Authority In the Church II*, no. 30 (1982), as cited in ARCIC II, *Mary: Grace and Hope in Christ* (Harrisburg, PA: Morehouse, 2005), 2–3, no. 2.
[31] ARCIC II, *Mary: Grace and Hope in Christ*, 48, no. 51.

than 'forward' from its beginning in fallen creation towards the future in Christ. This perspective offers fresh light in which to consider the place of Mary."[32] From this point of departure, ARCIC II is able to affirm both that Mary was uniquely set apart to be the mother of the Redeemer, and that she is "a pattern of anticipated eschatology . . . [now] fully present with God in Christ."[33]

This section next turns attention to the papal definitions regarding the immaculate conception and assumption of Mary.[34] Because the fortuitous wording of both dogmatic definitions points foremost to God's free and gracious action in the life of Mary without specifying the means of that action, the document of ARCIC II is able to state that "the teaching about Mary in the two definitions of 1854 and 1950, understood within the biblical pattern of the economy of grace and hope outlined here, can be said to be consonant with the teaching of the Scriptures and the ancient common traditions."[35] At the same time, because the dogmas lack clear scriptural warrant, they remain problematic for some Anglicans. The concluding remarks of this section express the hope that the agreed understanding of Mary's place in the economy of salvation will deepen the common faith and understanding of both of the churches.

The fourth section treats the distinctive place of Mary within the communion of the saints and the life of the church. The practice of invoking the saints is affirmed as being consonant with authentic Christian tradition, provided that it in no way "blurs the trinitarian economy of grace and hope."[36] Within this context, Mary's unique role as intercessor is affirmed:

> Among all the saints, Mary takes her place as *Theotókos*: alive in Christ, she abides with the one she bore, still "highly favoured" in the communion of grace and hope, the exemplar of redeemed humanity, an icon of the Church. Consequently she is believed to exercise a distinctive

---

[32] Ibid., 49, no. 52.

[33] Ibid., 54, no. 56.

[34] See Pius IX, *Ineffabilis Deus*, Papal Bull (December 8, 1854) in J. Neuner and J. Dupuis, *The Christian Faith in the Doctrinal Documents of the Catholic Church*, 6th rev. ed. (New York: Alba House, 1996), 260, no. 709; and Pius XII, *Munificentissimus Deus*, Apostolic Constitution (November 1, 1950), ibid., 262–64, nos. 713–15.

[35] ARCIC II, *Mary: Grace and Hope in Christ*, 58, no. 60.

[36] Ibid., 70, no. 70.

ministry of assisting others through her active prayer. Many Christians reading the Cana account continue to hear Mary instruct them, "Do whatever he tells you," and are confident that she draws the attention of her son to their needs: "they have no wine" (John 2:1-12).[37]

The fourth section goes on briefly to touch on devotional practices, including pilgrimages to sites of purported Marian apparitions. With proper catechesis, and an understanding of their optional and derivative nature, such practices are found to be "acceptable, though never required of believers."[38] The section then concludes with a statement that clearly illustrates how much progress these churches have made in their ecumenical understanding of Mariology:

> Affirming together unambiguously Christ's unique mediation, which bears fruit in the life of the Church, we do not consider the practice of asking Mary and the saints to pray for us as communion-dividing. Since obstacles of the past have been removed by clarification of doctrine, by liturgical reform and practical norms in keeping with it, we believe that there is no continuing theological reason for ecclesial division on these matters.[39]

Mary: Grace and Hope in Christ is a striking example of ecumenical convergence in an area of often highly controversial theology. It is important to note, however, that the reception of this document among Anglicans will likely not be uniform. Anglicanism, as the self-styled *via media* between Catholicism and Protestantism, embraces both traditions in all their richness; yet, individuals within the Anglican Communion frequently identify with one of the traditions over against the other. While some Anglican theologians will agree substantially with the conclusions of ARCIC II, the opinions expressed in the statement may be foreign to those faithful whose theological stance and piety is more in keeping with traditional Protestantism.[40]

---

[37] Ibid., 71, no. 71.

[38] Ibid., 73, no. 73.

[39] Ibid., 74–75, no. 75.

[40] Thus the General Secretary of the Church Society (an evangelical organization in the Church of England) comments: "If someone believes Roman Dogma concerning Mary to be true, they will so distort Scripture as to support their belief. However, to all others it is abundantly plain that Scripture does not teach these things, and that they were a later development. The ARCIC report fails miserably

Protestant Faith and Catholic Popular Culture:
The Virgin of Guadalupe

That Anglicans are affirming (together with more essential theological points) the acceptability of pilgrimage to Marian shrines as an optional devotional practice should come as no surprise.[41] Indeed, one of the great centers of Marian pilgrimage since the Middle Ages is located in England, at Walsingham—popularly styled "England's Nazareth." The shrine celebrates a series of apparitions of the Virgin Mary to Rechildis de Faverches, the Lady of Walsingham Parva manor, in the year 1061.[42] Dismantled in 1538 during the Dissolution of the Monasteries, interest in the Marian shrine was rekindled around the turn of the twentieth century.[43] It remains an ecumenical center of pilgrimage for Anglicans, Methodists, Roman Catholics, and Eastern Orthodox, all of whom maintain separate chapels in conjunction with the shrine.

In places where Anglicanism is known more in its Protestant passion than its Catholic conviviality, appreciation for the value of pilgrimage as a spiritual exercise may be negligible. Such is the case in Mexico, where Anglicans are often indifferent to the prepotent Marian piety, centered on the image of the Virgin of Guadalupe. Mexican Anglicans raise questions challenging the integrity of the history of the apparitions and the image and the centrality accorded to Guadalupe in Mexican culture. There is also a history of fighting and murder between Catholic and Anglican zealots: on December 12, 1878 (the feast of Our Lady of Guadalupe), twenty-two Anglicans were executed at Atzala, in the Mexican state of Puebla.[44] Their executioners are reported to have cried, "*Viva la Guadalupe!* Death to those who do not adore her."

---

to do justice to what Anglicans believe." See David Phillips, "ARCIC on Mary, or Things Vainly Invented," *CrossWay* 97 (Summer 2005): 1–3; here at 3.

[41] *Editor's note*: A recent example of this is certainly the September 2008 sermon preached by Rowan Williams, the Archbishop of Canterbury, at the famous site of the Marian apparitions to Bernadette at Lourdes, France, commemorating the 150th anniversary year of those apparitions. See http://news.bbc.co.uk/1/hi/uk/7631156.stm.

[42] Duckworth, *Mary*, 126.

[43] Roman Catholic efforts at reestablishing pilgrimage to Walsingham date to 1897; Anglican interest in the shrine was kindled with the appointment of the Rev. Alfred Hope Patton as Vicar of Walsingham in 1922.

[44] Ibid., 106–7.

Anglicans in Mexico are not the only non-Catholic Christians who struggle with the dominance of Guadalupe in Latino/a culture. Protestantism on the whole, and specifically in its "radical" or "Reformed" strands, tends to view culture generally in a negative light. In particular, "Latino Protestantism has had a tense relationship with Latino culture. It has dismissed many elements of the culture due to their connections with Catholicism."[45] As Mexican cultural identity is often inextricably bound up with the beliefs and practices of folk Catholicism—and specifically Guadalupan piety—Mexican Protestants (predominantly Evangelical and Pentecostal in affiliation) find their religious and cultural loyalties tensely divided. For example, within the Catholic-cultural milieu

> [religious] practices . . . center on saints and manifestations of the Virgin Mary. Churches bearing the names given to these manifestations—Carmen, Guadalupe, Soledad—feature large images of the Virgin. Through fiestas each locale celebrates its patron saint's day, with lively bands, dancing, drinking, fireworks and, often, a carnival-like atmosphere. Protestants censure such activities and have on occasion been arrested for failing to support them, since their refusal to buy candles or liquor or to otherwise join in the festivities is considered divisive and harmful to local economic interests.[46]

The rapid growth of Protestantism among Mexicans in particular,[47] and Latinos/as in general, enjoins consideration of an important question: can the Virgin of Guadalupe be recognized as a *cultural* symbol apart from Roman Catholic belief and practice? Alternatively, can the Virgin be appropriated as a denominationally neutral symbol, *both* Christian and cultural?

One approach toward resolving this tension would be to circumscribe the relationship between the apparitions at Tepeyac in 1521 and the prevailing "Catholic" culture, for the sake of emphasizing the Latino/a element. In this approach, Mary would be understood as coming to Juan

---

[45] Nora O. Lozano-Díaz, "Ignored Virgin or Unaware Women: A Mexican-American Protestant Reflection of the Virgin of Guadalupe," in Gaventa and Rigby, *Blessed One*, 85.

[46] Lynda K. Barrow, "Mission in Mexico: An Evangelical Surge," *Christian Century* 118, no. 7 (2001): 24.

[47] "[T]he Protestant rate of growth in this once-solidly Catholic country is striking. Government figures indicate that between 1970 and 1990 the number of Mexican Protestants grew by more than 280 percent" (ibid., 24).

Diego not in the image of the Catholic Spaniards' Maria, but above all as one of his own people. She did not identify with the established church; rather, in giving voice to the needs of the people, she made demands upon its attention, as:

> [s]he is not just the mother of the gods of the Indians' ancestors or the Ever-Virgin Mary of the Christians but is also the ever-present and listening mother of each and every inhabitant of the nations. Everyone can come to her without fear or hesitation. . . . She demands nothing of us; she asks only to be ever-present to respond to our cries and lamentations and remedy our ills.[48]

Comprehending the Virgin of Guadalupe in this way highlights her uniquely Latina quality (even as that quality transcends itself.) The temptation, however, to pit the cultural icon against the religious persists, completely rejecting the Catholic realization of the Marian symbol. Such an approach, it seems, would be inimical to the very character of Guadalupe:

> What most people who have not experienced the Guadalupe tradition cannot understand is that to be a Guadalupano/a (one in whose heart Our Lady of Guadalupe reigns) is to be an evangelical Christian. It is to say that the Word became flesh in Euro-Native America and began its unifying task—"that all may be one." In Our Lady of Guadalupe, Christ became American.[49]

An alternative to asserting the Latino/a element of the Guadalupe symbol while downplaying the attendant Catholic culture is the inculturation of Protestant Christianity within a matrix that is inseparably both Mexican/Mexican American *and* Catholic; that is, embracing the Virgin of Guadalupe as *both* a cultural and Christian symbol. Although some North American Anglicans and Lutherans would have no difficulty with such a proposition, such an arrangement would be antagonistic to much of the Protestantism (of whatever tradition) that has developed and continues to flourish in Central and South America. Justo L. González notes,

[48] Virgilio Elizondo, *Guadalupe: Mother of the New Creation* (Maryknoll, NY: Orbis, 1997), 68–69.
[49] Ibid., 113.

[i]t is true that in some rare Protestant Latino churches one may find an image of Our Lady of Guadalupe. But it is also true that still today for most Protestant Latinos—even those of Mexican origin—rejecting Guadalupe is an essential mark of being truly Christian. . . . The notion that Cuban Catholics and Protestants will come together around the image of [Our Lady of] Caridad, or Mexicans around Guadalupe, may be very beautiful, but is made less than credible by our own histories.[50]

In the United States, the situation seems to be developing along different lines. U.S. Hispanic Protestants—Episcopalians and Lutherans especially—seem to be exhibiting more openness to identifying with and celebrating the Virgin of Guadalupe. Thus, one can find numerous images of the Virgin of Guadalupe in Lutheran and Episcopal communities in California, as well as other places with high populations of Mexicans and Mexican Americans.[51] The Evangelical Lutheran Church in America (ELCA) can boast of the Iglesia Luterana Santa María de Guadalupe in Irving, Texas, and the Episcopal Church embraces communities under the Virgin's patronage in San Jose and Fresno, California; Waukegan, Illinois; Poughkeepsie, New York; and Wilson, North Carolina. In spite of such local developments, however, neither the ELCA nor the Episcopal Church includes the December 12 feast of the Virgin of Guadalupe on its national liturgical calendar.[52] Though celebrations of the Guadalupan feast will be marked with the character and popular traditions of the community celebrating (in terms both liturgical and cultural), "when the Virgin of Guadalupe is celebrated within Protestant Christian communities, there

---

[50] Justo L. González, "Reinventing Dogmatics: A Footnote from a Reinvented Protestant," in *From the Heart of Our People: Latino/a Explorations in Catholic Systematic Theology*, ed. Orlando O. Espín and Miguel H. Díaz (Maryknoll, NY: Orbis, 1999), 224–25. I am grateful to Professor Díaz for directing my attention to this reference.

[51] See M. E. Johnson, *The Virgin of Guadalupe*, 123 and 124.

[52] Ibid., 122. The relevance of such observances for these national church bodies is mounting, however, as the Hispanic population in both churches grows. In the Episcopal Church, local and regional celebrations will normatively precede the addition of a commemoration to the calendar of the national church. See "Guidelines and Procedures for Continuing Alteration of the Calendar in the Episcopal Church," in *Lesser Feasts and Fasts 2006* (New York: Church Publishing, 2006), 491–96, here at 492.

is really nothing to distinguish those 'Protestant' celebrations from Roman Catholic ones."[53]

In considering the place (or nonplace) accorded to the Virgin of Guadalupe among Protestants, what is ultimately at stake is the identity of persons. The theological and devotional concerns of the inherited Anglo-European Protestantism (as those of Anglo-European Catholicism) have often been treated as universal and normative outside the cultural context in which they developed. Is this situation necessarily beneficial? Can Latino/a Protestants identify fully with Hispanic culture (including the Virgin of Guadalupe) without betraying their religious tradition? Conversely, if as Protestants they choose not to esteem the Virgin of Tepeyac, do they thereby betray their cultural heritage? Any attempt at inculturating Protestant faith and Latino/a culture inevitably must confront the Guadalupan issue, namely,

> whether the narrative and image of the Virgin of Guadalupe has a message for Protestants in general, especially, but not exclusively, for those within those particular Protestant traditions like Lutheranism and Anglicanism that share with Roman Catholicism much of the common liturgical and sacramental heritage of Western Christianity.[54]

The answer to such a question will depend heavily on where one (individual or community) begins. What theological language about Mary will form the framework for discussion? How does the Guadalupe narrative relate to the scriptural revelation—how is *this* Mary understood in relationship to Christ?

As the Hispanic population in the United States grows, Christians of all church bodies are rapidly having to find ways of embracing Latino/a cultural expressions. Anglo-European Christian communities in the United States will soon have no choice but to confront (or to be confronted by) the dark-skinned, pregnant Mary dressed in red and veiled in blue-green, who herself was an alien—both in Egypt and in the Americas. With immigration reform remaining a priority among issues of domestic interest, Anglo-European Christians in the United States—Catholics as well as Protestants—have a unique opportunity to publicly witness to the unconditional hospitality that characterizes the reign of God.

---

[53] M. E. Johnson, *The Virgin of Guadalupe*, 126.
[54] Ibid., 137.

For the church being called into existence more than ever before in the United States is one called to be clearly multicultural and mestizo in form, and such a church appears to be already present proleptically in the mestizo face of the Virgin of Guadalupe. To gaze contemplatively upon her image, then, is to gaze at the future church in the making and to gaze at what we hope, by God's grace and Spirit, the Church of Jesus Christ, racially, culturally, and even ecumenically, will become.[55]

Conclusion

"[T]he Cold War between Protestants and Roman Catholics over Mary has ended."[56] What has ensued is an often surprising retrieval of Mariology among Protestants—holding much promise, both for the ongoing development of Protestant faith and devotion and for ecumenical dialogue with Catholic (and Orthodox) Christians. Yet such retrieval is also fraught with difficulty. As illustrated above, the major Marian models being appropriated by Protestant scholars are thoroughly biblical; yet none fully expresses the place of Mary in the life of Christ and of the church without complication. Although the work of the various ecumenical dialogues, ARCIC in particular, exhibit great promise, they remain vulnerable to contention and critique from within the participating churches, on both academic and popular levels. And although the theological and liturgical retrieval of the feast of the Virgin of Guadalupe (or the feasts of any locally revered and culturally identified Marian apparition) invite new expressions of Protestant piety and cultural pride, the extrabiblical origins of the feasts make them suspect to many of the Protestant faithful.

The turn to Mary, whether for Protestants, for Catholics, or for the Orthodox, must always be above all a turn to God in Jesus Christ the Lord. Mary "is who she is by pointing away from herself: her identity is caught up in leading to Jesus."[57] This is to say that who Mary is for Protestants is not, and cannot be, other than who she is for Catholics and Orthodox: the mother whose attention is *always* directed toward her son. At the same time, Mary cannot be other than what each human person is: one of God's creatures, a child by election and adoption, justified by grace

---

[55] Ibid., 184.

[56] McKnight, *The Real Mary*, 5.

[57] Rowan Williams, *Ponder These Things: Praying with Icons of the Virgin* (Franklin, WI: Sheed & Ward, 2002), 7.

through faith, and thereby brought into a new and living relationship with
God in Christ Jesus through the power of the Holy Spirit. As Protestants
wrestle with the mariological tradition, retrieving it from the recycling bin
of the Reformation, there will no doubt be challenging intellectual and
spiritual moments. Some traditions will be left behind, some images that
simply cannot be lived with will be jettisoned, and some metaphors will
be found devoid of power. Yet, there is also great potential for even more
discovery and the renewal of insights long forgotten in the two millennia
that have passed since she offered her *fiat* and began to point the way to
Christ for us all.

Whenever we emulate Mary's consent, or follow her direction, we
quickly discover ourselves on a new and exciting journey: to the Bethlehem where the Word becomes flesh among us in new and unexpected
ways; to the cross where, too often helplessly, we see Christ crucified in
the poor and the marginalized; to the upper room where over and over
we welcome the gusty wind and cleansing fire of God's Spirit, there learning to make heard the gospel in the language of contemporary culture. In
each of those places, Mary remains, silently pondering (see Luke 2:19),
caught up in prayer with and for the church. In this too we do well to
follow her lead. To that end, and by way of a conclusion, I offer a Litany
of Mary, drawn from the models and images discussed in this essay. Not
intercessory in the strict sense (that is, the invocations are not addressed
to Mary herself but to her Son), this prayer is given as a model that might
find a place in the devotional practices of many Protestants, and perhaps
also in ecumenical experiences of prayer and worship, particularly with
Roman Catholics.

God the Father, creator of the world	*have mercy on us.*
God the Son, Word made flesh	*have mercy on us.*
God the Spirit, fire of love	*have mercy on us.*
Holy Trinity, one God	*have mercy on us.*
With Mary, Mother of God	*we pray to you, Lord Christ.*
With Mary, Mother of the church	*we pray to you, Lord Christ.*
With Mary, the model of discipleship	*we pray to you, Lord Christ.*
With Mary, prophet of the Word	*we pray to you, Lord Christ.*
With Proud Mary,	
standing with her children	*we pray to you, Lord Christ.*
With Mary, touchstone of unity	*we pray to you, Lord Christ.*
With Mary, the Lady of Walsingham	*we pray to you, Lord Christ.*

With Mary, the Virgin of Guadalupe	*we pray to you, Lord Christ.*
With Mary,	
the Mother of the Americas	*we pray to you, Lord Christ.*
With Mary,	
champion of the marginalized	*we pray to you, Lord Christ.*
With Mary, model of inculturation	*we pray to you, Lord Christ.*
With Mary, face of the future church	*we pray to you, Lord Christ.*
With Mary,	
who points the way to you	*we pray to you, Lord Christ.*

Let us pray. God our Creator, look with love upon your sorely divided church, for whose sake the Word became flesh in the womb of the Blessed Virgin Mary. Grant us the faith that made her receptive to your Word, the hope that trusts in your promises of salvation, and the love necessary to overcome all division. With Mary as our model and our Mother, may we seek the way of unity together, and become an effective witness to your compassion in our world. Empowered by your Holy Spirit, we make our prayer through Jesus Christ our Lord. *Amen.*

4

Juan Diego:
A Psychohistory of a Regenerative Man

Carl C. Trovall

Broken Spears

Broken spears lie in the road;
we have torn our hair in our grief.
The houses are roofless now, and their walls
are red with blood.

Worms are swarming in the streets and plazas,
and the walls are splattered with gore.
The water has turned red, as if it were dyed,
and when we drink it,
it has the taste of brine.

We have pounded our hands in despair
against the adobe walls,
for our inheritance, our city, is lost and dead.
The shields of our warriors were its defense,
but they could not save it.

We have chewed dry twigs and salt grasses;
we have filled our mouths with dust and bits of adobe;
we have eaten lizards, rats and worms. . . .

They set a price on all of us
on the young men, the priests, the boys and the girls.

> The price of a poor man was only two handfuls of corn,
> or ten cakes made from mosses
> or twenty cakes of salty couch-grass.
> Gold, jade, rich cloths, quetzal feathers—
> everything that once was precious was now considered worthless.[1]

> Generativity . . . is the true archaic foundation of man. . . . Generativity sums up that in man which is most basic and most primitive. But it also points toward that which is the end and goal of all existence. If all of man's instincts propel him toward biological generativity, man's capacity for imagination, reason, and conscience make it possible and necessary for him to elevate this generativity to higher cultural, ethical, and religious levels.[2]

As the Protestant Reformation rapidly exploded from a fuse lit by Martin Luther in the early sixteenth century, changing the face and faith of Europe, Mesoamerica's faith was also being rapidly transformed at the hands of another, quite different, reformer: a poor, disenfranchised, and humble indigenous Náhuatl tribesman by the name of Juan Diego (1474–1548). One could say that the resolution of Luther's spiritual quest to find a gracious God and the eventual posting of Ninety-five Theses in October 1517 are for Protestants what the baffling occurrences of December 9–12, 1531, are for the Mexican people—a historic, defining moment that reshaped the religious and cultural identity of a whole people. The account of Juan Diego's experiences of December 9–12, 1531, called the *Nican Mopohua* ("It is Narrated"), that I use throughout this essay is a translation into English from the oldest known written copy originally written in Náhuatl. The document was prepared allegedly by Antonio Valeriano (1520–1605) who supposedly received the story by dictation from Juan Diego before Diego's death in 1548.[3]

---

[1] Miguel León-Portilla, *The Broken Spears: The Aztec Account of the Conquest of Mexico* (Boston, MA: Beacon Press, 1962), 137–38.

[2] Don S. Browning, *Generative Man: Psychoanalytic Perspectives* (Philadelphia, PA: Westminster Press, 1973), 146.

[3] *Editor's note*: On the authorship and date of the *Nican Mopohua* as well as contemporary discussion on the historicity of Juan Diego see Lisa Sousa, Stafford Poole, and James Lockhart, eds., *The Story of Guadalupe: Luis Laso de la Vega's Huei tlamahuiçoltica of 1649*, UCLA Latin American Studies, vol. 84 (Stanford, CA: Stanford University Press, 1998); and Eduardo Chávez, *Our Lady of Guadalupe*

The thesis of this psychohistorical study is that Juan Diego served as the *homo religiosus* for his own particular, tumultuous age of human history in Mexico. In particular, I explore how Juan Diego exemplified Erik Erikson's "generative man" for a whole generation of Mexican people as well as their descendants. To make this elaboration more manageable, I have chosen to use Don Browning's interpretation and description of Erikson's seventh stage of the human life cycle: Generativity versus Self-Absorption.

I admit from the outset that I am not interested in the scientific validity of the apparition of Guadalupe herself, which is a persistent topic of agnostic, Protestant, and Roman Catholic polemics. Edwin E. Sylvest expresses well my own attitude regarding the historicity of this event: "I do not challenge the historicity of the events of 9–12 December 1531. . . . The historian, on strictly historical grounds, cannot affirm or deny the nature of what was evidently a miraculously transforming experience for Juan Diego, his uncle, and an entire people."[4] What is crucial here is that something did "happen" that became a transformative experience not only for Juan Diego and his uncle but also for a whole culture, and remains so to this very day. The potent image of Our Lady of Guadalupe lives culturally in the day-to-day existence of all Mexicans. Even for those who may be genuinely skeptical of apparitions such as Guadalupe, this does not invalidate Juan Diego's genius. For if, on the one hand, the apparition of Nuestra Señora de Guadalupe was verifiably real, then we have a miracle on our hands and a unique man who found the courage to share his startling vision. If, on the other hand, the apparition was a conjuring of Diego's own psyche, it then only more pointedly confirms the incredibly perceptive religious imagination, genius, and ego strength of Juan Diego.

Psychohistory

Erik H. Erikson was the forerunner in the development of the "science" of psychohistory, believing it to be a helpful method of enriching biography by using the tools of psychology. Erikson's primary subjects for his psychohistorical biographies were "great" people, considered to be ideological

---

and *Saint Juan Diego: The Historical Evidence*, Celebrating Faith: Explorations in Latino Spirituality and Theology (Lanham, MD: Rowman & Littlefield, 2006).

[4] Edwin E. Sylvest Jr., *Nuestra Señora de Guadalupe: Mother of God, Mother of the Americas* (Dallas, TX: Bridwell Library, Perkins School of Theology, 1992), 42.

innovators for a whole age, such as Freud, Luther, and Gandhi.[5] In each of Erikson's major biographical studies, he chose iconic cultural figures who "succeeded in making the environment adapt to their special demands."[6] I view Juan Diego as standing in this line of ideological innovators, for he straddled the crossroads of ancient Mesoamerican Aztec culture and sixteenth-century Iberian Roman Catholic culture. The cultural synthesis in Juan Diego's account of Our Lady of Guadalupe is nothing short of remarkable. Through it Diego reworked and reimagined his own cultural environment of cruel Spanish oppression, adapting it to his own special psychological demands for identity, security, and meaning. Thus, in Erikson's psychohistorical spirit, I hope to honor this great, indigenous, and American ideological innovator.

For Erikson, the first rule for a psychohistorical study was that "the author should be reasonably honest about his own relation to the bit of history he is studying and should indicate his motive without undue mushiness or apology."[7] Let me, then, without sentimentality, relate my own interests and motives in this cultural project. My first motive arises out of the practical necessities of my ministry. Having personally encountered Guadalupismo (the cult of Guadalupe) among Mexican American people on the U.S.-Mexico border in Laredo, Texas, I discovered Our Lady of Guadalupe's image to be nearly ubiquitous, in living rooms and kitchens, in bars and businesses, on mantels and car windshields, tattooed on bodies, and, of course, in Roman Catholic churches. People adored and devoted themselves to her image and honor. As a Lutheran pastor, I asked myself: What attitude should I take toward this mystical icon, so central to a whole people's cultural and religious identity? Is it possible to affirm the cult while harboring skepticism? In short, how should I deal with Guadalupismo in sermons, table-talks, and counseling? Is Our Lady of Guadalupe a hindrance to or a resource for my own ministry?

A second motive for this study is a sheer delight and interest in Mexican religious, cultural, and intellectual history. In particular, Octavio Paz's *Labyrinth of Solitude*[8] moved me to see deeper psychological issues at work in the culture and struggles of the Mexican people as a whole. I cannot

---

[5] Paul Roazen, *Erik H. Erikson: The Power and Limits of a Vision* (New York: The Free Press, 1976), 73.

[6] Ibid.

[7] Erikson, as quoted in ibid., 74.

[8] Octavio Paz, *The Labyrinth of Solitude: Life and Thought in Mexico*, trans. Lysander Kemp (New York: Grove Press, Inc., 1961).

but interpret Juan Diego's encounter with Guadalupe as standing at the heart of that psychology as well as Mexico's national identity.

A third motive is simply the desire to be more aware of the Mexican demographic and cultural influence on the United States. The United States cannot but be enriched and reformed by this Mexican consciousness and yet it tends to ignore Mexican religious culture, to its diminishment. To understand a people we must understand their central narratives, especially this narrative recounted by Juan Diego. In the words of Richard Rodriguez, the image of Our Lady of Guadalupe "symbolizes the entire coherence of Mexico, body and soul . . . the unofficial, the private flag of Mexicans."[9]

Even with these three benevolent motives in mind, however, I admit that this psychohistory is severely limited. I am a moral theologian by training, not a behavioral or social scientist. Furthermore, this account is admittedly limited because, while Erikson had rich autobiographical material to draw on in Luther, we know almost nothing of Diego's youth or young adulthood. He was presumably a leader in the Náhua tribe and was converted to Christianity by the Franciscans. He burst onto history's stage, not because of a whole life's work of writing and teaching (as with Freud, Luther, and Gandhi), but because of a single event that lasted only a few days in his late adulthood. Nevertheless, I still believe that Juan Diego is worth examining in light of Erikson's developmental life stages because he shares the following with other Eriksonian "greats" (like Luther), because he solved a whole culture's identity crisis with his own individual patienthood.[10] Diego made a "lonely" discovery, which stood at the beginning of a new era.

Erikson's Generative Person

Erikson does not explicitly and systematically set forth in his writings a view of a human individual called the "generative person." Rather, he has written of "generativity" as a stage of adult maturity, which should be considered "the normative center of his thought."[11]

---

[9] Richard Rodriguez, *Days of Obligation: An Argument with My Mexican Father* (New York: Penguin Books, 1993), 16–20.

[10] Erik H. Erikson, *Young Man Luther: A Study in Psychoanalysis and History* (New York: W. W. Norton and Company, Inc., 1958), 67.

[11] Browning, *Generative Man*, 23–24.

Erikson writes that the Oedipal complex, as the concept is generally employed, "is only the infantile and often only the neurotic core of an existential dilemma which (less mythologically) may be called the *generational complex*, for it derives from the fact that man experiences life and death—and past and future—as a matter of the turnover of generations."[12]

If Browning is right in his interpretation of Erikson, there is common ground to be turned and fruitful possibilities to explore in comparing the religious genius to the generative person.

> To generate and maintain a world, but in such a way as to include and yet transcend one's own issue, one's own family, tribe, nation, and race—this is the essence of the generative man, the essence of his ethics and of his religious meaning. Generativity, for Erikson, is a process that stretches from man's most archaic and unconscious biological tendencies to the highest cultural products of his imagination and his reason. . . . Only the word *generativity* conveys that Erikson has in mind not only the results of man's "genitality and genes" but also the results of his "works and ideas," as well as the continuity between the two.[13]

To assist in understanding systematically Erikson's vision of the generative person, and to help apply this generative typology to Juan Diego, I will use Don Browning's helpful fourfold division of the generative person's relationship to self, to society, to time, and to the stranger or "other."[14]

Category 1: The Generative Person in Relation to Self

In order to grasp the fullness and complexity of the human being at the stage of generativity, we must understand Erikson's *epigenetic principle*. Patterned after the embryological model (that the fetus passes through certain critical stages in which there is either continued healthy development or a threat of malformation), Erikson taught that in human development,

> all [that] advances to the higher and later stages of development . . . must include and carry forward, while retaining, a lower level of

[12] Ibid., 147.
[13] Ibid., 145–46.
[14] Ibid., 31.

development. . . . Unless the high in man somehow includes and re-states the low, the high is weak, anemic, and unstable.[15]

Thus, individuals genuinely at the stage of generativity will include and carry forward in themselves the resolutions of conflicts encountered in their previous stages of development. "Full generativity is born out of a series of encounters with *mistrust, shame, guilt, inferiority, identity confusion* and *isolation*. Human strength and maturity, or generativity, come not so much from victory as from synthesis."[16] Maturity in the generative individual has come not because he or she has eliminated or overcome the threats to identity, but rather maturity comes through a successful resolution of those threats, resulting in a new equilibrium. Out of each of these progressive encounters and resolutions at each stage, corresponding virtues are developed in the human being. Thus, keeping both Erikson's stages and Juan Diego's Guadalupe account in mind, I search for clues of Diego's own successful negotiation of each of Erikson's developmental stages and evidence of a resultant virtue in Diego himself. We turn now to Erikson's first stage.

Stage 1. Trust versus Mistrust—Resulting Virtue: Hope

The generative person first possesses a basic *trust* in the world reflected in the virtue of *hope*. Browning says that this trust

> often finds its highest articulation in mature religious and philosophical world images and ideologies. This basic trust . . . grants one both a fund of positive feeling toward one's own inner needs and a faith in the capacity of the outer world to meet these needs. It gives generative man hope and faith that the dark denials, deprivations, and frustrations of life, as real as they are, will not in the end outweigh its satisfactions. This basic trust and hope of generative man makes a certain kind of receptivity, openness, and passivity the fundamental modality of his life.[17]

This basic trust allows a person to continue his or her own existence with some sort of meaning, as well as to possess hope and concern for the health and survival of the generations to come. This basic trust, openness, and

[15] Ibid., 22.
[16] Ibid., 180.
[17] Ibid., 182.

hope the generative man wants to pass along to his own community, but also to his future progeny. As we read in the *Nican Mopohua*:

> Ten years after the conquest of the city of Mexico, arrows and shields were put down; everywhere the inhabitants of the lake and the mountain had surrendered.
>   Thus faith started; it gave its first buds; and it flowered in the knowledge of the One through Whom We live, the true God, Téotl. (3–4)[18]

These opening lines of Diego's account aptly illustrate his fundamental attitude of hope. These words can hardly be appreciated unless one has a sense of the magnitude of the destruction of the city of Mexico.

> The most profound aspect of the conquest was the spiritual devastation of the Aztec people. With the destruction of their pride and their temples, as well as the killing of their people, came a feeling that the gods were angry with them and had deserted them. . . . The people had nothing to live for: as the Spaniards claimed, their gods were dead, it was better to allow them to die, too.[19]

For someone such as Juan Diego to survive and retain a fundamental trust in life, as well as to retain the desire to pass his hope along to succeeding generations after the havoc inflicted by the conquistadors is a testimony to Diego's having passed through this stage successfully! The second paragraph illustrates in picturesque language Diego's fundamental trust: "Thus faith started; it gave its first buds; and it flowered."

Stage 2. Autonomy versus Shame—Resulting Virtue: Will

The generative person possesses some form of *autonomy* and its corresponding virtue of *will*. The generative person "has learned to trust his own powers partially because he has first learned to experience the basic reciprocity between his powers and the powers of the external world."[20]

---

[18] All quotations from the *Nican Mopohua* are from the translation of Virgilio Elizondo, *Guadalupe: Mother of the New Creation* (Maryknoll, NY: Orbis, 1997), 5–22. See also appendix 1 below, pp. 185–200.

[19] Jeanette Rodríguez, *Our Lady of Guadalupe: Faith and Empowerment among Mexican-American Women* (Austin: University of Texas Press, 1994), 13.

[20] Browning, *Generative Man*, 183.

The individual at the stage of generativity realizes that the use of one's own power neither destroys the world's power, nor does that person seek to destroy the supportive nature of the world. Power and autonomy are used in service of the world.

> Generative man has learned to exercise his will and autonomy in such a way that his *holding* is not defiance or stubbornness and his *repudiations* are not violent destructiveness. All this means that generative man can accept the limitations of his will without losing his basic confidence in his right to exercise it. He can also assert limitations on the will of others without undue fear of destroying the other. His capacity to endure reasonable limitations without unmanageable shame or doubt makes it possible for him to submit both himself and his progeny to the prudent restraints of an institutionalized legal order.[21]

The *Nican Mopohua* notes that Juan Diego "heard that he was being called from the summit of the hill. He heard: 'Dignified Juan, dignified Juan Diego.' Then he dared to go to where he was being called. His heart was in no way disturbed" (13–14).

Juan Diego here "dared" to go to the source of the voice. He had an awareness of a power greater than himself with which he knew he had to negotiate. He had to submit to a greater order, a divine order. Yet, he was not disturbed. In his autonomy he could choose to go to the voice, or to run away. Then, in verses 29–55, Diego's autonomy is further tested. Diego could have taken the reverend bishop's challenging unbelief as God's will, accepted it, and kept the apparitional experience to himself for the rest of his days. But without personal shame, Diego trusts his own power, autonomously challenging the bishop without demeaning or undermining the bishop's power. This occurs not once but twice. In verse 59 the powers work against Diego's willingness through threats of severe punishment. But even then Diego confidently and persistently negotiates with the ecclesiastical authorities within the restraints of the institutional order, ultimately to succeed. Juan Diego as a generative individual seeks not to undermine the newly established ecclesiastical matrix of society, but rather seeks to transform it with new patterns of love, care, instruction, and training. Diego thus expresses his own fundamental trust in the need for institutions—a certain sign of the generative person.

[21] Ibid.

Stage 3. Initiative versus Guilt—Resulting Virtue: Purpose

Generative persons have the power to refine their autonomous will into a capacity for *initiative*, resulting in the virtue of *purpose*. Thus, the generative person has the capacity to simultaneously possess a freedom from (stage 2) to involve him- or herself in a freedom for. Purpose and initiative surpass the guilt imposed by the moralism of one's familial, tribal, and national customs. This freedom from tradition's constraining moralism empowers a freedom to be genuinely moral.

> Generative man will possess and respect those vestiges of inherited morality which inculcate the specific patterns of permissions and restraints characteristic of his native culture. But his morality will stop short of moralism—those blind and totalistic rejections of all people and experiences which cannot conform to his own customary ways. . . . Hence, certain aspects of his inherited prohibitions and of his inherited ideals will undergo revision, sometimes born out of considerable agony, with a new synthesis being the result.[22]

Resolution of this stage permits the generative person to pass along morality. While this morality will be different from the one he or she has received, it will still retain a flexible link with the past, offering to future generations a sense of rootedness in their own location and time. Thus, "the progeny of generative man will be liberated for the future and a wider universalism."[23]

Some might label Diego a coward for accepting Spanish rule rather than fighting against it. Yet, his choice was either to see his people become increasingly marginalized or exterminated at the hands of the Spanish, or to discover some new synthesis on which later generations might build a new future. What choice did he have? I believe Diego possessed a universalizing love of generations far off.

At one point, according to the text of the *Nican Mopohua*, Diego faces a conflicting obligation that has the potential to induce crippling guilt. His uncle, Juan Bernardino, fell very ill. Would Diego return in faithfulness to Our Lady ("Tomorrow in the afternoon, when the sun sets, I will return your thought and word to you, what the lord of the priests [has] answer[ed] me" [47]) or would he take care of his familial obligation of mercy? "On the next day, Monday, when Juan Diego was supposed to take

---

[22] Ibid., 186.
[23] Ibid.

something to be the sign by which he was to be believed, he did not return, because when he arrived home, one of his uncles, named Juan Bernardino, had caught the smallpox and was in his last moments" (60). How might Juan resolve this crisis, this conflict of initiative versus guilt? The Virgin then confronts Juan saying, "'My most abandoned son, where are you going? In what direction are you going?' Did he become embarrassed a bit? Was he ashamed? Did he feel like running away? Was he fearful?" (69–70). Humble Juan confesses to her, expresses deep love for his family and explains the dilemma in which he finds himself. Then, in gracious response, the Merciful Guadalupe absolves, honors, and rewards him:

> "Listen and hear well in your heart, my most abandoned son: that which scares you and troubles you is nothing; do not let your countenance and heart be troubled; do not fear that sickness or any other sickness or anxiety. Am I not here, your mother? Are you not under my shadow and my protection? Am I not your source of life? Are you not in the hollow of my mantle where I cross my arms? Who else do you need?" (75–76)

In a wondrous resolution, Juan Diego's guilt and conflict are resolved. The resulting virtue in Juan is a sharpened autonomy and purpose in his task.

> When Juan Diego heard the thought and word of the Lady from Heaven, he was very much consoled; his heart became peaceful. *He begged her to send him immediately to see the lord of the priests* to take him his sign, the thing that would bring about the fulfillment of her desire, so that he would be believed. (78; emphasis added.)

Stage 4. Industry versus Inferiority—Resulting Virtue: Competence

Generative individuals have a sense of competence about their work. The awareness of limitation does not result in absolute feelings of unworthiness. "Because his accumulated sense of limitation does not completely cripple his deeper initiatives and spontaneities, generative man has considerable capacity for *play*." For Erikson, meaningful play is the human being's most significant therapy on the road to wholeness. Whether child or adult plays, both use it "to regain a sense of ego integration, wholeness, and mastery; through play, both the child and adult attempt to convert the more capricious and obstinate aspects of life into something at least acceptable and manageable if not actively willed." The generative adult, thus, is one who can fill up his or her work with play—one who can "stand back from the reality situation of his work long enough to fantasize a more human way of coping with its confinements, tensions, and dichotomies."[24] In verses 79–84 we see a Juan Diego who, though ordered to go to "work" at the top of the hill, could also play. He could "stop to smell the roses" and pick them. The reality of the terrain and climate in central Mexico in December is not pleasant. Frosted rocks, thorns, cacti, prickly pear, and mesquite trees all inhabited the cold winter's abode (83–84). Yet, in this environment, Juan has time to seek, find, and pick the myriad of softly fragrant flowers. In verse 89, Juan arrives in Mexico City *happily*. Erikson's great cultural synthesizers (namely, Luther, Freud, and Gandhi) were "players," particularly in going about their work.

> All great historical syntheses are as much play as they are work. They are work because they are indeed attentive to the real contradictions and tensions that most people of a given historical period both sense and suffer. They are a result of play because the creative genius does not simply conform to, adjust to, and accommodate to these tensions. Instead, he bends and reshapes these tensions until they submit to a new synthesis, which not only enlivens and activates him but also enlivens and activates a whole people and an entire area.[25]

The synthesis that Juan Diego eventually was to accomplish establishes that he was this sort of creative genius. For Juan almost single-handedly restores the honor of the Náhuatl woman, the faith of the Náhuatl man, and restores dignity and playfulness to the lives of a people who were dead in the face of the devastating Spanish conquest. There is no longer any need for the conquered to feel inferior. Yet, even in the devastation, there is time to play and adapt. The humble Juan Diego was not worthy, but he was the chosen vessel through whom the Mesoamerican people could raise their heads in pride in a new cultural circumstance.

> The real turning point in conversion of the Aztecs to Christianity came with the miraculous appearance of the Indian Virgin of Guadalupe in 1531. . . . Only six years after the apparition . . . nine million Aztec people had been baptized into the Christian faith. . . . Guadalupan

---

[24] Ibid., 188–89.
[25] Ibid., 189.

Catholicism spread rapidly in central Mexico and became the focal point of Aztec culture.[26]

Stage 5. *Identity versus Role Confusion—Resulting Virtue: Fidelity*

It is in this period that, "from the point of the individual, ideology comes to meet the youthful striving for fidelity, confirming identities; but from society's point of view, it is the young who rejuvenate its institutions."[27] Generative individuals have learned to live with a sense of changing identity and have wrestled with and overcome their identity confusions in their encounter with a variety of ideologies. Out of a myriad of potential identities, the generative person's ego has formed a unity of them all into a unique identity.

> For Erikson the ego guards the person's indivisibility, and everything that underlies an ego's strength adds to its identity. . . . Identity refers not only to a conscious sense of individual uniqueness, but also to what Erikson stresses as the unconscious striving for continuity and sameness of experience.[28]

Thus, the generative person possesses a workable identity and

> can present himself to succeeding generations as a tangible identity from whom they can learn and against whom they can test their own emerging self-definitions. He can also present himself as one who can be trusted, just as he can help guide others to their own discovery of that which is worthy of their commitment and loyalty.[29]

That Juan Diego actually enables a lost people to recover its identity and commit to a future may not be fully appreciated. In the conquest, the Spanish humiliated the indigenous peoples. The former glory of Diego's people had been dimmed, if not extinguished. The despair and hopelessness that Juan Diego's people had experienced was fresh in their memories. Yet, even then, he attempts to convince them to believe his account of Our Lady of Guadalupe as the new identity-bestower of a once and future

---

[26] J. Rodríguez, *Our Lady of Guadalupe*, 45.

[27] Roazen, *Erik H. Erikson*, 115.

[28] Ibid., 24.

[29] Browning, *Generative Man*, 193.

people. Juan Diego presents himself (and the Virgin) as one who could be trusted and who could guide others in their search for a meaningful identity. In the apparition, Diego discovers not only his own identity but also an identity type for succeeding generations. He bears the name of a prophet, and he forth-tells for God.

> Juan Diego represents all the poor who lived before, who were alive at the time, and who were to live afterward, and not simply the historical Juan Diego. . . . Juan Diego was one of the first converts to Christianity in Mexico. His name before the coming of the Spaniards was Cuauhtla-toaxin, *he who speaks like an eagle*, that is, he who explains the wisdom of . . . God (the sun). The eagle is a symbol of the sun, which is in turn a symbol for God.[30]

Stage 6. Intimacy versus Isolation—Resulting Virtue: Love

The generative person has also worked through the young adult struggle between the tensions of intimacy and isolation, with the resulting virtue of *love* emerging. Sexual attraction and spouse selection particularly characterize this stage. The generative individual has overcome the fear that one's own fragile identity might be destroyed when opening up to share oneself or one's aspirations with another person. Generative individuals genuinely and intimately love others without the sense that they have lost themselves.

> By intimacy, then Erikson means the capacity for two people to develop a shared commitment without the loss of a sense of individual identity. Hence, intimacy requires a prior sense of identity strong enough to risk the development of a shared commitment without fear of self-loss in the process.[31]

Furthermore, intimacy and love complement one another. Intimacy reflects the capacity to receive; love reflects the capacity to give. While this love involves more than mere bodily pleasure, it is a love that is marked by the "capacity of giving and receiving complex patterns of bodily pleasure."[32]

[30] J. Rodríguez, *Our Lady of Guadalupe*, 52.
[31] Browning, *Generative Man*, 194–95.
[32] Ibid., 195.

Two aspects of Juan Diego's dictated story resonate with this stage. Diego's generativity is reflected, first, in his detailed description of the profound intimacy that existed between himself and Guadalupe. Bodily pleasure, although not erotic, does play a part in the relationship between Diego and Our Lady. For example, as Juan walks by he hears music. "For the Nahuatl, music was one-half of their dual expression of truth, beauty, philosophy, and divinity: flower and song together . . . manifested the presence of the Divine."[33] Diego utilizes the fullness of his bodily senses in his encounter with Guadalupe. Indeed, this is demonstrative of the fullness of their love for each other. Furthermore, the language used between Juan Diego and Guadalupe clearly reflects profound mutual intimacy and deeply shared love. Diego refers

> to Our Lady of Guadalupe as "my dear child" (two times), "my lady" or "dear lady" (five times), "lady and mistress" (one time), "heavenly lady" . . . (two times), "Holy Mary" (one time), and "precious Mother of God" (one time). In addition, given her physical appearance, Juan Diego most likely perceived Our Lady of Guadalupe as a member of his race. . . . Both Our Lady of Guadalupe and Juan Diego address each other in familial terms, right from the beginning. She addresses him as "Juanito," "Juan Dieguito," "the smallest of my children," and he addresses her as "my dear child" and "my daughter."[34]

Diego's generativity is also illustrated by his ability to define himself as distinct from the powerful love of Our Lady. There are always two individuals, intimately related, yet nevertheless distinct. Throughout the story, one never senses that their relationship fuses. Reciprocity of commitment—a mutual giving and receiving of love—remains consistent.

Stage 7: Generativity versus Self-absorption—Resulting Virtue: Care

Intimacy and love are never complete without moving beyond into a larger community with larger commitments. "This larger commitment is summarized by the capacity for *generativity* and by the virtue of *care* which are, finally, the central characteristics of generative man and the final culmination of the meaning of love in the wider and grander sense of

---

[33] J. Rodríguez, *Our Lady of Guadalupe*, 38.
[34] Ibid., 52.

the word."[35] Because the remainder of the essay elaborates this particular virtue, I will not examine this stage in any further detail here. Suffice to say that Juan Diego is missionally focused; he concerns himself most with the broader indigenous community that surrounds him. While deeply absorbed in the events themselves, he is not self-absorbed. Rather, noble concerns about family, church, and Guadalupe weigh heavy on his mind with their corresponding and conflicting responsibilities. Diego is no loner. Our Lady will not be privatized. Rather, she will be made public and universal. In fact, the account ends with this climatically universalizing close:

> And the lord bishop transferred to the major church the precious image of the Queen and Lady from Heaven; he took her from the oratory of his palace so that all might see and venerate her precious image.
>
> The entire city was deeply moved; they came to see and admire her precious image as something divine; they came to pray to her. They admired very much how she had appeared as a divine marvel, because absolutely no one on earth had painted her precious image. (122–24)

Category 2: The Generative Person in Relation to One's Society

Browning views Erikson's generative individual relating to society in two ways. Seeing human relationships as a mutual reciprocity of giving and receiving, the generative individual, first, has a generative politics of establishing, maintaining, and ritualizing the institutional fabric of society (creative ritualization). Second, the generative individual integrates religion, synthesizing its ideological and universal elements (religious integration).

Creative Ritualization

"Creative ritualization . . . sums up generative man's attitude toward his social world." The generative person is a creative ritualist, creative insofar as he is open to development and improvement, but a ritualist insofar as he respects the necessity of tradition. The generative person does not slavishly innovate or unthinkingly follow tradition. "Neither innovation nor tradition is his god. Yet he has an appreciation for the necessities of both." The generative person does not flee from the tasks and challenges

[35] Browning, *Generative Man*, 195.

of the contemporary. "For generative man, all human activities are to be judged from the perspective of what they contribute to the generative task itself, i.e., the establishment and maintenance of succeeding generations."[36] No human activity is an end in itself, but its purpose is ultimately to be expressive of and supportive of the future. Unlike Freud, who viewed society as a "foreign burden" on the ego, Erikson viewed society as an entity that helped limit and steer an individual's choices, confirming people in "the right life plan."[37] This is to say that the generative person is concerned with and trusts human institutions, large and small, because he or she sees them as essential to human identity, both individually and communally. For Erikson, the ego can only develop and remain strong as it interacts with cultural institutions. The generative individual creates and sustains institutions, gives birth to and cares for institutions, all while confining care and responsibility to healthy limits. For Erikson, ritualization protects individuality and produces genuine community because ritual is the agreed upon interplay between people at meaningful times and places. "Without a ritual fabric to life, community becomes conformity and individuality becomes normless privatism and destructive egoism."[38] Even the generative person has a need to follow rituals and to be a ritualist. "Without them [the virtues and strengths of youth], institutions wilt; but without the spirit of institutions pervading the patterns of care, love, instruction and training, no virtue could emerge from the sequence of generations."[39] Institutions ensure the passage of habits of care from one generation to the next, and so the generative individual strongly desires to establish and maintain the institutional fabric of society.

Religious Integration

The second characteristic of the generative person's relation to society is by means of the integration of religion, in which one tries to synthesize religion's ideological and universal elements. The regenerative person is religious and participates in a religion that offers people "a commanding world image and a vigorous ritual enactment which sums up, yet somehow

---

[36] Ibid., 23.

[37] Roazen, *Erik H. Erikson*, 34.

[38] Browning, *Generative Man*, 202.

[39] Erik Erikson, *Insight and Responsibility: Lectures on the Ethical Implications of Psychoanalytical Insight* (New York: W. W. Norton and Company, 1972), 155–56.

renews and enriches, the rituals of everyday life, both those of his children and of himself, and those of his own childhood."[40] The particularist ideological and universal elements of Our Lady of Guadalupe are manifest to Diego. Guadalupe affirms both Diego's historical beliefs concerning Tonantzin in the specificity of the Hill of Tepeyac and the rituals that surrounded the Náhuatl prior to the conquest. This Guadalupe is a sign for Juan Diego, for the Náhuatl, and for Mexico. At the same time, Our Lady of the indigenous also affirms her cosmic and universal role as mother of all nations, a religious universality that Diego fully affirms. "I am your merciful mother [particularity] and the mother of all the nations [universality] that live on this earth who would love me" (24–25).

Category 3: The Generative Person in Relation to Time

"Generative man has a discernible experience of time. The center of his time perspective is in the present, but it is a present that grows out of the past and actively leans toward the future."[41] Freed from the past, the generative man is free to use the past as a resource to define the present and guide the future.

The generative individual identifies with the past in two ways. First, the individual selectively forgets, falsifies, or idealizes portions of the past to fit the present. This, thereby, reshapes the past as a resource to take control of the present. Second, "the past provides a ground of renewal, an original beginning, which becomes a present source of strength for the ego." Thus, there is a sort of active passivity regarding the past and past experiences. There is a return to a "ground of trust," a higher matrix in the interest of recovering one's passivity. According to Erikson, Luther regained a passivity as Scripture served as that "ground of trust" or "motherly mode."[42] Juan Diego as a generative individual repeatedly finds comfort in passively receiving Guadalupe's ministry of mercy, redemption, encouragement, and protection. And in his reception and passivity, he regained power to become active. He thus exhibits an "active passivity."

Furthermore, regenerative individuals are active in orienting themselves for the future. In this stance, there is hope, a reaffirmation of the virtue of trust gained in the first stage of the life cycle. "One's hope for the future

---

[40] Browning, *Generative Man*, 205.
[41] Ibid., 197.
[42] Ibid., 198.

evolves out of a past where one has learned that the 'things' and 'people' of the world will reciprocate 'one's physical and emotional needs in expectable ways.'"[43]

In Diego's account, the time and dates of the apparitions are clear. The first apparition (7–28) is early in the morning (Spanish: *muy de madrugada*) on Saturday, December 9, 1531. Diego's generativity is clearly illustrated in the subtle use of time in the text. For if December 9 would represent the present time, "for the indigenous peoples, *muy de madrugada* . . . refers not only to daybreak, but to the beginning of all time."[44] Our Lady appears just as darkness gives way to light. The Virgin stands not only as the mother of all spiritual life, but as the mother who stands at the cosmic beginning of the world, giving life. Thus, Juan Diego, as religious genius and generative man, stands at the intersection of the primordial past, the present, and the future. Diego is the means by which his whole culture might live in this present, with hope toward the future, while incorporating and transforming the past.

Category 4: The Generative Person in Relation to the Other (the Stranger)

The final category is that of the generative person's relationship to the other—the stranger of another culture who, upon an encounter, must be incorporated into one's worldview in some way. In dialogical relationship with the other, the generative person respects and learns from the particularity of the other while aspiring for a transcendent and all-encompassing universal identity.

The generative person is both particular and universal. The generative person is first, a particularist. That is to say, the generative person is defined by the particularities of one's birth, ethnicity, class, geography, and history with a unique outlook on life that has been shaped by one's particular community and master narrative. At the same time, the generative person is also a universalist. That is to say, the generative person is aware that he or she has something in common with all human beings and their children no matter what their particularities are. This universalism is not "out there" abstracted into universal moral norms such as love, peace, and justice. Rather, these virtues can only be realized and expressed in particular and

---

[43] Ibid.

[44] J. Rodríguez, *Our Lady of Guadalupe*, 38.

individual human histories. The generative individual realizes that he or she cannot universalize all aspects of one's own perceived reality. There must be plurality. The generative individual thus is not threatened by the other, but can allow the other to be other. The generative person takes the stranger, and the stranger's world, seriously and attempts to see the universal elements in that stranger's world.

> Because of his twofold commitment to the pseudospecies of which he is immediately a part as well as to the larger species of which he is genuinely a part, [the generative man] refuses to regard the specializations of others as mere chaos, evil, or threat. In the same vein, he is able to accept his own inherited specializations without undue remorse or pride. . . . At all points, then, generative man finds in the "other" a particularity that contains a truth which is often complementary to his own partial truth.[45]

The search for a more inclusive identity is the search of the generative man at a cultural level.

Juan Diego's Guadalupe is an astounding synthesis of those elements, which were universal to both the Spanish and the indigenous people of central Mexico. In Spanish Roman Catholicism Juan Diego finds partial truths, which are complementary to his own indigenous partial truths. Between the foreign conquistadors and the indigenous Náhuatl, Diego stands at the intersection of the two worlds that are "other" to each other. Diego seeks to synthesize their universal elements while affirming their distinctive elements. Through Diego, two worldviews are introduced and made to fit each other—for the sake of the subsequent cultural resynthesis, survival, cultural identity, growth, and generational succession. Some might argue that Diego betrayed his Náhuatl community and heritage; others might argue that he saved it from extinction. Yet, are not generative people, particularly those of the *homo religiosus*, often viewed as betrayers of their own worlds for the sake of a greater vision?

Erikson's own studies of Native American tribes taught him that not every group of people has the adaptive ability to confront major social change in a positive way. In fact, Erikson expressed concern that radical social and historical alterations pose "the threat of a traumatic loss of ego identity."[46] The resources on which Juan Diego drew must have been re-

---

[45] Browning, *Generative Man*, 208–11.
[46] Roazen, *Erik H. Erikson*, 43.

markable, as his vision forged a whole new culture, typically called *mestizo* (mixed) in Mexico. The Mexican people have proudly viewed themselves as a positive cultural and biological synthesis (Spanish: *mestizaje*) of Meso-american indigenous peoples and Spanish Europeans. Juan Diego through Our Lady of Guadalupe helped to forge that particular self-conception with which nearly all Mexicans identify themselves.

> In short, native peoples who had lost their "mother" [*Tonantzin*] in the destruction of their culture, found another in that of the conquer-ors. . . . Since the traditional symbols and rituals related to *Tonantzin* were suppressed, it was natural that people needing the succor of a powerful mother would have responded when they found one in Chris-tian piety. Reluctant to preach devotion to the Christian Mother of God, the friars' own pious practices inadvertently spoke even more powerfully and directly to the native peoples.[47]

Consider the following amazing and complementary parallels, outlined by Jeannette Rodríguez, in Diego's account and Guadalupe's image, which demonstrate Diego's universalizing tendency in an effort to synthesize two worldviews.

> *The Account*. The Náhuatl version of the account is full of parallel im-agery using the symbolic imagery of the Náhua.

- Guadalupe identifies herself with the "true God for whom one lives." This is also one of the names of the Náhuatl gods.

- Náhuatl numerology considers four to be symbolic of cosmic totality.

- Juan Diego in the text asks four questions.

- Juan Diego looks to the east when he hears music and the voice. The Náhuatl believed that life came from the east.

- The hill upon which the Christian Mother of God appears is the ancient site of the Náhuatl mother goddess, *Tonantzin*.

- The text says that Our Lady of Guadalupe is standing up, a symbol of humility, restoring dignity to the conquered. Aztec and Span-ish nobility normally received people sitting down, symbolizing domination over others.

---

[47] Sylvest, *Nuestra Señora de Guadalupe*, 14.

- Our Lady is described as being covered with the radiance of the sun. For the Náhuatl the sun is symbolic of God.

- Guadalupe identifies herself with five names. These five names were known to be names of Náhuatl gods.

The Image. The mysterious image on Juan Diego's *tilma* also impacted the indigenous peoples of the area. Consider these parallels:

- The face held great importance for the indigenous people because they felt they could come to know the inner person. Guadalupe's image has a subtle smile of compassion. She also had a dark face, indicating her identification with the indigenous.

- The eyes of Our Lady look humbly downward, yet she was personal.

- Infrared photos have detected in Guadalupe's eyes an image of a bust believed to be Juan Diego. Her eyes, thus, look upon human beings . . . demonstrating her compassion for humanity.

- Our Lady of Guadalupe's hands are not in the Western prayer position, but in an indigenous manner of offering.

- The fingers on her hands are short, indicating that they are hands of an indigenous woman.

- The objects in the picture, such as stars, gold, rays of the sun, moon, and angel are all related to some aspect of Aztec divinity.[48]

Conclusion

Homo religiosus . . . makes his own patienthood and cure into a universal drama which activates and gives meaning to the people of his day. Part of the cure is likely to be a playful new ideological synthesis which combines both old and new religious, political, humanitarian, and economic patterns with present states of knowledge. Hence, the religious man is a cultural worker who creates, out of the conflicts of his time, a new identity for his age.[49]

Luther wrote, "A theologian is born by living, nay dying and being damned, not by thinking, reading or speculating." The peasant Juan Diego

[48] J. Rodríguez, *Our Lady of Guadalupe*, 22ff.
[49] Browning, *Generative Man*, 149.

spent little of his time engaged in formal theological reflection, reading, or speculating. Rather, trusting his encounter with Guadalupe, he risked his reputation among his indigenous kin and his reputation with the Spanish Roman Catholic authorities. As Luther performed his transformative spiritual task in Europe, I believe Juan Diego was early Mexico's *homo religiosus* who performed his epic task in his own generative stage. Juan Diego created a new identity for his age and culture in Mexico. He did this not by rejection of his indigenous past. On the contrary, as a generative man, Diego embraced a new future that uniquely synthesized his Náhuatl past and his Spanish Roman Catholic future. Guadalupe's revelation to Diego would be an act of gracious revelation. Like a Gandhi or a Luther, Juan Diego was a religious genius in his own right. As Erikson notes, "In some periods of his history, and in some phases of his life cycle, man needs . . . a new ideological orientation as surely and as sorely as he must have air and food."[50] Juan Diego knew well his ancient religion. Equally well did he understand the new state of knowledge, power, spirituality, and culture under the conquest of the Spanish. Juan Diego, with his vision of Our Lady of Guadalupe, forged a new and noble identity for the people of his age who would be called "Mexican."

Extending an Imaginative Welcome

I return now to the guideline that Erikson himself suggested at the outset, namely, that "without undue mushiness or apology" an author honestly indicate the motive behind his or her historical exposition. These were my questions: What attitude should I take toward this mystical icon, so central to a whole culture's cultural and religious identity? Is it possible to affirm the cult while harboring skepticism? How should I deal with Guadalupismo in sermons, table-talks, and counseling? Is Our Lady of Guadalupe a hindrance or resource in my own ministry?

An idea expressed by C. S. Lewis reflects my own present stance toward Guadalupe: "A man who disbelieved the Christian story as fact but continually fed on it as myth would, perhaps, be more spiritually alive than one who assented and did not think much about it. . . . We must not, in false spirituality, withhold our imaginative welcome."[51] I was taught at an

---

[50] Erikson, *Young Man Luther*, 22.

[51] C. S. Lewis, "Myth Became Fact," in *God in the Dock: Essays on Theology and Ethics*, ed. Walter Hooper (Grand Rapids, MI: Eerdmans, 1970), 67.

early age that a myth is not false. Or, even more precisely, "What flows into you from the myth is not truth but reality (truth is always *about* something, but reality is that *about which* truth is)."[52] I refuse to choose whether the Guadalupe event "really" happened. That would only diminish my own imaginative welcome. But, reality most certainly flows into me from Juan Diego's account. Through Guadalupe, I continue to welcome her, Juan Diego, and the embrace of Mexican American people into my spiritual life. In fact, Guadalupe's own welcoming invitation provokes and inspires my own openness and hospitality to the "other." What continues to draw me to Guadalupe is the solidarity she permits me to have with the biblical world of Mary, the Mother of Jesus, and with all people of Mexican heritage with whom I live and labor.

Our Lady of Guadalupe brings together worlds I have spent a lifetime trying to reconcile and bridge. For example, Guadalupe has helped me as a Lutheran more deeply trust other cultures through social and historical solidarity. The image of Guadalupe hanging on my office wall provokes regular conversation and dialogue among colleagues, students, parishioners, and staff that I serve. Some know my office as a safe place. Guadalupe permits me as pastor and theologian to participate in the Mexican American community as an equal, not simply as a stranger. Pastorally, Our Lady empowers and renews, functioning as a proclaimer of Good News, a type of pure Gospel (as opposed to "law" in a Lutheran vernacular). Our Lady of Guadalupe offers a way to establish a deeper ecumenism, especially with my Roman Catholic brothers and sisters. Guadalupe offers me an opportunity to appreciate the feminine aspects of the divine and the human. And, ethically, Guadalupe inspires me as she plays the role of comforter, helper, liberator, servant, and hope of the impoverished and oppressed.

My own theology has been deeply grounded in incarnational manifestations of God's grace in water, table, cross. It has always seemed incumbent in ministry to take a people's history seriously, and to find connections between the narratives of Scripture and a people's cultural metanarratives and myths. Making the Gospel intelligible in the people's own symbols and metaphors is of first priority, and the missionary will use those accounts and images in ways that ultimately permit transformation and human fulfillment. Paul's efforts at the Areopagus in Athens to explain the identity of the liberating "unknown God" to his hearers parallels my

---

[52] Ibid., 66.

own embrace of Guadalupe. Her narratives are powerful insofar as they establish solidarity with a people and point to an opportunity to share the goodness of a universal God who created heaven and earth. In a Lutheran hermeneutic, Guadalupe clearly functions culturally as a manifestation of "Gospel," of what God does to rescue humans: Our Lady is *Theotokos* who promises to "give all life, compassion, help, and protection." She is "merciful mother." She listens to lamentations and promises a remedy to all "miseries, afflictions and sorrows." From Luther I have learned to welcome and listen to the Scriptures. In a similar way, from Juan Diego, I have learned to welcome and feed upon the apparition of Guadalupe as a powerful and most incredible sign, a theological narrative that speaks a deep truth of affirming welcome for the poor, the outcast, the struggling, the dying, and all of us who reside in the Americas. Guadalupe's inclusive nature and message of welcome of all reflect her universality. Historically, Guadalupe may have come chronologically after the incarnation of Christ in the Virgin's womb, but mythologically, Guadalupe stands both before and after Mary. Lewis argues that myths such as these "ought to be there" in the world, in all cultures.[53] They permit us to recognize both reality and God's active work in the world. It takes the religious genius of a Juan Diego to see these deep accounts and synthesize them, share them, and use them for a type of personal, communal, and ultimately universal transformation. No one should be surprised by a religious genius such as Diego who can take this encounter for what it is—an opportunity to affirm both the past and the future, the rich and the poor, the old world and the new, the indigenous and the European.

[53] Ibid., 67.

5

Beyond Word and Sacrament: A Reformed Protestant Engagement of Guadalupan Devotion

Rubén Rosario Rodríguez

 U.S. Latino/a theology, while recognizing its indebtedness to Latin American liberation theology, has struggled to create its own distinct identity as a North American theological movement. Some Latino/a theologians maintain that at this point in history, U.S. Latino/a theology needs to move beyond the narrow walls of confessional theology in order to strive for a "wider sense of human solidarity across racial, cultural, and ideological lines."[1] In this search for political solidarity, Latino/a theologians have downplayed significant doctrinal differences between Protestants and Catholics for the sake of creating a unified movement. While U.S. Hispanic-Latino theology defines itself as an intentionally ecumenical movement, it is important to engage the beliefs and practices of particular communities of faith. Accordingly, when confronted by certain essentialist claims about ethnicity and theological identity from U.S. Latino/a theologians, it is important to question such claims or risk undermining the intellectual

---

[1] Benjamin Valentin, "Nuevos Odres para el Vino: A Critical Contribution to Latino/a Theological Construction," in *Journal of Hispanic/Latino Theology* 5, no. 4 (May 1998): 44.

credibility of the movement. For example, Virgil Elizondo projects a particularly Mexican American and Roman Catholic popular religiosity as normative for *all* Latino/a Christians when he writes, "I do not want to say that every Hispanic has to remain a member of the Roman Catholic Church in order to be a Hispanic, but I am saying that when a Hispanic ceases to be catholic (to participate in the religious-cultural expressions of our people), he or she ceases to be a Hispanic."[2] He thereby overlooks the many Hispanic Protestants who consider some aspects of popular Catholicism—especially the apparition of (and subsequent devotion to) Our Lady of Guadalupe—as superstitious and therefore antithetical to the Gospel of Jesus Christ.

In the spirit of the thirty-year history of cooperation across confessional boundaries, I am arguing that for U.S. Hispanic-Latino theology to mature as an emergent movement in North American theology, it must engage in critical self-analysis. This essay, Protestant in its perspective, develops a constructive approach for crossing the borders between Protestant and Catholic Latino/as by exploring the doctrinal significance of Guadalupan devotion. Specifically, I evaluate and critique Virgil Elizondo's contribution to the Christian doctrine of creation in *Guadalupe: Mother of the New Creation* (1997), in such a way that Reformed/Calvinist Protestants might come to appreciate the strong christological focus and profound doctrinal insights of Elizondo's interpretation of the Guadalupe narrative.

Utilizing Guadalupe as a case study for the encounter between Christ and culture, this article (1) defends Elizondo's interpretation of the Guadalupe myth as a legitimate manifestation of Guadalupan devotion in light of Stafford Poole's historical critique, (2) traces the Reformed Protestant discomfort with and objections to Guadalupan devotion to iconoclastic tendencies among sixteenth-century Protestant Reformers and the strict Christocentric understanding of divine revelation in the theology of John Calvin, (3) recovers resources within the Reformed theological heritage that allow Protestants to approach Guadalupe as a vehicle of divine self-communication (that is, a new cultural manifestation of the Gospel), (4) argues that Elizondo's interpretation of the Guadalupan tradition is compatible with a Reformed Protestant Christocentric theology, and (5) suggests constructive directions in which a Reformed doctrine of creation can creatively incorporate Elizondo's interpretation of Guadalupe.

[2] Virgilio Elizondo, foreword to Justo L. González, *Mañana: Christian Theology from a Hispanic Perspective* (Nashville, TN: Abingdon, 1990), 17.

Recognizing the power of images to communicate sacred truth as well as foster ideological transformation, I employ Guadalupe in order to identify potentially harmful tendencies in Reformed doctrine, while preserving the uniqueness and primacy of the Christ event for the Christian faith.

Why Guadalupe?

Further discussion is warranted among U.S. Latino/a theologians concerning the role of popular Catholicism, and in particular Guadalupan devotion, in the formation and preservation of U.S. Latino/a culture. Given the diversity of national origins among U.S. Latino/a theologians, the strong focus in the theological literature on Guadalupe is surprising, especially since the image of the blessed Virgin has manifested itself in similar ways in other Latino/a cultural contexts, such as Our Lady of Charity in Cuba and the Virgin of Montserrat in Puerto Rico.[3] Virgil Elizondo, considered by many to be the progenitor of U.S. Hispanic-Latino theology, often treats Guadalupe as *the* generative event for *mestizo*[4] identity and links the 1531 apparition of Our Lady of Guadalupe to the birth of Hispanic Christianity as "the beginning of a new creation, the mother of a new humanity, and the manifestation of the femininity of God—a figure offering unlimited possibilities for creative and liberating reflection."[5] For, unlike other Latin American Marian cults, Guadalupe is a wholly indigenous tradition in which the Virgin appeared in the traditional clothing of the region and her image resembled an Indian or *mestiza*. In order to understand Elizondo's claims about Guadalupe's centrality for Hispanic Christianity—an event he describes as "the indigenous account of the real

---

[3] See Miguel H. Díaz, "Dime con quién andas y te dire quién eres: We Walk with Our Lady of Charity," in *From the Heart of Our People: Latino/a Explorations in Catholic Systematic Theology*, ed. Orlando O. Espín and Miguel H. Díaz (Maryknoll, NY: Orbis, 1999), 153–71.

[4] The terms *mestizo* and *mestizaje* refer to the process of cultural and racial mixing of Spanish and Amerindian peoples. Originally a denigrating label, *mestizaje* has been transformed and appropriated by Latino/as as a term of self-identity and cultural pride. The term *criollo* refers to the children of Spaniards born in America.

[5] Virgilio Elizondo, *Guadalupe: Mother of the New Creation* (Maryknoll, NY: Orbis, 1997), xi.

new beginnings of the Americas"[6]—it is important to first understand Elizondo's methodological commitment to the study of popular religion as a privileged means of evangelization.

Elizondo's interest in popular religion arose in the context of his pastoral work as a priest and educator in San Antonio, Texas, where he learned to value and respect popular forms of Catholicism. From his earliest works to the present, Elizondo, while recognizing its limitations, has viewed popular religion as a privileged source for theology; he does not seek to supplant official doctrine but is a tireless defender of the people's faith as authentically Catholic. Elizondo argues for the methodological incorporation of popular religion into the church's theological reflection because it is both a legitimate way of being Catholic (arguably the way in which the majority of the world's Catholics express their faith) and a way in which the official tradition may be positively transformed.[7] In other words, popular practices that do not originate in official church teaching and that thrive without the presence of clergy—often arising out of a communal desire to "supplement" or even "correct" official teaching—are in fact vessels through which God speaks to the church and the world. Thus, popular religion interprets and transforms received doctrine while also giving voice to religious experiences not yet articulated in doctrine.[8]

---

[6] Ibid., xviii.

[7] While Elizondo speaks primarily about popular Catholicism, his insights are applicable to any form of Christianity that thrives in popular belief and practice though not always recognized by official doctrine. A proper understanding of tradition cannot ignore the role of popular beliefs and practices in the formation of official doctrine, as evidenced by the trinitarian and christological controversies of the early church. See J. N. D. Kelly, *Early Christian Doctrines*, 5th rev. ed. (New York: Harper & Row, 1978); Aloys Grillmeier, *Christ in Christian Tradition*, trans. John Bowden, 2nd ed. (Atlanta, GA: John Knox Press, 1975); and Jaroslav Pelikan, *The Emergence of the Catholic Tradition (100–600)*, vol. 1 of *The Christian Tradition* (Chicago, IL: University of Chicago Press, 1971).

[8] This synopsis of how Virgilio Elizondo understands and employs popular religion is gleaned from various works, especially *Galilean Journey: The Mexican-American Promise* (Maryknoll, NY: Orbis, 1984); *Religious Practices of the Mexican American and Catechesis* (San Antonio, TX: Mexican American Cultural Center Press, 1974); *Christianity and Culture: An Introduction to Pastoral Theology and Ministry for the Bicultural Community* (Huntington, IN: Our Sunday Visitor, 1975); and his doctoral dissertation, published in English as *Mestizaje: The Dialectic of Cultural Birth and the Gospel* (San Antonio, TX: Mexican American Cultural Center Press, 1978).

Elizondo not only views popular religion as the primary means of Christian evangelization but also understands popular Catholicism as a key element for preserving a distinctly Latino/a cultural identity—whether one is Catholic, mainline Protestant, Pentecostal, agnostic, or atheist—due to Catholicism's influence in the historical and cultural development of Latin America and Latino/a communities in the United States. It is with this understanding of the "Catholic" cultural context of Latino/a experience that I now consider Elizondo's theological reflections on Our Lady of Guadalupe. According to Elizondo, interpreting the Guadalupe event "through the Mariological practices and theologies of the West will lead to misunderstanding and error. Such a process would impose a meaning that would not correspond to the true meaning it has for the people."[9] Instead, Elizondo demonstrates great pastoral sensitivity to both the community's lived faith and the broader Christian tradition by articulating a prophetic theology grounded in the popular beliefs and practices of Guadalupanos and Guadalupanas. Thus, *Guadalupe: Mother of the New Creation* is not just Elizondo's account of the theophany of the Virgin of Guadalupe at Tepeyac but also an exploration of its theological significance for contemporary ecumenical Christianity.

The importance of the Guadalupe event for *all* Latino/as is linked to the violent conquest of the Americas that resulted in the racial, ethnic, and cultural *mestizaje* of its people. Her symbolic power is attributed to (1) the appearance of the Virgin to a lowly Indian or *mestizo* laborer rather than a Spanish ruler or church official, (2) the Virgin's physical appearance resembling an Indian or a *mestiza*,[10] and (3) the location of her apparition on Mount Tepeyac, the ancient site of Tonantzin worship, the mother goddess of the Aztecs. Ultimately for Elizondo, the Guadalupe

---

[9] Virgilio Elizondo, "Mary and the Poor: A Model of Evangelizing Ecumenism," in *Mary in the Churches*, ed. Hans Küng and Jürgen Moltmann (New York: Seabury Press, 1983), 59.

[10] In Elizondo's works there remains an ambiguity as to whether Guadalupe is *mestiza* or an indigenous woman. The Guadalupe tradition has long identified Guadalupe and Juan Diego as indigenous persons, yet in Elizondo's various writings he sometimes refers to Guadalupe as Indian and at other times as *mestiza*. Of greater importance for understanding Elizondo is that Juan Diego, while biologically an Indian, nonetheless embodies cultural *mestizaje*. Accordingly, throughout this essay I refer to both Guadalupe and Juan Diego as *mestizos* insofar as they represent for Elizondo the genesis of a new humanity that transforms the history of conquest into salvation history.

event marks the cultural, biological, and religious union of the conqueror and the conquered, a *mestizaje* that symbolizes the birth of a new humanity. Therein lies the importance of the Guadalupe event as culturally and theologically significant for the people of Mexico, Mexican Americans, and many other Latino/a Christians throughout the Americas.

Historical Critiques of Popular Guadalupan Devotion

In Robert Ricard's classic text, *The Spiritual Conquest of Mexico* (1966), the author argues that the cult of Guadalupe is an invention "born, and it matured and triumphed, under the active influence of the episcopate . . . in the midst of Dominican and Augustinian indifference, and despite the hostile anxiety of the Franciscans."[11] Elizondo acknowledges these suspicions and dismisses them by pointing out that (according to the earliest documentation) church officials tried to suppress Guadalupan devotion among the Indians as a threat to their own missionary and evangelical efforts.[12] Whether or not the roots of the Guadalupe myth lie in popular devotion or ecclesial manipulation, evidence of strong Franciscan opposition to the Guadalupan devotion among the indigenous population exists in the form of a 1556 sermon by a Franciscan friar denouncing the cult of Our Lady of Guadalupe as a "disguised idolatry."[13] If understanding and interpreting the social significance of Guadalupe for the formation of a distinctively Latino/a (specifically Mexican and Mexican American) culture allows Elizondo to defend the role of popular religion as a locus for theological reflection, his unpacking of the Guadalupe narrative also allows him to interpret it as a symbol of liberation: "I do not know of any other event since Pentecost that has had such a revolutionary, profound, lasting, far reaching, healing, and liberating impact on Christianity."[14] While Virgil Elizondo overstates the significance of this event within the history of ecumenical Christianity, such hyperbolic statements reveal his

---

[11] See Robert Ricard, *The Spiritual Conquest of Mexico: An Essay on the Apostolate and the Evangelizing Methods of the Mendicant Orders in New Spain: 1523–1572*, trans. Lesley Byrd Simpson (Berkeley: University of California Press, 1966), 302; also see 35–38, 188–91.

[12] Elizondo, *Guadalupe*, 84.

[13] Ricard, *The Spiritual Conquest of Mexico*, 189.

[14] Elizondo, *Guadalupe*, xi.

deep commitment to the Guadalupe narrative as the guiding myth for Latino/a self-understanding.

Still, in spite of the privileged role Elizondo grants Guadalupe as the hermeneutical key for understanding Latino/a theology and culture, any scholarly engagement of the Guadalupe event must address certain historical-critical questions. First and foremost, the historical verity of this event is still debated, with some critics dismissing the story as a fabrication of the *criollo* ruling class to foment nationalism in their struggle for independence from Spain.[15] Stafford Poole, who provides the most thorough critical historical analysis of the Guadalupe myth in the English language, concludes, in effect, that no historical foundation exists for authenticating the Guadalupan apparitions: "The fundamental question here is whether a sign or a symbol can exist apart from an underlying reality."[16] He contends that, as a Mexican national and religious symbol, Guadalupe was not "born" at Tepeyac in 1531, but was the result of a growing *criollo* independence movement that linked the indigenous apparition story to the birth of Christianity in the New World in order to eliminate their dependence on Catholic Spain. In other words, contra Elizondo, Poole contends that the cult of Guadalupe has its origin in Spanish/*criollo* interests, not within Indian or *mestizo* religiosity, and notes that "there is no evidence of mass conversion of the Indians after 1531" and "almost nothing is known about

---

[15] Miguel Sánchez, author of *Imagen de la Virgen María, Madre de Dios de Guadalupe: Milagrosamente aparecida en la Ciudad de México, celebrada en su historia, con la profecía del capítulo doze del Apocalipsis* (Mexico City: Imp. Vidua de Bernardo Calderón, 1648), is considered by many critics the "inventor" of the *criollo* Guadalupe myth, in which he compares the Mexican Guadalupe to the European Our Lady of Remedios by employing the typology of Naomi and Ruth (Guadalupe is the native-born Naomi while Remedios is the foreign-born Ruth). D. A. Brading's exhaustive history of the Guadalupe tradition, *Mexican Phoenix: Our Lady of Guadalupe: Image and Tradition across Five Centuries* (Cambridge: Cambridge University Press, 2001), challenges Poole's conclusion that the Guadalupe myth was a *criollo* creation of the seventeenth century by proposing the thesis that there are two distinct yet interrelated Guadalupe traditions—one indigenous dating back to the sixteenth century, the other *criollo* and linked to Miguel Sánchez's 1648 publication. Still, Brading argues that even if Sánchez did not initiate the Guadalupan devotion, this first published account of the apparition at Tepeyac determined the direction of both traditions, eventually converging into today's recognizable devotion.

[16] Stafford Poole, *Our Lady of Guadalupe: The Origins and Sources of a Mexican National Symbol, 1531–1797* (Tucson: University of Arizona Press, 1995), 214.

the devotion among the Indians in the seventeenth century."[17] Of course, when applying Poole's standards of historiography to the origins of Christianity the same lack of evidence surrounds the resurrection story, which for many is the central doctrine of the Christian faith and is accepted as a historical event in spite of a lack of evidence. So, rather than undertake a critical history of the Guadalupan devotion or trace the origin and redaction of the Guadalupe narrative, I grant Poole's evaluation of Elizondo's interpretation of Guadalupe as historically inaccurate (according to certain canons of scholarship), yet important for understanding popular practices among Mexican Americans, since Elizondo "exemplifies a contemporary Catholic attitude toward Guadalupe."[18]

Flor y Canto: The Postmodern Rediscovery of Mystery

Recognizing the complex history of the various interpretive controversies underlying the transmission of oral and written Guadalupe traditions, I choose to focus on Elizondo's interpretation of contemporary Guadalupe devotion in an effort to explore his contributions to Christian theology. Unlike Poole, who characterizes Elizondo as manipulating the Guadalupe myth to meet "the needs of contemporary agendas,"[19] I contend that such instances of Guadalupan devotion need not document their historical relationship to the first three centuries of Guadalupan devotion in order to be studied as legitimate manifestations of the Guadalupe myth. The well-documented history of this sort of manipulation demonstrates the cultural importance of the Guadalupe myth. It is, however, Poole's other critique—that Guadalupe has not been widely embraced as a symbol of liberation by liberation theologians—that most challenges Elizondo's reading of the Guadalupe tradition.[20]

As recently as 1987, Andrés Guerrero recognized that historically, "with a few exceptions, the symbol of Guadalupe has not been proclaimed as a liberating symbol."[21] Whether or not Guadalupe has been or can become a symbol for liberation depends on the person defining Guadalupe. In the

---

[17] Ibid., 216–17.

[18] Ibid., 13.

[19] Ibid.

[20] Ibid., 13–14.

[21] Andrés G. Guerrero, *A Chicano Theology* (Maryknoll, NY: Orbis, 1987), 115.

past, the institutional church has used Guadalupe "to placate the Indians and the Chicanos," but Guerrero challenges these received traditions by asking, "How do we redefine Guadalupe as a symbol of liberation as opposed to a symbol of placation and passivity?"[22] He exposes the manipulation of the Guadalupe myth by the church hierarchy as a means of social control in order to contrast it with popular devotion, especially among indigenous peoples and *mestizos*, for whom Guadalupe is often a source of dignity and group pride in the face of conquering powers. Contra Poole's generalization, both Virgil Elizondo in the North American context and Latin American liberation theologian Leonardo Boff (writing on the eve of the quincentennial of the Spanish-Catholic conquest and evangelization of the Americas) have proffered the Guadalupe event as a model of evangelization, liberation, and cross-cultural interaction for the Latin American church.[23] Still, Poole dismisses precisely this kind of creative retrieval and reconstruction of the Guadalupe tradition because such approaches disregard historical accuracy in order to meet "the needs of contemporary agendas."[24] Is it possible to retrieve a liberating reading of the Guadalupe myth that remains true to the "facts" as Poole has presented them? Allan Figueroa Deck, in a review of Stafford Poole's work, asserts, "No ultimately satisfactory assessment of the Guadalupe phenomenon can be made outside the framework of the faith of the living community in dialogue with Scripture and the ongoing Christian tradition."[25] In other words, while the kind of thorough deconstructive analysis of tradition undertaken by Poole

[22] Ibid., 116.

[23] For examples of Guadalupe as a liberating symbol other than the work of Virgil Elizondo, see Leonardo Boff, "The Amerindian Gospel: The Liberating Method of Our Lady of Guadalupe," in *SEDOS Bulletin* 23, no. 2 (February 1991): 42–45; Susan D. Buell, "Our Lady of Guadalupe: A Feminine Mythology for the New World," in *Historical Magazine of the Protestant Episcopal Church* LI, no. 4 (December 1982): 399–404; Nora O. Lozano-Díaz, "Ignored Virgin or Unaware Women: A Mexican-American Protestant Reflection on the Virgin of Guadalupe," in *A Reader in Latina Feminist Theology: Religion and Justice*, ed. María Pilar Aquino, Daisy L. Machado, and Jeanette Rodríguez (Austin: University of Texas Press, 2002); and Jeanette Rodríguez, *Our Lady of Guadalupe: Faith and Empowerment among Mexican-American Women* (Austin: University of Texas Press, 1994).

[24] Poole, *Our Lady of Guadalupe*, 13.

[25] Allan Figueroa Deck, review of *Our Lady of Guadalupe: The Origins and Sources of a Mexican National Symbol, 1531–1797*, by Stafford Poole, *Journal of Hispanic/Latino Theology* 3, no. 3 (February 1996): 64.

is important, religious worldviews cannot be reduced to a collection of historical facts. Accordingly, Deck commends David Tracy's postmodern theological project for its ability to hold "critical reason in tension with a profound sense of wonder and mystery."[26]

The disputed events at Tepeyac are central to Elizondo's interpretation of the Guadalupe myth, despite the brutal historical events that gave birth to *mestizaje* and during which the Virgin of Guadalupe appeared, because the birth of this new humanity is a source of hope—a new way for human beings to relate one with another that transcends relationships of domination. This last point is evidenced by Elizondo's emphasis on reconciliation throughout his analysis of the conquest of the Americas and attempts to understand, without completely condemning either, the cultural and historical factors that shaped both the Iberian conquerors and the various pre-Columbian indigenous peoples:

> In the Nahuatl text (v. 19), Juan Diego hears Our Lady's thought and her word, which he finds to be "exceedingly re-creative, very ennobling, alluring, producing love." This is a perfect description of the effects that the word of God brings about in the person who hears and receives it. In our response to the word of God, we are totally re-created into new being. This is salvation. The old, defeated, victimized, "inferior," humiliated, "worthless," self ceases to exist, and a new, confident, noble, self-assured, joyful human person arises. Through faith, we are totally rehabilitated in our humanity as men and women. This new person will have no need of becoming like the victimizing conquistador (the ongoing curse of the creole and mestizo) but will be him/herself in a radically new way. This is redemptive birth. This is the beginning of the truly "new church" of the eventual new humanity of the New World, which was just beginning to dawn at Tepeyac.[27]

Granted, Elizondo does not wish to diminish the sinfulness of the genocidal atrocities committed by the Spanish conquerors (and tacitly condoned by the church), but his analysis also recognizes how several aspects of the indigenous cultures contributed to the Spanish takeover.

The Aztecs dominated other Náhuatl peoples by means of a strong military and a rigid aristocratic order; consequently, they were hated and feared by subjugated groups, especially for their religious obsession with

[26] Ibid., 65.
[27] Elizondo, *Guadalupe*, 121.

human sacrifice. Elizondo does not condemn either culture, believing that "each civilization produced its own language, philosophies, artistic works, sophisticated crafts, and complex religion. Each had its unique ways of approaching truth, expressing beauty, and communicating with ultimate reality."[28] The latter point—the genuine *mestizaje* of two very different theological perspectives—Elizondo finds most fascinating and instructive for the twenty-first-century church:

> Guadalupe brings about what even the best and most sensitive mission-ers would not have wanted or even suspected as salutary: the mutually enriching dialogue of the Christian notions of God with the Nahuatl notions of God. In this Guadalupan synthesis, the good news of new life breaks through. This is not a juxtaposition or a coexistence of opposing notions of God but the real *birth* of something new. The two religions need not kill one another and should come together as in the conjugal relation to produce a new offspring—in continuity with both yet trans-formative of both into something new. This new creation receives life from both but is not a mere extension or simple continuity of either. It is a new child, a new humanity, a new church.[29]

While according to Stafford Poole, the Guadalupe devotion did not play a crucial role in the sixteenth-century evangelization of the Indians, Elizondo traces the origins of Latino/a Christianity to the unsubstantiated events of 1531. Why? Because he is committed to giving voice to the religion of the people and believes, in the face of scant historical evidence, that the events at Tepeyac gave birth to a Guadalupe tradition that has survived in the popular collective consciousness in spite of official church resistance.

Notwithstanding the lack of historical evidence, the fact remains that as early as 1556 Franciscan friars were preaching against some form of popular Guadalupe devotion. While there is no historical evidence that the sixteenth-century Guadalupe tradition embraced both the appari-tions at Tepeyac and the pre-Christian worship of Tonantzin, subsequent manifestations of Guadalupe devotion incorporated both strands into one tradition with its spiritual nascence at Tepeyac (despite its suspect historical origins). Thus, in spite of Poole's concerns, Virgil Elizondo gives voice to a form of popular Guadalupan devotion with legitimate links to the first three hundred years of Guadalupe history. This gap in standard

[28] Ibid., xiv.
[29] Ibid., 127.

historiographical evidence does not necessarily imply the manipulation of facts for the sake of a contemporary agenda; it can also point to the suppression of an alternative history—a history of resistance that Elizondo reclaims through his work on popular religion.

Reformed Protestant Engagement of Guadalupan Devotion

Elizondo's championing of Our Lady of Guadalupe may appear, from a classical Reformed perspective,[30] to undermine Christian doctrine given his proclaiming of her as "the beginning of a new creation, the mother of a new humanity, and the manifestation of the femininity of God."[31] The role we give to various cultural symbols (like Guadalupe) reveals much about our hermeneutical perspective. Is the Bible a record of the acts of God in human history that provides (somewhat) reliable knowledge about the character and nature of God, or is the Bible a collection of narratives from the collective human religious imagination that gives meaning to some (but not all) people's existence? For the most part, Reformed theology has always presumed that theological statements are possible because God first reveals God's self. God not only reveals God's self, but God is the only means by which humans can know God with any degree of reliability. Yet, while the event of revelation is at the heart of all our human talk about God, we only have access to interpretations of this event, not the event itself. As the dominant forms of Christian theology (in this particular case

[30] See Daniel L. Migliore, "Woman of Faith: Toward a Reformed Understanding of Mary," in *Blessed One: Protestant Perspectives on Mary*, ed. Beverly Roberts Gaventa and Cynthia L. Rigby (Louisville, KY: Westminster John Knox, 2002), 117–30, for a brief overview of John Calvin's views on Mary's role in Christian devotion. I also want to thank Timothy Matovina for introducing me to the work of Maxwell E. Johnson, *The Virgin of Guadalupe: Theological Reflections of an Anglo-Lutheran Liturgist*, Celebrating Faith: Explorations in Latino Spirituality and Theology (Lanham, MD: Rowman & Littlefield, 2002), which to my knowledge is the only book-length theological reflection on Guadalupe from a Protestant perspective. Johnson describes his project as "a Protestant-Catholic Mestizaje, a synthesis of popular Guadalupanismo and Protestant theological convictions" (174). It is in the same spirit that I offer these reflections on Guadalupe, complementing Johnson's Lutheran emphasis on justification by grace alone through faith with a Reformed/Calvinist Christocentric theology that also emphasizes the freedom of God to act in new ways.

[31] Elizondo, *Guadalupe*, xi.

I am speaking specifically about the Reformed/Protestant perspective) encounter and critically engage popular and indigenous forms of religion, like the Guadalupan devotion, we must ask: Is our doctrine of the Word of God broad enough to include new theophanies? New revelations? Or is God's act of self-revelation circumscribed by the biblical witness?

Protestant Discomfort with Sacred Images

John W. de Gruchy, a South African liberation theologian rooted in the Reformed tradition, suggests Protestant discomfort with sacred images like Guadalupe is partially attributable to iconoclastic tendencies prevalent during the Reformation. The question of sacred images was only part of Protestantism's polemic with Rome: "The cult of the Virgin, prayers to the saints and pilgrimages to their relics, passion plays, the endowments of masses for the dead, indeed, the mass itself, along with the veneration of images, were, for the Reformers, all part of the same popish parcel."[32] Granted, John Calvin drew on the ancient Iconoclastic Controversy in his own anti-idolatry polemic by linking the decline of early Christianity to the introduction of images.[33] Still, while forbidding the use of images in worship, Calvin affirms human creativity, including sculpture and painting, as a gift from God that can—in the proper context—give pleasure.[34] In fact, de Gruchy commends Calvin's exegetical principle of accommodation,[35] by which God bridges the gulf between creator and creature, as a possible avenue for Reformed theology to recover the aesthetic as theological locus.[36]

[32] John W. de Gruchy, *Christianity, Art, and Transformation: Theological Aesthetics in the Struggle for Justice* (Cambridge: Cambridge University Press, 2001), 37.

[33] John Calvin, *Institutes of the Christian Religion*, ed. John T. McNeill, trans. Ford Lewis Battles, 2 vols. (Philadelphia, PA: Westminster Press, 1960), 112–14 (1.11.13).

[34] Ibid., 1.2.12; 2.2.16.

[35] See Ford Lewis Battles, "God Was Accommodating Himself to Human Capacity," in *Interpretation*, vol. 31 (January 1977), 19–38.

[36] Still, de Gruchy concludes the chief contribution of Calvinism "has been in the field of music, hymnody and poetry, that is, the arts that appeal to the ear and add enrichment to the Word," not the visual arts (*Christianity, Art, and Transformation*, 44).

Christianity, Art, and Transformation, is de Gruchy's attempt to bring together social justice concerns with theological aesthetics by analyzing the role of art in social transformation. Specifically, de Gruchy explores the contributions of visual images in resisting apartheid (while acknowledging similar developments in Latin American Christianity) to argue that the arts may play prophetic and redemptive roles in the struggle for justice. Echoing Calvin's conviction that humankind is fallen and inevitably misuses God's gifts, de Gruchy both recognizes that images are extremely powerful and can be easily manipulated for oppression as well as liberation and cautions not to "confuse the glory and power of God with images that invariably reflect or reinforce our own interests, whether personal, national, ethnic or class. Iconoclasm in this regard is a necessary outworking of the prophetic trajectory in the biblical tradition."[37] Nevertheless, de Gruchy maintains that "recovery of aesthetic experience is of considerable importance for the renewal of the church and its mission in the world, and that its neglect has serious consequences to the contrary."[38] That theological aesthetics has become a pressing concern given the changing face of world Christianity is evidenced by the often tragic history of European and American missionary encounters with "alien" cultures that have embraced sacred images.

While de Gruchy identifies the use of sacred images in non-Western cultures as the primary source of discomfort for Reformed/Protestant theology, I believe the strong Christocentric conception of divine revelation inherited from John Calvin presents a greater obstacle to cross-cultural understanding. Specifically, I contend that by focusing on the issue of images in worship and theological reflection, Protestant theologians risk misrepresenting both Calvin's theology and the Guadalupe tradition. The central issue for sixteenth-century iconoclasm is the potential for idolatry when images created by human hands—i.e., the product of human imagination—are used in the context of worship. Considering Calvin's principle of accommodation as an avenue for greater aesthetic appreciation, an honest interpretation of Calvin's theology recognizes that—even when Calvin identifies both the beauty of God's creation and the product of human creativity as vehicles of divine revelation—Scripture and the incarnation are the only reliable instances of God accommodating God's self to our human limitations (because of humanity's tendency toward

---

[37] Ibid., 243.
[38] Ibid., 254.

idolatry). As Ford Lewis Battles concludes, "surely the incarnation, to which (for the Christian) all this evidence points and from which it takes its meaning, must be the accommodating act par excellence of our divine Father, Teacher, Physician, Judge, and King," since, "after the Fall, there is no salvation apart from the Mediator."[39]

Guadalupanos and Guadalupanas do not view the image of *Nuestra Señora de Guadalupe* as the creation of human hands but as a direct and unmediated revelation from God. This raises a fundamental concern: does Christian theology allow for "new" revelations from God, or is "Christian" religious experience necessarily a remembering and retelling of the formative and unique Christ event? From a systematic perspective, it is necessary to determine whether theophanies like Guadalupe are "new" revelations or culturally specific variations of the same mariological event. As a Reformed theologian, when I consider Virgil Elizondo's interpretation of popular Catholicism (a pastorally sensitive and accurate representation of his community's devotion to Guadalupe), I have to ask whether the theological commitments arising from this devotion—especially the belief that Guadalupe's image originates in an act of divine revelation—are harmonious with the broader Christian tradition. Granted, more research is needed to determine whether the typical Guadalupano/a understands *Nuestra Señora de Guadalupe* as something new—as a new church, a new revelation from God—or if the popular beliefs and practices of the people have stronger mariological and/or christological components than many Latino/a intellectuals are willing to acknowledge. Nonetheless, Elizondo's own claims about the uniqueness and "newness" of the Guadalupe event appear to stand as a barrier to mutual understanding between Protestants and Catholics. How (if at all) should Protestant and Pentecostal churches embrace the various cultural manifestations of the Virgin?

Overcoming Iconoclastic Objections

Although Elizondo does not seek to supplant official doctrine, his language suggests that the Guadalupe event is a new theophany—a new manifestation of the divine communicating a new revelation—and thus problematic to any understanding of Christian doctrine that grants the Christ event unique revelatory status. Is a Christocentric theology necessarily at odds with theologies receptive to new revelations from God *not*

---

[39] Battles, "God Was Accommodating Himself," 36, 38.

mediated by Christ, or is it the case that the Guadalupe event—while a
new cultural expression of the divine—is nonetheless a manifestation of
the Christ event? As I read Elizondo, the Guadalupe event is a new cultural manifestation of the Christ event, calling the church to repentance
and conversion because the church has strayed from original Christianity.
Hence, it is not a new revelation, but a strong christological critique of
the dominant (European and Anglo-American) forms of the Christian
religion rooted in the original Gospel witness yet incarnated in new and
different ways.

Jeanette Rodríguez, who has written extensively on Guadalupe, notes
that there is an evolution in Elizondo's writings on Our Lady of Guadalupe, from Guadalupe as the foundational event of Mexican Catholicism,
to Guadalupe the protector and liberator of the poor as evangelizer of
the church and the Americas, and most recently, Guadalupe as the beginning of a new creation and feminine manifestation of God.[40] Several
key passages in his most recent book on the subject, *Guadalupe: Mother
of the New Creation* (1997), reveal a move away from a Marian reading
of Guadalupe to a more christological interpretation, which bolsters my
position that the Guadalupe theophany is not a new revelation from God
but a different cultural manifestation of the central Christian revelation.
By outlining the traits of the Guadalupe event that make it similar to, or
continuous with, the Christ event—even while manifest in new cultural
forms—I appeal to Elizondo's strong Christocentric interpretation of the
Guadalupe theophany in order to counter Protestant objections to the
use of Guadalupe as a source for Christian theology.

Virgil Elizondo's Christocentric Guadalupe

According to Elizondo, "the Lady is in effect speaking about the reign
of God that was the core of the life and message of Jesus. Guadalupe is
thus a good Náhuatl translation of the New Testament reality of the reign
of God as revealed by Jesus."[41] Consequently,

---

[40] See Jeanette Rodríguez, "The Common Womb of the Americas: Virgilio
Elizondo's Theological Reflection on Our Lady of Guadalupe," in *Beyond Borders:
Writings of Virgilio Elizondo and Friends*, ed. Timothy Matovina (Maryknoll, NY:
Orbis, 2000), 109–17.

[41] Elizondo, *Guadalupe*, 129.

Our Lady of Guadalupe is not just another Marian apparition. Guadalupe has to do with the very core of the gospel itself. It is nothing less than an original American Gospel, a narrative of a birth/resurrection experience at the very beginning of the crucifixion of the natives, the Africans, and their mestizo and mulatto children. The condemned and crucified peoples of the Americas were homeless, alone, and without protection. But God would triumph. . . . In Our Lady of Guadalupe at Tepeyac, God pitched a tent and came to dwell among us. The Word became flesh in the Americas through Our Lady of Guadalupe and dwells among us truly as one of us.[42]

Without question, Elizondo understands the events of 1531 on Mount Tepeyac as a genuine manifestation of the one God—God incarnate as Indian or *mestiza*—and not a competing revelation. Rather, Guadalupe properly understood is a call to repentance and a return to the original Gospel witness. Still, Elizondo is aware there is much resistance within the broader Christian tradition to embrace Guadalupe as a christological theophany:

What most people who have not experienced the Guadalupe tradition cannot understand is that to be a Guadalupano/a (one in whose heart Our Lady of Guadalupe reigns) is to be an evangelical Christian. It is to say that the Word became flesh in Euro-Native America and began its unifying task—"that all may be one." In our Lady of Guadalupe, Christ became American. Yet because the gospel through Guadalupe was such a powerful force in the creation and formulation of the national consciousness and identity of the people as expressed, understood, and celebrated through their art, music, poetry, religious expression, preaching, political discourse, and cultural-religious celebrations, its original meaning—that is, the original gospel of Jesus expressed in and through native Mexican terms—has become eclipsed. This has led to some modern-day Christians—especially those whose Christianity is expressed through U.S. cultural terms—to see Guadalupe as pagan or as something opposed to the gospel.[43]

A careful reading of the parallels between Elizondo's interpretation of the Guadalupan event (as recorded in the *Nican Mopohua*)[44] and the gospel

---

[42] Ibid., 134–35.

[43] Ibid., 113–14.

[44] Ibid., 3–4. (See also appendix 1 below.) I am relying on Elizondo's own English translation of the Spanish translation of Siller Acuña's text of the *Nican*

narrative will underscore its christological content and perhaps challenge those Protestant Christians who dismiss Guadalupe as pagan to come to terms with their prejudices.

Elizondo's reading of the New Testament witness identifies several key themes: (1) God's preferential option for the poor and oppressed, (2) a new inclusive vision of community where all people—including *mestizo/as* and other outcast and marginalized persons—are valued as *imago Dei*, and (3) the ongoing incarnation of the Christian Gospel in new cultural contexts. The early Christian movement embraced the poor and disenfranchised because Christ himself ministered to those on the margins of society: "The Spirit of the Lord is upon me, because he has anointed me to bring good news to the poor. He has sent me to proclaim release to the captives and recovery of sight to the blind, to let the oppressed go free, to proclaim the year of the Lord's favor" (Luke 4:18-19). Jesus preached to the poor and outcast and in his words they discovered their place as children of God made in the image of God (Gen 1:27). His parables confronted the dominant culture and challenged listeners to question and reevaluate their most basic beliefs, as in the case of the good Samaritan—a member of a despised ethnic minority whom Jesus praises for his actions in contrast to the religious hypocrisy of the priest and Levite (Luke 10:25-37). In *Galilean Journey*, Virgil Elizondo compares the Galilean context of Jesus' earthly ministry and subsequent crucifixion to the cultural situation during the christianization and conquest of the Americas by identifying the *mestizo* peoples born from violent rape with the earliest converts to the way of Jesus:

> In the new universal fellowship from below, based on the "little stories" of Jesus of Nazareth, a new identity and status emerged that would transcend the previous identity struggles and dehumanizing divisions between men and women; Greeks, Jews, and Romans; masters and slaves; intellectual elites and the ignorant rabble; saints and sinners; citizens and foreigners; legals and illegals—for beyond those worldly classifications, they were all first and foremost creatures of the one Creator. . . . A new fellowship could now be formed wherein all would truly be esteemed and respected brothers and sisters in the one family, all welcomed members of the one household, all sharing a common body and

Mopohua, fully aware of the controversy over the origins of this text (first published in 1649, over one hundred years after the events at Tepeyac) given that popular devotion claims that the *Nican Mopohua* dates back to the sixteenth century.

blood that were far greater and more noble than the flesh and blood of any earthly royalty. This was the beginning of the new culture brought about through the power of the Spirit.[45]

In fact, Jesus himself is identified as culturally *mestizo*:

The God of Jesus cannot be known unless Jesus is known . . . yet we cannot really know Jesus of Nazareth unless we know him in the context of the historical and cultural situation of his human group. Jesus was not just a Jew, he was a Galilean Jew and throughout his life he and his disciples were identified as Galileans. In order to know Jesus, efforts must be made to know the Galileans of his day. It is only in their identity that the identity of the Word of God, made flesh, is to be found.[46]

Recalling the history of the region—Galilee was a land route connecting great empires like the Assyrians, Babylonians, Persians, and Egyptians whose people had been conquered numerous times—Elizondo concludes that Galilee was a land of mixed peoples and that the image of the Galilean Jew in the minds of the Jerusalem Jew is comparable to the image of the *mestizos* in the minds of the Spanish conquerors. And—according to the Guadalupan devotion—just as God became the flesh-and-blood Jesus of Nazareth in first-century Galilee, God became manifest in Our Lady of Guadalupe, a *mestiza*, in sixteenth-century America.

According to Elizondo, the text of the *Nican Mopohua*, like the Gospel, first takes root among the poor and marginalized: "First she allowed herself to be seen by a poor and dignified person whose name is Juan Diego."[47] He also suggests that the author of the Guadalupe narrative situates the events during a time when the brutal reality of the Spanish conquest was not just a distant memory but a still-bleeding wound ten years after the conquest of the city of Mexico. Elizondo comments that it "was very much like St. Luke wanting to situate the birth of the Savior of the world at the very precise moment of the census ordered by Caesar Augustus."[48] Before commencing the historical narrative of Juan Diego's encounter with Our Lady, however, the author presents a brief and highly symbolic creation

[45]Elizondo, *Galilean Journey*, 101.
[46]Ibid., 47.
[47]Elizondo, *Guadalupe*, 5.
[48]Ibid., 25.

narrative—overtly linking the cosmic creation at the dawn of time to the liberating events at Tepeyac:

> Juan Diego, a low-class mission Indian, appears out of the darkness of the night. It is not just the physical darkness before dawn. It was the darkness of one who has been made ashamed of one's very being, who is bent over with the weight of hard work and humiliating treatment. . . . But when Juan Diego arrives at Tepeyac, there is a radical new beginning—from the darkness of nothingness to the darkness of expectation. Juan Diego leaves his home "when it was still night" but arrives at Tepeyac while "it was already beginning to dawn" (v. 8). Tepeyac will be the site of the new creation. It is here that a new humanity will begin. This will not be a new conquest but a new creation.[49]

A similar strategy was employed during the earliest period of Christian theology when the affirmation that God is one—Creator and Redeemer—became the first article of "orthodox" faith. For example, the second-century Christology of Irenaeus reconciled the radical monotheism of the Hebrew Scriptures with the bitheism implied by the salvific work of Jesus Christ by articulating a doctrine of recapitulation in which the Redeemer is the Creator. Correcting the teachings of Arius—who argued that no creature can redeem another, and since Jesus is a creature, Jesus cannot redeem humanity—Athanasius (c. 296–373 CE) affirms that Jesus is God incarnate. Therefore, since only God can save, and we know from Scripture (and from personal experience of grace) that Jesus Christ saves, we must conclude that Jesus Christ is God (making the act of redemption inseparable from the act of creation).

According to Elizondo's interpretation, the author of the *Nican Mopohua* defends the theological "orthodoxy" of the narrative by identifying the theophany at Guadalupe with "the Ever-Virgin Holy Mary, Mother of God" (1). Still, this raises questions about the origins of this written narrative, which according to scholarly consensus dates to the seventeenth century, and which, even if attributable to an indigenous sixteenth-century oral tradition, has been indelibly shaped by Miguel Sánchez and other *criollo* theologians advancing their own nationalistic agendas. Without minimizing the importance of historical criticism, I suggest that Elizondo—who is well acquainted with the breadth of Guadalupe scholarship—is attempting to explicate the text for the purposes of

[49] Ibid., 33.

the reader's edification, not historical accuracy. Furthermore, regardless of the complex history of Spanish evangelization, coerced acculturation of the indigenous populations, or how many redactions the *Nican Mopohua* (and its underlying oral tradition) has undergone, the fact remains that today the Guadalupe event is embraced by millions of people as a genuine Christian revelation.[50]

Thus, when Tonantzin/Guadalupe introduces herself to the Indian or *mestizo* peasant Juan Diego saying, "I am the Ever-Virgin Holy Mary, Mother of the God of Great Truth, Téotl, of the One through Whom We Live, the Creator of Persons, the Owner of What Is Near and Together, of the Lord of Heaven and Earth" (22), she is not the manifestation of some competing divine pantheon but the action of the one God in a new cultural context. By introducing herself as the Mother of the true God (Téotl) she subsumes the God of the Náhuatl into the triune God of Western Christianity:

> She is the mother of both and as such is the mother of the new children of these lands. She is the mother of the new *mestizaje* of the Americas. In her we move from the radical opposition of the two religions to a new synthesis that will occur in the new life that she is about to give birth to—the new Christianity of the new humanity of the Americas. She will be the compassionate and listening mother of all who come to her.[51]

As the translation of Christ's Gospel into a new cultural and historical context, Our Lady of Guadalupe represents for many millions "the temple in whom and through whom Christ's saving presence is continually incarnated in the soil of the Americas."[52] It is through Guadalupe's mediation that Latino/a people come to know God's liberating message previously communicated in the *Magnificat* of Mary: "He has shown strength with his arm; he has scattered the proud in the thoughts of their hearts. He has brought down the powerful from their thrones, and lifted up the lowly; he has filled the hungry with good things, and sent the rich away empty"

---

[50] Jacques Lafaye, *Quetzalcóatl and Guadalupe: The Formation of Mexican National Consciousness, 1531–1813* (Chicago, IL: University of Chicago Press, 1976), 238–300. Lafaye points out that Guadalupe became the central religious symbol of the poor centuries before it became the symbol of Mexican independence.

[51] Elizondo, *Guadalupe*, 67.

[52] Virgilio Elizondo, "Our Lady of Guadalupe as a Cultural Symbol," in Matovina, *Beyond Borders*, 124.

(Luke 1:51-52). Ultimately, for Elizondo, the Guadalupan epiphany points away from itself to the liberating work of Christ through whom we come to know the true God. Thus, in spite of the historical development of the Guadalupan devotion into a national and cultural symbol, it is first and foremost a witness to the person and work of Jesus Christ.

Elizondo points out that the Lady names herself "the Mother of God" but never explicitly identifies herself as the mother of Jesus. Rather, it is Juan Diego who recognizes her as Mary the mother of Jesus and so names her in his conversation with the bishop (53). This detail is significant because it demonstrates affinity between the Gospel taught by Spanish missionaries and the Gospel proclaimed at Tepeyac:

> She never tells him that she is the mother of Jesus, but Juan Diego recognizes her as such. This is probably the first theological reflection (versus simple memorization) of the Americas, for Juan Diego combines what he has heard from the friars about Jesus Christ with what he has heard and seen at Tepeyac and deduces that she is the mother of our Lord and Savior Jesus Christ.[53]

Yet, it is the Lady's actions that fully confirm her divine mission, by restoring to health Juan Diego's dying uncle. Furthermore, her gift of healing is accompanied by the miraculous transformation of creation, confirming that the truth of God is at hand: "All over the place there were all kinds of exquisite flowers from Castile, open and flowering. It was not a place for flowers, and likewise it was the time when the ice hardens upon the earth" (81).

In his concluding reflections to *Guadalupe: Mother of the New Creation*, Elizondo identifies five theological loci he associates with the Guadalupe event: (1) it is about ultimate truth, (2) it is about evangelization and faith, (3) it is about God, (4) it is about Christ and the New Humanity, and (5) it is about the triune God. He confirms that the Guadalupe theophany "is not something totally new, for it is simply the ideal of the kingdom of God as lived and proclaimed by Jesus"; the same good news "that is recorded in the Gospels and lived and celebrated by Christians, especially in the Eucharist."[54] Nonetheless, there is something unique and new about Guadalupe. As the *mestizaje* of the Náhuatl cosmic religion with the Christianity of the Spaniards, Guadalupan devotion

---

[53] Elizondo, *Guadalupe*, 68.
[54] Ibid., 115.

introduces us to a more comprehensive and open-ended concept of God—a mestizo God. In Our Lady, the Spanish and Nahuatl concepts of God are beautifully combined to present us with an understanding of God that is fuller than either one of them had suspected. Guadalupe purifies both notions of God, takes nothing away from their original manifestation, and enriches both. But Our Lady does not present two gods. There is only one God who is known in various ways, and Our Lady is the mother of that God. She stimulates new ways to think about God—for instance, she challenged the patriarchal Christianity of that time with the reality of the femininity of God.[55]

While Guadalupe points beyond itself back to the original Christian Gospel, it can also become an impediment to faith for Christians from other—sometimes vastly different—traditions. Elizondo attributes much of this resistance to certain views of human rationality that dominate Western theological reflection: "Guadalupe is not an isolated abstract, doctrinal truth; neither is it legal or moralistic truth."[56]

Guadalupe, as the *mestizaje* of Western and Náhuatl perspectives, "merges the two into a new metaphysics that recognizes the interconnectedness and interdependence of all creation while equally recognizing the uniqueness and value of the individual within the cosmic."[57] At its core, Guadalupan devotion is grounded in the ecstatic experience of the religious believer in mystic communion with God. Without dismissing the need for doctrine, catechetical instruction, and critical reflection, Elizondo nonetheless challenges the church to experience the divine in ways that have long been ignored or marginalized within the Western tradition. The truth revealed by Guadalupe "cannot be obtained or arrived at through observation, rational analysis, and argumentation alone, but can only be fully grasped through the beauty of sight and sound followed by critical questioning."[58] Accordingly, he challenges the church to embrace mystical experience as a legitimate source of theological reflection since "dreams and visions are as much a part of the process of discovering and knowing as critical observation and analysis of reality."[59] However, not every believer knows and experiences God in this manner. If Elizondo's theology

---

[55] Ibid., 124.
[56] Ibid., 116.
[57] Ibid., 117.
[58] Ibid.
[59] Ibid.

is going to "convert" the ecumenical church to the Lady's beautiful vision of universal *mestizaje*, in which all the world's people are welcomed and included and the dehumanizing actions of racism, sexism, and classism are reversed, then U.S. Latino/a theologians must articulate this vision not just in terms of mystical participation but also in terms of a theology of the Word.[60]

A Constructive Protestant Engagement of Guadalupe

Having demonstrated the strong christological focus of Virgil Elizondo's interpretation of the Guadalupe encounter, I argue that dominant theological traditions can benefit from an open and receptive encounter with different, even apparently incompatible, perspectives. Theological reflection about the Guadalupan understanding of creation teaches us to (1) view the whole creation as interconnected and interdependent, (2) affirm an inclusive theological anthropology that views all human beings—but especially the marginalized and oppressed—as *imago Dei*, and (3) incorporate historical liberation into our understanding of divine providence. Contextual theologies originate within a local community but are relevant to the whole of Christianity. While each and every Christian community does not share all the same beliefs and practices, a major task of theology has always been to preserve the diachronic and synchronic unity of the church in the face of such pluralism by identifying those doctrines and practices without which a tradition cannot name itself Christian. In this continuing theological conversation, the task of marginalized perspectives is often to correct historical errors by emphasizing neglected or silenced aspects of doctrine—not to supplant one perspective with the other—but in order to articulate a richer, more authentic comprehension of divine mystery. Thus, while not every Christian community need embrace the

---

[60] For a discussion of the two prevalent forms of religious expression, "manifestation" and "proclamation," see David Tracy, *The Analogical Imagination: Christian Theology and the Culture of Pluralism* (New York: Crossroad, 1981), 202–18. The author argues that the Catholic and Orthodox forms of Christianity emphasize sacramental participation in divine manifestation, whereas Protestant Christianity is distinguished by its emphasis on word and "a sense of radical non-participation" in the divine life (203). In other words, a theology of proclamation is one in which God is understood as radically transcendent and knowledge of God an act of God's grace to overcome the "infinite qualitative difference" between God and the creation.

Guadalupan devotion, every Christian community can broaden its understanding of God by listening to what Guadalupe teaches us about creation
and liberation.

The Interconnectedness of All Creation

By identifying Guadalupe as the "Mother of the New Creation" Elizondo
highlights several important, often neglected, aspects of the doctrine of
creation. First, by embracing the Náhuatl metaphysical perspective that sees
creation as an interconnected and interdependent organic system, Elizondo
seeks to counterbalance the dominant Western theological perspective,
which has tended to focus almost exclusively on humanity as the pin-
nacle of the creation. While the worldwide ecological crisis has caused the
Western church to reconsider traditional understandings of the doctrine of
creation,[61] European and North American culture since the Enlightenment
has tended to view the earth and its resources as objects for human manipulation and control instead of as gifts from God to be faithfully nurtured
and protected. Guadalupe calls the church back to the original Gospel of
Jesus Christ, in which the whole creation is mysteriously involved in the
work of redemption. According to the biblical witness, both humanity and
the nonhuman world are included in God's promises. In fact, the earliest
covenant between God and humanity—the divine covenant with Noah—
includes all of creation in God's promise of redemption: "As for me, I am
establishing my covenant with you and your descendants after you, and
with every living creature that is with you" (Gen 9:9-10).

Nahum M. Sarna's commentary on Genesis notes that numerous elements in the Noah story "are artful echoes of the Creation narrative. . . .
Noah's ark is the matrix of a new creation, and, like Adam in the Garden
of Eden, he [Noah] lives in harmony with the animals."[62] In much the same
way that the Genesis account attributes the undoing of God's creation via
the flood to human sinfulness and the renewal of the creation to God's
covenant with Noah, the Guadalupe event inaugurates a new creation:

[61] See Jürgen Moltmann, *God in Creation: A New Theology of Creation and the
Spirit of God*, trans. Magaret Kohl (San Francisco, CA: Harper & Row, 1985); and
Kathryn Tanner, *God and Creation in Christian Theology: Tyranny or Empowerment?*
(New York: Blackwell, 1988).
[62] Nahum M. Sarna, *The JPS Torah Commentary: Genesis* (New York: The Jewish
Publication Society, 5749/1989), 49–50.

"Her presence begins to reverse the devastation of the conquest."[63] Biblical religion has always acknowledged that evil has disrupted the natural order of creation and envisions God's redemption in terms that transcend a personal notion of salvation to encompass all of creation: "Then I saw a new heaven and a new earth; for the first heaven and the first earth has passed away, and the sea was no more. . . . And the one who was seated on the throne said, 'See, I am making all things new'" (Rev 21:1, 5). Hopefully, greater emphasis on the cosmic dimension of the doctrine of creation will allow Christian theology to embrace the radical interdependence of all life by embracing creation's absolute dependence on God as Creator.

Imago Dei *and Radical Inclusion*

Second, by appearing as a *mestiza*, God utilized the Guadalupe event to reverse the dominant theological anthropology of the time. No longer can the racially "other" be viewed as less than human given the Virgin's "introduction of the new paradigm of partnership" in which the Indian Mother sends the *mestizo* child (Juan Diego) to call the European Christian father (the bishop) to conversion: "The integrity of the Mother, the rebirth of the conquered Indian, and the repentance of the conquering bishop . . . will be the basis of mestizo spirituality: openness to everyone without exception."[64] Consequently, a central aspect of the New Creation is a conception of the *imago Dei* that embraces and values *mestizaje*. Furthermore, as a feminine manifestation of the divine, Guadalupe challenges the church to embrace the full humanity of women: "It is a declaration that the women will no longer remain silent, passive, and subject to abuse."[65] As liberation theology broadens its scope to consider all forms of social oppression, Latinas continue to expose the gender bias underlying our patriarchal culture and reinterpret the Bible in ways that reveal the inherent dignity of women as men's equals: "So God created humankind in his image, in the image of God he created them; male and female he created them" (Gen 1:27). As Christians with a firm belief in a benevolent and omnipotent God, Hispanic theologians attempt to understand the intolerable realities of poverty, racism, and sexism in our society. Accordingly, any discussion of liberation must come to terms with the fact that

[63] Elizondo, *Guadalupe*, 74.

[64] Ibid., 107. See note 10 above for a discussion of Elizondo's ambiguous use of *mestizaje* in reference to Guadalupe and Juan Diego.

[65] Ibid.

the greatest challenge facing U.S. Latino/a theology today is the sexism ingrained in our culture. Nonetheless, many in the church still have a difficult time accepting that women are not subordinate to men, but share equally in the *imago Dei*. In the contemporary social context one of the ways in which our faithfulness to the covenant with God can, and must, be measured is by the way in which women are treated in our society.[66]

Thus, Elizondo's Guadalupe reminds the church that contemporary conceptions of the *imago Dei* must contend with the realities of racism and sexism within the church and offer society an alternative model of community. Traditional reflections on the *imago Dei* provide us with tools to resist relationships of domination by emphasizing that (1) we are created in God's image insofar as we possess rationality, (2) we are created in God's image insofar as we have the freedom and capacity to transform the world through our work, (3) we are created in God's image insofar as we share in the capacity for self-transcendence, and (4) we are created in God's image insofar as we share in the capacity to care for others. The biblical witness understands creation as an act of divine grace, and values humanity by virtue of the fact that we are created to live in covenant with God. As an act of grace, the gift of life is unmerited, and our value as God's creatures is independent of our moral choices, our physical and mental abilities, or our social status. Theologically speaking, the value and dignity given to us as a gift in the act of creation can never be lost or taken away. Granted, the *imago Dei* is distorted by sin, yet our faith rests on the promise that through Jesus Christ God will redeem us. Therefore, our inherent dignity as creatures in the image of God does not depend on our moral worth, and this fact prescribes how we must treat others and how we can expect others to treat us.

Simply put, there are ways of relating to others that violate the covenant between God and God's creation since the value and dignity we possess as God's creatures entitles each and every human being to be recognized as the image of God and treated with the appropriate respect and care. Hence, Elizondo's theological anthropology (clothed in the Guadalupe myth but echoing a biblical understanding of creation) reminds the church that our identity as creatures made in the image of

---

[66] Sadly, Elizondo remains silent on a pressing issue of gender discrimination within the Catholic Church: the prohibition on ordaining women to the priesthood. In my opinion, Guadalupe as a female incarnation of God counters arguments that the priesthood must remain exclusively male because of the doctrine of *in persona Christi*.

God necessarily includes the "other" historically marginalized because of race or gender. Elizondo writes:

> In the events of Tepeyac, the process of unjust and dehumanizing segregation by sex, race, class, and ethnicity is totally reversed not by providing a finished humanity but by initiating a new process by which a truly new humanity recognizing the legitimacy, beauty, and dignity of each and every human group might gradually develop and come to be. Within the new process, *mestizaje* will be transformed from a source of shame and dislocation to a source of belonging and pride.[67]

Theological reflections that consider the Guadalupan event seriously must strive to find doctrinal support for multicultural diversity and a liberating praxis of inclusion that breaks down historical barriers between human groups.

From Imago Dei *to* Imago Christi

Finally, the doctrine of creation interpreted through a Guadalupan lens must incorporate human liberation into the unfolding of God's plans. Christian theology has always recognized the purposive character of creation—that is, there is an order and a goal to the creation toward which all things point and this purpose is revealed to us in the person and work of Jesus Christ: "He is the image of the invisible God, the firstborn of all creation; for in him all things in heaven and on earth were created, things visible and invisible, whether thrones or dominions or rulers or powers—all things have been created through him and for him. He himself is before all things, and in him all things hold together" (Col 1:15-17). And just as through Christ God first ordered creation, so through Christ God promises to redeem creation. The messianic promise of the Gospel is that of a new creation in which injustice and suffering are replaced with fellowship and celebration: "See, the home of God is among mortals. He will dwell with them; they will be his peoples, and God himself will be with them; he will wipe every tear from their eyes. Death will be no more; mourning and crying and pain will be no more, for the first things have passed away" (Rev 21:3-4).

In much the same way, Guadalupe restored the sick to health and transformed broken relationships into Christian fellowship. Comparing

---

[67] Elizondo, *Guadalupe*, 113.

and contrasting the evangelization of the Native peoples by the Spaniards to the new evangelization embodied in Guadalupe, Elizondo writes, "Our Lady prefers to offer us a foretaste of heaven. This is the new method, which is actually the method of Jesus and which is supposed to be lived out in the Eucharist."[68] Although grounded in a mystical experience that is difficult to express through language, this foretaste of heaven leads to concrete emancipatory praxis:

> Salvation is not just about the hereafter. It begins in the here and now— for instance, with the healing of Juan Bernardino. . . . Our Lady never speaks about the soul or about eternal salvation or damnation. She is interested in the immediate salvation of her people. Her presence is to have immediate results, and the people are to experience her saving powers in their very flesh.[69]

Consequently, a doctrine of creation that embraces the interdependence of all God's creatures, by definition desires the liberation of creation from sin and death. Led by the Holy Spirit, we are called to be God's partners (1 Cor 3:9) in liberation (understood holistically to include spiritual salvation and historical liberation) by continuing the ministry of reconciliation begun by Christ, a ministry that clearly involves the transformation of unjust social structures (Luke 4:18-19).

I have argued that, at its core, Elizondo's interpretation of the Guadalupe event is a christological critique of dominant forms of Christianity that have strayed from the original liberating ministry and message of Jesus Christ. Theological reflection is "Christian" insofar as it acknowledges the centrality of Jesus Christ in God's plan for salvation. Christ's saving work, properly understood through the lens of *mestizaje*, embraces all humanity and resists racist theologies and ideologies. Thus, in spite of Protestant discomfort, Guadalupan devotion and other forms of Latino/a popular Catholicism stand well within the orthodox Christian tradition while articulating a culturally unique witness to the person and work of Christ.

[68] Ibid., 119.
[69] Ibid., 90–91.

6

Wesleyans and Guadalupans:
A Theological Reflection

Edgardo A. Colón-Emeric

 When Elvira Arellano, an undocumented immigrant facing deportation, sought refuge within Adalberto United Methodist Church in Chicago, she set off a media maelstrom. Probably for most people following the mainstream news coverage, this was a story about church and state relations. But for Hispanic and Latin American Protestants watching the numerous television interviews, what caught their eye was not the image of Ms. Arellano valiantly standing by the pulpit of the church where she had found sanctuary, but rather the large statue of the Virgin of Guadalupe prominently displayed next to her.[1] It was this latter image that stirred profound sentiments of confusion and even resentment among Spanish-speaking Protestants, particularly Methodists, both in the United States and abroad.[2] Hispanic Methodist pastors responded to this incident by emphasizing the uniqueness of a Hispanic Methodist identity and reject-

[1] See Jason Byassee, "Sanctuary," *Christian Century* 123, no. 22 (2006): 10–11. The presence of the statue of Guadalupe at Adalberto UMC was part of a strategy of congregational development for welcoming Hispanics.

[2] The presence of the Virgin of Guadalupe in this United Methodist church in Chicago prompted some Methodists in Mexico to withdraw their church membership, even though the Methodist Church of Mexico is autonomous from the United Methodist Church.

ing the use of Roman Catholic popular religiosity as an evangelism tool. The response from the United Methodist episcopal leadership was more equivocal. While affirming traditional Methodist rejection of the adoration of images, they allowed for the use of the image of the Virgin as a sign of hospitality. In short, the Virgin of Guadalupe could be displayed near the entrance of the church but not near the altar.

For many theologians, the image of the Virgin of Guadalupe is rich in ecumenical potential. In the words of Catholic theologian Virgil Elizondo, "Guadalupe, properly understood, can become the deepest source of unity not only of Christians but also of people of all religions."[3] Maxwell E. Johnson's work in plowing this ecumenical field has been pioneering.[4] His lead has been followed by Methodists like Paul Barton[5] and Presbyterians like Rubén Rosario Rodríguez.[6] The collection of essays in this present book further tills this ground.

Nevertheless, as the controversy sparked by the Arellano incident shows, the Virgin of Guadalupe is a sign of contradiction. For many Latino Protestants, the face of this brown-skinned Virgin, *La Morenita*, does not present a maternal image but a sinister specter. At times, the devotees of the Virgin of Guadalupe, the Guadalupanos, have manifested the arrogance of the conquistadors instead of the humility of Juan Diego. In the mid-twentieth century, Mexican Methodist theologian Gonzalo Báez-Camargo linked revivals in Guadalupan fervor with anti-Protestant crusades: "As usual, the feelings aroused about a revival of intolerance. All the windows in a Protestant church, which

---

[3] Virgil Elizondo in the preface to Maxwell E. Johnson's *The Virgin of Guadalupe: Theological Reflections of an Anglo-Lutheran Liturgist,* Celebrating Faith: Explorations in Latino Spirituality and Theology (Lanham, MD: Rowman & Littlefield, 2002), ix.

[4] See M. E. Johnson, *The Virgin of Guadalupe;* and idem, "The Feast of the Virgin of Guadalupe and the Season of Advent," *Worship* 78, no. 6 (2004): 482–99. See also below, pp. 141–57.

[5] Paul Barton, "Guadalupe in Theology and Culture (panel): A Hispanic Response to Nuestra Señora de Guadalupe," *ATLA Proceedings* 59 (2005): 142–48. In Barton's opinion, "Guadalupe represents an authentic revelation of the Gospel that has been kept from Latino/a Protestants due to the anti-Catholic message of Protestant missionaries. . . . My belief is that Guadalupe has a message for Latino/a Protestants as well as Catholics and that it is a difficult journey for Latino/a Protestants to arrive at the point of embracing Guadalupe, or being embraced by Guadalupe" (142). His main point is that until Guadalupe is personally encountered she remains an abstraction that one knows about (*saber*) without knowing intimately (*conocer*).

[6] See the previous essay in this collection.

the pilgrims had to pass on their way to the basilica were broken, and other Protestant chapels in the neighborhood were damaged."[7] As in the days of Father Hidalgo (the "Father of Mexico," d. 1811), Guadalupe served as both an icon of unity and a battle standard. In this fight, Protestants have been far from passive. Hispanic and Latin American Protestants have raised opposition to the Virgin of Guadalupe to something on the level of dogma. In addition to distributing tracts purporting to expose the fraud of Tepeyac, Protestant groups have encouraged conspiracy theories like the one linking Guadalupanismo with Spanish fascism. Given this history, far from promoting the cause of Christian unity, the Virgin of Guadalupe remains a cause of division. As Justo González avers, "The notion that Cuban Catholics and Protestants will come together around the image of Caridad, or Mexicans around Guadalupe, may be very beautiful, but is made less credible by our own stories."[8]

In the present essay, I propose to engage in a Wesleyan reading of the Virgin of Guadalupe. My ultimate purpose is to suggest that a serious engagement with the sources of Wesleyan theology prepares the way for a Methodist reception of Guadalupe, a Wesleyan Guadalupanismo. Even if my argument is less than convincing on historical and sociological grounds, as long as it clears some of the significant theological obstacles hindering such devotion, then I will consider my work a success. My argument is divided into two parts. First, I will lead us in a very brief historical-theological survey of the state of the Marian question in Methodism. Second, I will engage in a Wesleyan reading of the mission of the Virgin of Guadalupe. I will consider the sending of the Virgin to Juan Diego at Tepeyac by applying a Wesleyan stamp to classic Catholic criteria for judging the authenticity of Marian apparitions. Finally, I will offer some remarks on the prospects for a Wesleyan Guadalupanismo.

Mary among Methodists

Marian reflection was not a significant theme of John Wesley's theology. Unlike Martin Luther, who preached numerous sermons on the occasion

---

[7] Gonzalo Báez-Camargo, "Mexico Recrowns Guadalupe Virgin," *Christian Century* 62, no. 47 (1945): 129.

[8] Justo L. González, "Reinventing Dogmatics: A Footnote from a Reinvented Protestant" in *From the Heart of Our People: Latino/a Explorations in Catholic Systematic Theology*, ed. Orlando O. Espín and Miguel H. Díaz (Maryknoll, NY: Orbis, 1999), 217–29, 224f.

of Marian festivals, not one of Wesley's 151 published sermons is based on a Marian text.[9] Wesley knew of Roman Catholic belief in the assumption of Mary, and he was aware of some of the titles bestowed on her like "gate of heaven" and "advocatrix." He knew of these things and was perplexed by the amount of attention that Roman Catholicism gave to one "whose acts on earth, and whose power in heaven, the Scripture doth very sparingly relate, or is altogether silent in."[10]

Wesley sincerely believed that Catholics worshiped Mary along with the saints and holy angels.[11] Commenting on Mark 3:34, where Jesus brushes aside his earthly family's solicitude on his behalf, Wesley states:

> In this preference of his true disciples, even to the Virgin Mary, considered merely as his mother after the flesh, he not only shows his high and tender affection for them, but seems designedly to guard against those excessive and idolatrous honours which he foresaw would in after ages be paid to her.[12]

Wesley knew of the distinction between *dulia* and *latria*, but he saw it as an illicit and inadequate distinction.[13] He was convinced that Catholic devotion to Mary was irredeemably idolatrous.[14] Thus, whenever Wesley

---

[9] David Butler, "The Blessed Virgin Mary in the Protestant Tradition" in *Mary Is for Everyone*, ed. William McLoughlin and Jill Pinnock (Leominster: Gracewing, 1997), 64.

[10] John Wesley, "A Roman Catechism with a Reply," in *The Works of John Wesley*, ed. Thomas Jackson, vol. 10 (Grand Rapids, MI: Baker Book House, 1984), 103. When citing John Wesley I will rely, when possible, on the critical text of the Bicentennial Edition of *The Works of John Wesley*, ed. Albert Outler et al. (Nashville, TN: Abingdon, 1984) henceforth referred to as WJW. Otherwise I will use the Jackson Edition of *The Works of John Wesley*, ed. Thomas Jackson (Grand Rapids, MI: Baker Book House, 1984), henceforth referred to as WW.

[11] WW 10:103, 105, 107, "A Roman Catechism with a Reply."

[12] John Wesley, *Explanatory Notes Upon the New Testament* (London: Epworth Press, 1976), 150. Significantly, these comments appear to be Wesley's own and not Bengel's, the main source for his commentary on the New Testament. Cf. Butler, "The Blessed Virgin Mary," 64.

[13] WW 10:110, "A Roman Catechism with a Reply."

[14] Cf. Butler, "The Blessed Virgin Mary," 56–67. According to Butler, "The main problem for John Wesley (1703–1791) with Catholic devotion to the Blessed Virgin is that she is not merely held in reverence but worshipped. . . . In Nicaea II the distinction was made between 'veneration' and 'adoration', (in the original

turned his attention to Mary it was usually for the purpose of giving an admonition: "Little children, keep yourself from idols" (1 John 5:22).

Wesley's views on Mary, conventional for his time and place, were bequeathed to his followers by way of his abridgment of the Anglican Articles of Religion, which stated among other things that:

> The Romish doctrine concerning purgatory, pardon, worshipping, and adoration, as well of images as of relics, and also invocation of saints, is a fond thing, vainly invented, and grounded upon no warrant of Scripture, but repugnant to the Word of God.[15]

The assessment of Catholic piety, including its Marian devotion, expressed in this statement remains the dominant view among Spanish-speaking Methodists. For some, anything that gives a whiff of being "liturgical" or "ecumenical" is resisted because it smells Catholic. In fact, in many Methodist churches in Latin America it is by no means clear that even the cross belongs in the sanctuary.[16]

In spite of the overwhelmingly negative tenor of early Methodist Marian thought and devotion, Wesley did make some positive statements about Mary. To begin with, Wesley affirmed the virginity of Mary ante- and postpartum.[17] At times, Wesley spoke appreciatively of the zeal that Catholics showed in their devotion to Mary.[18] For instance, Wesley tells the story of how a penitent drunk professed his newfound faith at a love feast by inviting the congregation to join in singing "Mary's song," the *Magnificat*.[19] Sometimes, Wesley was accused of being a secret Marian

---

Greek '*proskunesis*' and '*latreia*', while confusingly in Latin '*adoratio*' and '*latria*'). One wonders whether the confusion in Wesley and others at this point is not caused by the ambiguous use of '*adoratio*' which looks like 'adoration' and yet is translated 'reverence'" (62).

[15] *The Book of Discipline of the United Methodist Church* (Nashville, TN: The United Methodist Publishing House, 2008), 62f.

[16] Cf. Diana R. Rocco Tedesco, "Un episodio iconoclasta en la Iglesia Metodista Argentina (abril–setiembre de 1953) y la organización de ALMA (Asociación Laica Metodista Argentina - 1954–1959)," *Cuadernos de Teología* 14, no. 2 (1995), 93–109. Rocco recounts the painful cycle of recriminations and membership loss sparked by bringing a cross into a Methodist church.

[17] WW 10:81, *A Letter to a Roman Catholic*.

[18] WJW 20:319, Journal 8, January 29, 1750.

[19] WJW 21:418, Journal 13, June 17, 1763.

devotee himself, a charge so absurd as to not even merit a rebuttal.[20] Methodists do not worship Mary, but they "honour the blessed Virgin as the mother of the Holy Jesus, and as a person of eminent piety."[21] Wesley does not spell out what kind of practices would honor the Virgin without committing idolatry, but at the very least he allows for the possibility of an authentically Wesleyan Marian piety.

Methodists have not quenched Wesley's generosity of spirit. Side by side with the aforementioned anti-Catholic sentiment so prevalent within early (and not so early) Methodism, there emerged a tradition of theological inquiry that, while fixed on the essentials of Christian orthodoxy, is willing to think and let think on matters not touching the root of Christianity. It was this "catholic spirit" that led the United Methodist Church to adopt an official resolution, which qualified the anti-Catholic Articles of Religion.[22] The United Methodist Church retained the aforementioned Article but underscored its particular historical provenance and insisted that it must be interpreted according to our best ecumenical understanding. Specifically, on the question of Mary, Methodist theologians have meditated on the role of Mary in salvation from an intentionally Wesleyan perspective.[23] A hopeful sign of the vitality of the catholic spirit among Methodists is a joint study of the British Methodist-Catholic dialogue, titled *Mary, Mother of the Lord: Sign of Grace, Faith and Holiness*.[24] Though brief, this

---

[20] WJW 19:298, Journal 5, September 24, 1742.

[21] WW 10:147, "Popery Calmly Considered."

[22] Resolution 97, "Resolution of Intent—With a View to Unity," in *The Book of Resolutions of the United Methodist Church* (Nashville, TN: The United Methodist Publishing House, 2004) states "that we declare it our official intent henceforth to interpret all our Articles, Confession, and other 'standards of doctrine' in consonance with our best ecumenical insights and judgments. . . . This implies, at the very least, our heartiest offer of goodwill and Christian community to all our Roman Catholic brothers and sisters, in the avowed hope of the day when all bitter memories (ours and theirs) will have been redeemed by the gift of the fullness of Christian unity" (273).

[23] Cf. David Carter, "Mary—Servant of the Word: Towards Convergence in Ecclesiology" in McLoughlin and Pinnock, *Mary Is for Everyone*, 157–70. David Butler, "The Blessed Virgin Mary in the Protestant Tradition" in ibid., 56–67. Geoffrey Wainwright, "Mary and Methodism" in *The Ecumenical Moment: Crisis and Opportunity for the Church* (Grand Rapids, MI: Eerdmans, 1983), 169–88.

[24] *Mary, Mother of the Lord: Sign of Grace, Faith and Holiness* (London: Methodist Publishing House, 1995). The statement has not been without its critics. Cf. Edward Ball, "Mary, Mother of the Lord," *Epworth Review* 24, no. 4 (1997):

document treats most of the relevant mariological loci: grace, election, the immaculate conception, Mary's fiat, Mary's assumption, and significant Marian titles. Curiously, one lacuna in this document and in most ecumenical reflections on Mary is the phenomenon of Marian apparitions. Even a Methodist as open to expressions of Marian piety as Neville Ward (after all, he wrote a book on praying the rosary which was very popular among English Catholics[25]), has been less than enthusiastic in his attitude toward Marian shrines and visions.[26]

In sum, the state of the Marian question among Methodists varies diachronically and synchronically. From the earliest days of Methodism to the present, anti-catholic sentiments and a catholic spirit have coexisted, but their respective intensity has waxed and waned throughout geography

---

25–34. At one level, Ball's critique is methodological: "[W]e note a characteristic way these controversial doctrines are handled in this ecumenical document: Methodists, it is said, may not be able to accept the doctrines themselves, but can affirm together with Catholics the 'spiritual truth' underlying them. . . . So how organic, how theologically necessary, is the link to Mary?" (32). At a deeper level, his critique is material: "First, we must ask whether ultimately the emphasis on Mary's role does not betoken a sense of the insufficiency in God's saving work of the *humanity* of Christ himself, not least as the assurance of that work's being brought to completion? . . . This brings us to the second point, which is ultimately, I think, the key to the whole discussion. If, as we have seen, Mary is understood as an 'icon' of the church, then a claim is being made that the church itself already participates fully in some sense in the eschaton. The idea appears in respect of the other Marian doctrines, too" (32). In my judgment, Ball's critique is evidence of an underdeveloped eschatology ill-suited for a Wesleyan theological framework that is built on Christian perfection.

[25] J. Neville Ward, *Five for Sorrow, Ten for Joy: A Consideration of the Rosary* (Cambridge, MA: Cowley, 1985).

[26] Cf. Neville Ward, "Mary: Intercessor," *One in Christ* 19, no. 3 (1983): 282–90. In this essay while arguing for an intercessory role for Mary, Ward confesses his own sense of alienation from at least this aspect of popular Marian piety. He admits, "I wish I could be more excited about visions like those of Lourdes and Fatima than I am. It may well be that inhibition inherent in the tradition in which I have learned Christianity slows me down. I am quite ready to acknowledge the possibility of genuine glimpses into the unseen, though I would certainly expect inadequacies and various kinds of spiritual and intellectual clumsiness in the attempts to describe them. On the other hand, I can easily imagine the possibility of someone being so stirred by the image of our Lady that love and longing should produce hallucinatory satisfaction of one sort or another" (288).

and history. Openness to Marian reflection is a relatively new experience for Methodists, and it is largely localized in the English-speaking world. Openness to Guadalupan reflection is at a different stage altogether, and it is to the consideration of the Virgin and Juan Diego that we now turn.

A Wesleyan Reading of the Virgin of Guadalupe

Wesley betrays no knowledge of the events surrounding the apparition of the Virgin of Guadalupe. With one significant exception to which I will return later, Wesley is not very interested in the happenings of Mexico during the time of the conquest. For this reason, a Wesleyan reading of Tepeyac cannot start with Wesley. Instead, I wish to engage in an ecumenical exercise where I attempt to listen to what God might be saying through Guadalupe. Through long experience with these matters, Roman Catholics have developed criteria for answering these questions. According to the eminent Mariologist René Laurentin, in assessing the authenticity of an apparition the church considers the adequacy of information concerning the event itself, the orthodoxy of the message, the evidence of supernatural signs, and the fruits of the event.[27] I intend to apply these criteria in order to discern the veracity and significance of Guadalupe from a Wesleyan perspective.

First, assessing the historical evidence for the apparition of Guadalupe is of primary importance. The historical-critical study of the textual and oral sources of the Guadalupan story and the scientific examination of the image, even when inconclusive, play a vital and necessary role in theological reflection on Guadalupe. Whether one agrees with his conclusions or not, no theologian can ignore the kinds of questions raised by Stafford Poole on the dating and origins of the Guadalupan tradition.[28] Nor can one ignore discussions on the genre of the apparition narratives. Theologians would do well to heed Maxwell Johnson's comments on Miguel Sánchez's *Imagén de la Virgen María* and Luis Laso de la Vega's *Nican Mopohua* and

---

[27] René Laurentin, *The Apparitions of the Blessed Virgin Mary Today* (Dublin: Veritas Publications, 1990), 39–42.

[28] Cf. Stafford Poole in *Our Lady of Guadalupe: The Origins and Sources of a Mexican National Symbol, 1531–1797* (Tucson: University of Arizona Press, 1995). For a contrasting account, see Eduardo Chávez, *Our Lady of Guadalupe and Saint Juan Diego: The Historical Evidence*, Celebrating Faith: Explorations in Latino Spirituality and Theology (Lanham, MD: Rowman & Littlefield, 2006).

treat these as theological portraits rather than as eyewitness, scientific accounts.[29] Yet even if the Guadalupan traditions share more in common with the genre of gospel than with newspaper columns, the search for the historical Juan Diego, so to speak, is indispensable. Theological appreciation for Guadalupe will not be compelling if it easily elides questions of history and practice as if these were in some secondary position to the beautiful message of Guadalupe. Among various contemporary appraisals of the Virgin of Guadalupe (from Catholics and Protestants alike) there lurks a regrettable tendency to separate the authenticity of the apparition from the significance of its message. Appreciation for the liberationist themes in the Virgin's appearance to Juan Diego is coupled with indifference about this event's actual historic basis. The result of such an approach is that Guadalupe becomes an abstract symbol unrecognizable to Guadalupanos and Methodists. Rapprochement between these two groups will not be attained without careful study of the documentary evidence.

A firm judgment concerning the authenticity of the sending of the Virgin of Guadalupe to Juan Diego on Tepeyac, however, exceeds the competence of the theological task. What theologians can do is reflect a posteriori on the appropriateness or fittingness of an event occurring in a certain way, at a certain time and place.[30] For example, since according to

[29] Johnson's argument is persuasive and instructive: "Hence, for example, if Archbishop Juan Zumárraga (whose own writings, to be fair, have not all survived) did not, in fact, play historically the central episcopal role accorded to him in the official Guadalupan narratives, this does not need to be any more of a problem than the equally problematic worldwide census under Emperor Augustus narrated as part of the birth of Jesus in Luke 2 or other similar questionable historical details throughout the New Testament writings" (M. E. Johnson, *The Virgin of Guadalupe*, 54).

[30] Cf. Francisco Raymond Schulte, *Mexican Spirituality: Its Sources and Mission in the Earliest Guadalupan Sermons* (Lanham, MD: Rowman & Littlefield, 2002). Schulte's study of the earliest Guadalupan sermons uncovers a profound theology of history that seeks to answer the question of the timing of Guadalupe by arguments from fittingness or *convenientia*. In the words of the Dominican Fray Juan de Villa y Sánchez, from a sermon preached in 1733 and quoted by Schulte, "Do you know, O Mexico, why God did not send Apostles to these lands before? Because the Most Holy Virgin who appeared at Guadalupe, and is portrayed in this her miraculous Image, had to be—as indeed she was and is—the Missionary of this entire new World. Say now: It was actually advantageous that the lights of the Gospel took so long to reach our America, if they were meant to dawn in the Dawn [*Aurora*] of Mary" (35).

Thomas Aquinas one of the main purposes of apparitions is the stirring of hope,[31] how appropriate that these events took place in 1531, a time when conscientious Christians despaired of the future of the church's mission in the Americas! How fitting that the Virgin who sang about how God had scattered the proud appeared to Juan Diego rather than to Bishop Zumárraga! How proper that she manifested herself as *mestiza* and that she participated in the birth of Mexico as a *mestizo* people! Wesley himself did not shy away from engaging in these kinds of explorations in theology of history. One need only read his remarks on Methodism's providential purpose to see that Wesley considered theological interpretation of historic events as a legitimate theological exercise. As a Wesleyan theologian, I can appreciate the efforts of the early Guadalupan theologians in interpreting the encounter in Tepeyac; their work should inspire Methodists to humbly plow the field of theology of history in order to discern God's purpose in raising the people called *metodistas*.

Second, can a Methodist read the message of Tepeyac as orthodox? In a real sense, the theological coherence of the revelation of Guadalupe with traditional Christian doctrine is more fundamental than the evidence of historic documents, miraculous signs, or changed lives. Is the message of the Virgin in accord with the message of Jesus Christ? For, to quote Paul, "even if we or an angel from heaven should proclaim to you a gospel contrary to what we proclaimed to you, let that one be accursed!" (Gal 1:8).

The message of Guadalupe is not simply the words of the Virgin but her very appearance at Tepeyac.[32] Can a Methodist read the appearance of the Virgin as a sign (*semeia*) from God or must it be automatically dismissed as a lying wonder (*terata pseudos*) of the devil? Wesley believes that in the communion of saints, "it is certain human spirits swiftly increase in knowledge, in holiness, and in happiness, conversing with all the wise and holy souls that lived in all ages and nations from the beginning of the world."[33] In heaven, saints grow in happiness as they commune with each

---

[31] René Laurentin, *Pilgrimages, Sanctuaries, Icons, Apparitions: A Historical and Scriptural Account* (Milford, OH: The Riehle Foundation, 1994), 91.

[32] Salvatore M. Perrella, "Le 'mariofanie': presenza segno e impego della Vergine glorificata nella storia," *Marianum* 67 (2005): 51–153. Citing De Luna, "Il *messaggio*, spesso orale, non si limita a una semplice comunicazione verbale della Vergine al veggente o ai veggenti che dovranno poi trasmetterla al popolo. L'apparizione è di per sé un messaggio: incarnando la realtà invisibile dell'ordine soprannaturale, ne rivela l'esistenza" (117).

[33] WJW 4:192, "On Faith."

other, but the communion of saints is not merely a heavenly club. The communion of saints above increases in holiness and happiness as it interacts with the communion of saints below. For this reason, Wesley muses: "may we not probably suppose that the spirits of the just, though generally lodged in paradise, yet may sometimes, in conjunction with the holy angels, minister to the heirs of salvation?"[34] Indeed, "how much happiness will that add to the happiness of those spirits which are already discharged from the body, that they are permitted to minister to those whom they have left behind!"[35] God does not need the help of creatures in order to accomplish his purposes. By means of his almighty power, God spreads the Gospel to all lands and brings all the nations into his fold. And yet it pleases God to work his designs through the participation of secondary agents. As Wesley explains, "The grand reason why God is pleased to assist men by men, rather than immediately by himself, is undoubtedly to endear us to each other by these mutual good offices, in order to increase our happiness both in time and eternity."[36]

Applying Wesley's logic to the issue at hand, may we not suppose that the Blessed Virgin Mary, "though generally lodged in paradise, yet may sometimes, in conjunction with the holy angels, minister to the heirs of salvation"? Is she not at the very least, a just spirit? Would it not add to her happiness to be permitted to be a mother to someone like Juan Diego? From a Wesleyan perspective the sending of Mary to Juan Diego is a theologically intelligible event. I deliberately use the word "sending" because no saint in heaven is an independent agent acting on his or her own initiative.[37] From the beginning of the gospel, "The 'acts of Mary' are the Acts of the Spirit."[38] Hence, any authentic Marian apparition must originate from a divine mission. Obviously, that God could send the Blessed Virgin

---

[34] WJW 4:191, "On Faith."

[35] WJW 4:197, "On Faith."

[36] WJW 3:15, "Of Good Angels."

[37] Richard Rutt, "Why Should He Send His Mother? Some Theological Reflections on Marian Apparitions," in McLoughlin and Pinnock, *Mary Is for Everyone*, 274–91. As Rutt helpfully observes: Mary is sent. "Common parlance tells of our Lady as though she appears of her own volition. I have deliberately spoken of her as being sent. As a saint in eternal glory her will must be so united to the Will of God, and so far beyond the space-time continuum, that she can appear only if God wills it; and since God's will is prior to ours in all things good, it is better to speak of her as being sent by God" (280).

[38] *Mary, Mother of the Lord*, 9.

to Juan Diego does not mean that God in fact did. But the message of her appearance need not be summarily dismissed, by a Wesleyan, as a lying wonder. Instead, given the theological coherence of a divine sending of Mary, we need to consider the content of her mission.

Ostensibly, the purpose of the Virgin's mission is the building of a Marian shrine on the hill of Tepeyac. This message is not exactly congenial to Methodist ears. A shrine is a container for the sacred and as such a point of destination for a pilgrimage. However, Jesus' ministry devalued the spiritual significance of geography. God is not bound to the temple in Jerusalem (John 4:21). The true Christian temple is not "made with human hands" (Acts 7:47-50). Christian life is indeed a pilgrimage, but one whose final destination is heaven. And yet, Methodists cannot completely dismiss the role of shrines in Christianity because Jesus was not above making pilgrimages himself. From the time he was a child to the time of his crucifixion, Jesus joined his people in their yearly processions to Jerusalem; he made the psalms of ascent his own. What does this mean for the orthodoxy of the Lady's request for a shrine? It means at the very least that the request is not irredeemably heterodox. Granted, Wesley did not have anything good to say about Muslim pilgrimages to Mecca or Catholic ones to Loreto.[39] He feared that on the way of salvation, earthly shrines are distractions or even temptations. This fear is not without its basis. Opportunities for abuse abound. A shrine can upset the balance of centripetal and centrifugal forces in Christianity. The church exists for mission not for pilgrimages. Nevertheless, *abusus non tollit usum.*[40] Hans Urs von Balthasar's judgment on the role of shrines in Christianity offers a helpful correction to the abuses while preserving the possibility of right uses: "Catholic shrines have the grace of sending pilgrims away with the certainty that this grace is not bound to any one place. Having established their credentials, they efface themselves."[41] The Basilica of Our Lady of Guadalupe as a place of sending is a message that a Methodist could appreciate. From this perspective, the shrine would serve as a landmark along the way of salvation, a place to get one's bearings before moving on. If the message of Guadalupe is heard in this way, then the pilgrim-

---

[39] WJW 11:273, *A Farther Appeal to Men of Reason and Religion, Part III.*

[40] This is a distinction that Wesley knew and employed when considering the authenticity of the violent physical phenomena associated with some conversions (Cf. WJW 21:234ff., Journal 11, November 25, 1759).

[41] Hans Urs von Balthasar, *In the Fullness of Faith: On the Centrality of the Distinctively Catholic* (San Francisco, CA: Ignatius Press, 1975), 116ff.

age to Guadalupe for the feast of December 12 might be interpreted as something analogous to "watchnight" services, which Methodists celebrate on December 31. The purpose of the gathering is for the sake of being sent back into the world with a renewed commitment to walk in holiness. Such an interpretation of the message of Guadalupe would dovetail nicely with David Chapman's suggestions for a Methodist approach to Marian piety.[42] Mary's *fiat* sums up the Methodist covenant prayer, she fully embodies the promises and petitions that Methodists make during the "watchnight" services. As such, Mary can be approached as an icon of the covenant that Methodists are trying to live into, and if an icon, then "Mary is both an inspiration to follow and a worthy recipient of our devotion and veneration (*dulia*)."[43] Such bold statements require that we consider another aspect of the Guadalupan message—the image of the Virgin on Juan Diego's cloak or *tilma*.

Often it is said that the medium is the message. This is very much the case when it comes to the message of Tepeyac. The Guadalupan cult is built around an image that was not made by human hands. The Virgin's request for a shrine is precisely for the sake of the integrity and preservation of this message. Theologians like Virgil Elizondo have helpfully discussed how the rich message written on Juan Diego's *tilma* is born from the *mestizaje* of Aztec and Christian symbols.[44] Like the woman of Revelation 12, she appears clothed with the sun and standing on the moon. Like the people of Mexico, the Virgin is brown-skinned. And she wears a band around her waist like that worn by pregnant *Mexica* women. In brief, Mary appears as the *Theotokos* who offers Christ to Juan Diego. Much more could be said about the symbolism of the image. I mention these few details in passing to illustrate the thickness of this message.

Wesley's understanding of the role of images in the church is more limited than that affirmed by other Christian traditions. Images have a legitimate place in the church when they bear a Gospel message.[45] Some images have been commissioned by God, and God works miracles through some images. Think of the seraphs resting on top of the ark of the covenant or of Moses' bronze serpent. But the role of images in Christianity has become confused throughout church history. "[W]hat were at first designed

---

[42] David Chapman, "Mary, Icon of the Covenant: A Methodist Perspective," *One in Christ* 33, no. 1 (1997): 55–66.

[43] Ibid., 65.

[44] Cf. Elizondo, *Guadalupe*.

[45] WW 10:175, "The Origin of Image Worship among Christians."

as monuments of edification, became the instruments of superstition."[46]
Not that want of images immunizes one to the dangers of idolatry. Wesley
is careful to warn Protestants about the perils of spiritual idols.

> Let the blind sons of Rome bow down
> To images of wood and stone;
>   But I, with subtler art,
> Safe from the letter of thy word,
> My idols secretly adored,
>   Set up within my heart.[47]

Nevertheless, Wesley saves his sternest remarks for the images of wood and
stone. Even in the case of images through which miracles were worked, the
moment that an image or relic becomes an object of worship it should be
destroyed in the same way that King Hezekiah destroyed Moses' bronze
serpent when the Israelites began to make offerings to it.[48]

In spite of these negative comments on images, I do not think that being
a Wesleyan means being an iconoclast. Images can serve as *libri laicorum*.
Whatever else it may be, the image of Guadalupe is a book that tells a
story. Thus, one Wesleyan response to this image would be to engage in
a patient reading of its message. If the message is orthodox and edifying
then the viewing of this image could be considered a prudential means
of grace, but the image must not be confused with grace itself. The image
is at most a means, and as such it cries *noli me tangere*. On this point, we
would do well to listen to von Balthasar's comments on the place of relics
and images in Christian life: "[T]he relics of the saints are entrusted to us
only conditionally: they are more properly part of their resurrection reality
and, like the Lord, they tell us not to hold on to them. At best they are a
memento of the Spirit who indwelt them and who is as alive as ever in
the Lord's Eucharist."[49]

Third, can a Methodist acknowledge miracles at Tepeyac? The Guadalupe story overflows with supernatural signs from the apparition of the
Virgin to the out-of-season flowers to the image on Juan Diego's *tilma*. The
healing of Juan Bernardino is the first of many miracles associated with

---

[46] WW 10:175-177, "The Origin of Image Worship among Christians."
[47] WW 11:193, "A Word to a Protestant."
[48] WW 10:147, "Popery Calmly Considered."
[49] Von Balthasar, *In the Fullness of Faith*, 116.

Guadalupe.[50] Whether this event is a genuine miracle is not something that I can competently adjudicate as a theologian. What I can do is offer a Wesleyan perspective on the theological significance of miracles.

Contrary to the views expressed by some of his contemporaries, Wesley believed that God still worked miracles even in eighteenth-century England. Indeed, Wesley claimed to have witnessed cures that came about in supernatural ways and also recorded the visions witnessed by some of his followers.[51] Yet, whereas in the early church the purpose of miracles was to make manifest the holiness of the apostolic community, in the eighteenth century these signs made manifest the sovereignty of God. In other words, the purpose of miracles in the modern era is to confound deists who deny that God still acts in the world. Surprisingly, Wesley found such signs of the supernatural in tales of ghosts and witches. As Wesley states, "With my latest breath will I bear my testimony against giving up to infidels one great proof of the invisible world; I mean, that of witchcraft and apparitions, confirmed by the testimony of all ages."[52]

Nonetheless, Wesley found evidence of the invisible realm not only in its infernal manifestations but also in a more hopeful phenomenon—miracles at shrines. In his journal, Wesley recounts the story of Montgeron, a deist miraculously converted to Christianity during a visit to a Jansenist shrine in Paris:

> I read, to my no small amazement, the account given by Monsieur Montgeron, both of his own conversion, and of the other miracles wrought at the tomb of Abbe Paris. I had always looked upon the whole affair as a mere legend, as I suppose most Protestants do; but I see no possible way to deny these facts, without invalidating all human testimony. I may full as reasonably deny there is such a person as Mr. Montgeron, or such a city as Paris, in the world. Indeed, in many of these instances I see great

[50] Cf. Fernando de Alba Ixtilxóchitl, *Nican Motecpana* in *La Protohistoria Guadalupana*, ed. Lauro López Beltrán (México: Editorial Jus, 1966), 173–91.

[51] WJW 9:214, "The Principles of a Methodist Farther Explained." See also Wesley's account of the vision of the crucified Jesus experienced by a young woman of his acquaintance (WJW 20:246, Journal 7, August 29, 1748). Wesley records other visions in his journals but withholds judgment on their authenticity or significance (Cf. WJW 21:28, Journal 10, September 7, 1755).

[52] WW 14:290, "Preface to a true Relation of the Chief Things which an Evil Spirit did and said at Mascon, in Burgundy." (Cf. WJW 22:135, Journal 15, May 25, 1768.)

superstition as well as strong faith. But the "times of ignorance God" does "wink at" still; and bless the faith, notwithstanding the superstition.[53]

Wesley is aware that Montgeron's account is not free from superstitions and defects. Yet, Wesley is not willing to close his mind to the evidence of miracles at a Catholic (Jansenist) site. The insistence on the importance of supernatural phenomena for the coherence and confidence of Christian witness places Wesley on the same side as Laurentin and over against ecclesial deists who confine miracles to the primitive church. True, Christians walk by faith and not by sight, but miracles and apparitions play a vital role in keeping the church from closing in on itself.[54] In short, there is a need to find a golden mean between a radical skepticism that, as Laurentin states, "leads to asphyxia of the faith" and a credulous simplicity that "leads to superstition, illuminism and distortion of focus."[55]

Consider for a moment, what if God never sends anyone? What if there is no intercourse of humans and spirits (separate or otherwise)? Is not closing the door on Guadalupe giving up "one great proof of the invisible world"? Should we allow "this weapon to be wrested out of our hands" because some people have mishandled it?[56] If the evidence of witchcraft, ghosts, and demons is enough to storm the bastions of deism, atheism, and materialism, what could the evidence of Marian intercessions accomplish?

Fourth, can a Methodist enjoy the fruits of Tepeyac? What are the fruits of the mission of Guadalupe? In Marian apparitions, the fruits test usually examines the transformation of the lives of those who encountered the

---

[53] WJW 20:317 Journal 8, January 11, 1750.

[54] René Laurentin, "Fonction et statut des apparitions," in *Vraies et fausses apparitions dans l'Eglise*, ed. Bernard Billet (Paris: Editions P. Lethielleux, 1973), 149–96. According to Laurentin, miracles and apparitions matter. "C'est important, pour que la liberté de la communication avec Dieu ne se trouve pas remplacée par un système clos formé d'éléments et organisations terrestres" (160).

[55] René Laurentin, *The Apparitions*, 31. Wesley was aware of the need to steer between this particular Scylla and Charybdis. As his remarks on the genuineness of spiritual manifestation show: "The danger *was* to regard *extraordinary* circumstances too much, such as outcries, convulsions, visions, trances; as if these were *essential* to the inward work, so that it *could not* go on without them. Perhaps the danger *is* to regard them too little, to condemn them altogether; to imagine they had nothing of God in them, and were an hindrance to his work" (WJW 21:234, Journal 11, November 25, 1759).

[56] See note 53.

Virgin (or her shrine). The first fruits of Guadalupe are the faith, hope, and love of Juan Diego. As I said earlier, Wesley seems to be wholly ignorant of the apparition of Mary in Mexico. The closest that Wesley comes to the Guadalupana is through his reading of the life of Gregory Lopez. Wesley regarded Lopez as a prime exemplar of the doctrine of Christian perfection. So highly did he think of this poor, Catholic mystic that Wesley published an abridgment of Lopez's biography for the meditation and imitation of the Methodist people. From this abridged work, we learn that Gregory Lopez's resolve to travel to Mexico in 1542 followed a miraculous encounter with Christ during a visit to the shrine of the Virgin of Guadalupe in Extremadura, Spain. It is unlikely (though not impossible) that Lopez became a Guadalupano in New Spain. We do know that one of Wesley's points of contention with Lopez is that his Catholic biographer "ascribed all [Lopez's] virtues to the merits and mediation of the Queen of Heaven."[57] Little wonder that Wesley referred to Gregory Lopez as "that good and wise (though much mistaken) man."[58]

What would it take for a Methodist to say at least that much about Juan Diego? From a Methodist viewpoint, Juan Diego's biography is full of problematic beliefs and practices. But is Gregory Lopez's case much better? Lopez was a Spanish Catholic solitary mystic—all damning descriptions for an eighteenth-century Anglican. And yet Wesley held up Lopez as an example of holiness because holiness is more a matter of the heart than of the head. We call people saints not because they are right but because they are good. As Wesley affirms, "Without holiness, I own, no man shall see the Lord; but I dare not add, or clear ideas."[59]

A Methodist need not gloss over troublesome aspects of Juan Diego's biography to find aspects of his life that are worthy of imitation. Juan Diego's willingness to approach Bishop Zumárraga with the Lady's request demonstrates a holy boldness, with which early Methodists could have identified. His willingness to give up on a future family and earthly goods for the sake of serving in the shrine at Tepeyac is an act of self-denial, which though incongruent with Methodism's missional priorities is still admirable in its complete dedication to the work of God. If Methodists patiently read and meditated on the life of Juan Diego, they might be able to join one of his biographers and exclaim, "May we serve [Christ] as he did and

---

[57] WJW 19:294, Journal 5, August 31, 1742.
[58] WJW 19:294, Journal 5, August 31, 1742.
[59] WJW 4:175, "On Living without God."

withdraw from all the distracting things of this world so that we might also attain the eternal joys of heaven!"[60] If Juan Diego could be recognized by Methodists as an exemplar of Christian perfection then much of the way would be paved for an authentically Wesleyan Guadalupanismo. A Methodist life of Juan Diego "that good and wise (though much mistaken) man" might be the best remedy for the bitter taste left in the mouth of Methodists from the years of abuse suffered from "Guadalupanos."[61]

Wesleyan Guadalupanismo

The contradictory responses to the presence of the Virgin of Guadalupe at Adalberto United Methodist Church in Chicago signal the need for further reflection. I believe that the range of Methodist responses to *La Morenita* is not limited to outright rejection, naïve acceptance, or, worst of all, cynical tolerance. In this essay, I have attempted to begin clearing the ground for a different kind of response. I have sought to plow the fields of Methodist history and theology in order to discern a Wesleyan way to honor Juan Diego and Our Lady. Admittedly, the fields are not exactly ripe for the harvest. The obstacles that have to be removed to make way for a possible Wesleyan Guadalupanismo are considerable. One of the chief difficulties facing the appropriation of Guadalupe in a Hispanic

---

[60] Fernando de Alba Ixtilxóchitl, *Nican Motecpana* in *La Protohistoria Guadalupana*, 191. The original Spanish reads: "¡Ojalá que así le sirvamos y que nos apartemos de todas las cosas perturbadoras de este mundo, para que también podamos alcanzar los eternos gozos de los cielos!" It is not clear from the Spanish whether the antecedent to "le sirvamos" is Christ, the Virgin, or even Juan Diego. But for a Methodist, the best way to read the text is to make Christ the antecedent.

[61] In the nineteenth century, Guadalupanismo sparked murderous rampages such as the execution of twenty-two Anglicans in Puebla on December 12, 1879. Allegedly, the executioners' cry was: ¡Viva la *Guadalupana*! (Cf. Cody C. Unterseher's essay, "Mary in Contemporary Protestant Theological Discourse," above, pp. 29–50). In this connection, one might recall the wisdom of George Lindbeck's words on the necessity of an intrasystematic coherence for a statement to be true: "The crusader's battle cry '*Christus est Dominus*,' for example, is false when used to authorize cleaving the skull of the infidel (even though the same words in other contexts may be a true utterance)" (*The Nature of Doctrine: Religion and Theology in a Postliberal Age* [Philadelphia, PA: Westminster Press, 1984], 64). In other words, the persons who cried "¡Viva la *Guadalupana*!" as they martyred the Anglican congregants lied.

Methodist context is that Catholic-Protestant injuries are not "of old, unhappy, far-off tales and battles long ago" but freshly inflicted wounds.[62] No essay can overcome this painful living record. Instead, I have directed my efforts to clearing some of the theological obstacles to a Wesleyan reception of Guadalupe.

Followers of Wesley should have no problem in acknowledging the possibility and benefit of apparitions, miracles, and visions. It pleases God to work in these ways to confound the proud and also to keep Christianity from turning into a closed system. Of course, Methodists would want to insist that the most important visitation is the invisible indwelling of the Holy Trinity and the most important miracle conversions. The graces that Christians are to seek earnestly and pursue are the sanctifying graces. We are to aspire not only for those gifts that inform us about God (prophecies, miracles, and tongues) but also for those that conform us to God (faith, hope, and love).

For a Methodist, the clearest way into the Guadalupan mystery is through Juan Diego and hymnody. On the one hand, if Charles Wesley could write a hymn about Mary Magdalene being sent to disciple the apostles of humankind, is it completely unimaginable that a Wesleyan could write a hymn about Juan Diego being sent to disciple the Spanish missionaries?[63] On the other hand, if John Wesley could learn about Christian perfection from Gregory Lopez, could not Methodists learn about the universality of God's call to holiness from Juan Diego? Sadly, the difficulty of discerning genuine exemplars of holiness from aspirants and counterfeits has led many Methodists to abandon the attainment of sanctity as impracticable. My point is that only a Methodist Church that is able to recognize saints like Juan Diego will be capable of welcoming miracles like Guadalupe.[64]

---

[62] Resolution 97, "Resolution of Intent—With a View to Unity," in *The Book of Resolutions*, 273.

[63] Cf. Charles Wesley, *Hymns for Our Lord's Resurrection*, "Hymn 3."

[64] For Roman Catholics, the status of canonizations and apparitions are related but distinct. "Si le Saint-Siège a solennisé les canonisations, il ne les impose pas sous peine d'anathème, mais les propose plutôt comme une fête accordée aux souhait des fidèles. Quant aux apparitions, le Saint Siège a pris soin de déclarer de manière plus nette et plus explicite qu'il ne les imposait pas, mais les proposait seulement à l'adhésion des chrétiens" (René Laurentin, "Fonction et statut des apparitions," 186).

This is not to say that all Latinos must be Guadalupanos. For Roman Catholics, even when the most careful, judicious investigation is conducted and the Catholic Church renders a positive judgment on the status of an apparition like Guadalupe, the "yes" is neither infallible nor universally binding.[65] Catholics are free to dissent from the church's judgment on an apparition as long as their dissent is marked by humility and respect. Methodists should not be held to a higher standard. If one can be a faithful Mexican Catholic without being a Guadalupano, then surely one can be an authentically Hispanic Protestant without being devoted to *La Morenita*. Still, some Methodists might find that the way of salvation leads them through Tepeyac.

---

[65]Cf. ibid., 149–96. According to Laurentin, "En ce qui concerne les apparitions (auxquelles, encore une fois, la théologie classique n'a jamais accordé la même certitude qu'aux canonisations), la garantie du magistère s'entend de même : le jugement autorisé porte, au premier chef, sur l'orthodoxie du message, en second lieu sur l'authenticité du mouvement collectif de prière et de conversions qui en découle, en fin sur les miracles, dont on juge selon un processus analogue à celui des canonisations" (185). "Bref, les encouragements que des papes ont prodigués avec ferveur à Lourdes et à d'autres sanctuaires d'apparitions ne semblent pas changer le statut fondamentalement précisé par Benoît XIV : un statut qui propose les apparitions à la liberté, à la générosité, à l'engagement du croyant, mais ne l'impose pas comme prescription et obligation" (188).

7

The Virgin of Guadalupe from a Latino/a Protestant Perspective: A Dangerous Narrative to Counter Colonial and Imperialistic Power

José David Rodríguez Jr.

 My reading of Maxwell E. Johnson's book on the Virgin of Guadalupe was not only an informative experience regarding the uses and abuses of this important expression of our Christian heritage but also a challenge to explore the role of this narrative of faith for the ministry and mission of Lutheran and other Protestant believers. Most provocative was Johnson's proposal to add the celebration of the Virgin of Guadalupe to our Christian liturgical calendars as a contribution of the faith of our Latino/a people.[1] While the debate about this proposal has not yet had a formal or intentional hearing in the Evangelical Lutheran Church in America,[2] a goal of this study and the publication of this book are to keep this conversation alive.

---

[1] Maxwell E. Johnson, *The Virgin of Guadalupe: Theological Reflections of an Anglo-Lutheran Liturgist*, Celebrating Faith: Explorations in Latino Spirituality and Theology (Lanham, MD: Rowman & Littlefield, 2002), 14.

[2] Nor have I heard of a special meeting from representatives of Protestant groups in the United States purposely designed to address this matter.

My proposal in this vital debate is to suggest that from a Latino/a Protestant perspective, the story of the Virgin of Guadalupe confronts us with
a powerful and important challenge for the mission and ministry of the
church. This story constitutes an important link in a provocative memory
of an ancient biblical tradition that even today witnesses to the power
of God that emerges from weakness.[3] For Martin Luther and Christian
believers of all times, this type of power was made evident in Mary's song
of the *Magnificat*. Contemporary theologians find in Mary's witness the
continuation of a narrative of faith empowering the liberation struggles
of oppressed and excluded sectors of society. For an increasing number of
believers who claim our heritage of faith and cultural identity from the
sixteenth century in these lands called the Americas, this divine power
was also reflected in the story of the Virgin of Guadalupe. This popular
expression of Mary's witness dating from the sixteenth century in Mexico
constitutes an important symbol of our tradition of faith to resist the forces
that throughout time and space, intend to oppress our people and tear
down our human dignity.

In the spring of 2004 a group of more than sixty representatives of
various Lutheran national churches in the Caribbean and South America,
along with Latino/a leaders of the Evangelical Lutheran Church in America
and Mexico, gathered at the Lutheran Center in Mexico City to explore
our Lutheran identity from the Latin American context. With that goal in
mind, theologians, church leaders, educators, historians, and representatives
of community organizations led the group in exploring these topics. In
addition, the group visited projects developed by the Mexican Association
for Rural and Urban Renewal (AMEXTRA), the Anthropological Museum
at Chapultepec, and the Basilica of Our Lady of Guadalupe in Tepeyac.
Two valuable studies by distinguished Latino/a Lutheran scholars focused
on the role of the Virgin Mary for Latino/a spirituality will form part of a
forthcoming publication edited by Carmen M. Rodríguez Rivera and this
author,[4] to provide a glimpse of this experience to a wider audience.

In one of these studies written by my father, now a retired Lutheran
pastor and educator both at various theological seminaries (in the United

[3] See an earlier reflection I produced on the significance of the Virgin of
Guadalupe in José D. Rodríguez Jr. with Colleen R. Nelson, "The Virgin of Guadalupe," *Currents in Theology and Mission* 13, no. 6 (December 1986): 369–70.

[4] Carmen M. Rodríguez Rivera and José D. Rodríguez Hernández, eds., *Lutero
Descalzo: Meditaciones sobre la identidad luterana desde el contexto latinoamericano*
(San Juan: Editorial de la Universidad de Puerto Rico, forthcoming).

States, Mexico, Puerto Rico, Argentina, Nicaragua, Costa Rica, etc.) and at the University of Puerto Rico, he reflects on what he describes as "an Evangelical perspective of Mary, the Mother of Our Lord."[5] For him, the overwhelming expression of Marian devotion in Catholicism, particularly by Latino/a people, has led in Protestant circles to an attitude of indifference, or a forthright sectarian intolerance regarding the role of Mary in the order of salvation. Faithfulness to the Gospel, as well as to the apostolic and catholic nature of our faith demands, according to Rodríguez, the recovery of an evangelical view of Mary, based on the Scriptures and led by the power of the Holy Spirit. His examination of the gospels from a christological perspective leads him to affirm an evangelical view of Mary in which her relationship to Jesus, the church, and God's reign is described.

According to Rodríguez, the Mary of the gospels always expressed her condition of believer. She understood herself as part of God's people that believes, praises, and blesses God, and not as an object of worship and devotion in the biblical sense. Mary's will was surrendered to her God and savior. As God's self was revealed in the person of Jesus, she totally committed herself to him. In this sense, the centrality of Jesus in the narratives of the four gospels leads us to describe Mary as a believer whose will was totally committed to her son. This might also direct us to conclude that Mary's true relationship with Jesus lies in the faithfulness she always expressed to the Word of the living God. Following this tenet, the form by which we can best express the rightful recognition we owe to Mary is by her witness of faith in obedience to her Son Jesus Christ.

In view of the Second Vatican Council's assertion in which Pope Paul VI declared Mary "Mother of the Church" (*Mater Ecclesiae*), Rodríguez argues that with this statement, far from claiming a condition of divinity (or almost a divine nature) for Mary, which would contradict the gospel's narrative since she never claimed that condition for herself, the gospels present Mary as a paradigm, as a symbol of humanity that places all her trust in God, her savior, and thus worthy of honor from all believers. Viewed in this way, the title of "Mother of the Church" would express the living image of the evangelical Mary.

Finally, for Rodríguez, Mary's role in the promise of God's reign takes place because in keeping with the gospels, she was chosen as God's vessel

---

[5] José D. Rodríguez Rivera, "María la Madre del Señor: Una perspectiva evangélica," in *Lutero descalzo*.

to make donation of God's Son for the salvation of all creation. To be sure, her selection for this role was not based on any special merit of her own.[6] Rather, she was chosen because of her faith. We therefore need to remember that Mary's call to fulfill this role is a product of God's gracious initiative.[7]

It is Rodríguez's contention that, while we should abstain from accrediting Mary divine attributes, we ought to recognize that she displayed in her life those gifts granted by the Holy Spirit to all those who, like Mary, believe and live their lives committed to God's Word. Mary's life embodied true faith, love, and hope. By faith she opened her life to God, thus becoming an efficacious instrument of God's plan for the salvation

---

[6] Here it is valuable to recall Martin Luther's commentary on the *Magnificat* where he states, "From this we may learn how to show her the honor and devotion that are her due. How ought one to address her? Keep these words in mind, and they will teach you to say: 'Oh Blessed Virgin, Mother of God, you were nothing and all despised; yet God in his grace regarded you and worked such great things in you. You were worthy of none of them, but the rich and abundant grace of God was upon you, far above any merit of yours. Hail to you! Blessed are you, from thence forth and forever, in finding such a God.' Nor need you fear that she will take it amiss if we call her unworthy of such grace. For, of a truth, she did not lie when she herself acknowledged her unworthiness and nothingness, which God regarded, not because of any merit in her, but solely by reason of his grace." (*The Magnificat: Luther's Commentary*, trans. A. T. W. Steinhaeuser [Minneapolis, MN: Augsburg Publishing House, 1967], 38. The original version of this paperback edition published for the celebration of the 450th year of the Reformation is found in *Luther's Works*, ed. Jaroslav Pelikan, vol. 21 [St. Louis, MO: Concordia Publishing House, 1956], 295–355.)

[7] Again Luther states, "As the wood [of the cross] had no other merit or worthiness than that it was suited to be made into a cross and was appointed by God for that purpose, so her sole worthiness to become the Mother of God lay in her being fit and appointed for it; so that it might be pure grace and not a reward, that we might not take away from God's grace, worship and honor by ascribing too great things to her. For it is better to take away too much from her than from the grace of God. Indeed, we cannot take away too much from her, since she was created out of nothing, like all other creatures. But we can easily take away too much from God's grace, which is a perilous thing to do and not well pleasing to her. It is necessary also to keep within bounds and not make too much calling her 'Queen of Heaven,' which is a true-enough name and yet does not make her a goddess who could grant gifts or render aid, as some suppose when they pray and flee to her rather than to God. She gives nothing, God gives all" (ibid., 44–45).

of all people. It was God's love mediated through Mary that sent God's only Son so that all who believe in him will not perish but have everlasting life (John 3:16).

According to Rodríguez, the fact that a humble young woman from Galilee became the vessel for the incarnation of God's Word will continue to be a mystery of God's gracious initiative. To highlight the unity of the two natures of Jesus Christ (human and divine), the Council of Ephesus (431 CE) established the dogma that declares Mary the Mother of God (*Theotokos*). Yet we also need to understand that rather than a Marian dogma, this is an eminent christological teaching. Mary is not just the mother of the historical Jesus, but also of the incarnate God, and in Jesus Christ the humanity and the divinity are present in perfect integrity, without distortions or confusions. For this reason it is right and salutary that we incorporate in our evangelical liturgy the angel's greeting to Mary, "Greetings, favored one! The Lord is with you" (Luke 1:28), along with the words of her cousin Elizabeth, full of God's Spirit, who exclaimed to her with a loud cry, "Blessed are you among women, and blessed is the fruit of your womb" (Luke 1:42), and to conclude with the hymn that the church added at a later time "Holy Mary, Mother of God, pray for us sinners now and at the hour of our death. Amen," for we believe that the saints on earth and those in heaven are joined in the same communion and we need to pray for each other.

As in the case of the work of Johnson earlier mentioned, Rodríguez's effort is aimed at clarifying some misunderstandings prevalent in Protestant circles regarding the role of the Virgin Mary. For that reason he provides an *evangelical* perspective of Mary, which he contends is demanded by our faithfulness to the Gospel as well as to the apostolic and catholic nature of our faith. To do otherwise might lead us to a type of narrow and selective affirmation of faith characteristic of sectarian movements that throughout the history of the church have led to division and heresy.[8]

---

[8] It is interesting to note that the etymological meaning of "heresy" implied the reduction of the content of a belief already established by a group. "The word 'heresy' comes from the Greek, αἵρεσις, and the Latin transliteration *hairesis* (from αἱρέομαι, *haireomai*, "choose"), which means either a *choice* of beliefs or a *faction* of believers, a course of action or a school of thought. The word appears in the New Testament and was appropriated by the Catholic Church to mean a sect or belief that threatened the unity of Christian doctrine. *Heresy* is frequently regarded as a departure from *orthodoxy*. See *Webster's New International Dictionary*, 2nd ed. (Springfield: G. & C. Merriam Company Publishers, 1957), 1167–68.

The author of the second study mentioned above is Dr. Suzanne E. Hoeferkamp Segovia, who argues that the role of Mary, specifically her song of the *Magnificat*, plays an important role in the emergence of a new consciousness of a Hispanic-Latino/a Lutheran spirituality. This spirituality is characterized by an awareness of the surprising inversion of the order of things that God's visit, actualized by the dynamic of love—a dynamic that witnesses to God's creative, redeeming (liberating), and sanctifying initiative—establishes as a foundation from which all the expressions of our hope and existence as God's people emerges. This experience of faith, which has its culminating expression in the cross and resurrection of Christ, gives rise to a new order of things that establishes a striking contrast to the one characteristic of this world. In this new order the weakest becomes the strongest, and the humiliated turns into the most privileged. According to this author, Mary impels us to become aware of the novelty that takes place in the crossing between our Lutheran spirituality and our Latino/a identity. This novelty consists of a new consciousness of what Luther had already recovered as the core of the gospel: that in the cross God identifies with our condition of suffering to transform it into the power that emerges from weakness.[9] This power, discerned by faith in the created Word of God becomes the foundation of our hope and victory in the midst of our present condition of suffering and affliction.[10]

[9] In the introduction of his commentary on the *Magnificat*, Luther argues that one of the most important contributions of Mary's song to the believers of all times is her witness, by the power of the Holy Spirit, to God's unique expression of working salvation in her and in all creation by the power that emerges from weakness: "When the holy virgin experienced what great things God was working in her despite her insignificance, lowliness, poverty, and inferiority, the Holy Spirit taught her this deep insight and wisdom, that God is the kind of Lord who does nothing but exalt those of low degree and put down the mighty from their thrones, in short, break what is whole and make whole what is broken. Just as God in the beginning of creation made the world out of nothing, whence he is called the creator and the Almighty, so his manner of working continues unchanged. Even now and until the end of the world, all his works are such that out of that which is nothing, worthless, despised, wretched, and dead, he makes that which is something precious, honorable, blessed, and living" (*The Magnificat*, 11).

[10] Suzanne E. Hoeferkamp Segovia, "La espiritualidad luterana latina: Una nueva consciencia," in *Lutero descalzo*.

Thus, faithfulness to the Word of the living God through an *evangelical* view of Mary (Rodríguez), and consciousness of the power that emerges from weakness in the cross and resurrection of Jesus Christ projected in Mary's song of the *Magnificat* (Hoeferkamp Segovia), are two of the most important contributions that, according to these authors, a Protestant view of the Virgin Mary has in establishing the foundations for a Hispanic-Latino/a Lutheran spirituality. In this study, however, I want to move a step forward and explore not only the relevance of Mary but also the significance that the story of the Virgin of Guadalupe has for our Lutheran Latino/a identity.

To be sure, for Luther, Mary witnesses in the *Magnificat* to the power and wisdom of God manifested in the redemptive work of Jesus Christ, grasped by faith, and stimulated by the Holy Spirit that works salvation for all creation. Yet the provocative nature of this divine initiative turns out as a stumbling block and foolishness for human wisdom (see 1 Cor 1:17-31).

The revolutionary character of this "New Testament song of liberation,"[11] evoking the powerful memory of God's continuing actions throughout history to redeem the lowly, including the speaker herself and all marginal and exploited people, has led some contemporary theologians to describe Mary's witness as a "dangerous memory." One of these distinguished theologians is Elizabeth A. Johnson, whose study about Mary offers a provocative challenge to the church to empower its mission and ministry.[12]

[11] Jane Schaberg, "Luke," in *The Women's Bible Commentary*, ed. Carol A. Newsom and Sharon H. Ringe (Louisville, KY: Westminster John Knox Press, 1992), 284.

[12] Elizabeth A. Johnson, *Dangerous Memories: A Mosaic of Mary in Scripture* (New York: Continuum, 2004). Johnson appropriated this concept from the German theologian Johannes Baptist Metz who describes the practice of remembrance found in the New Testament and during the age of the early martyrs promoting a companionship in Christ between the living and the dead as a type of "dangerous" remembrance. Johnson writes, "Why dangerous? Because it interrupts the present moment, which can be all-absorbing, and discloses that something more is possible. . . . In situations of injustice, it challenges the status quo, saying: you can resist the course of things. By bringing 'something more' into view, it reminds us of a future worth struggling for and sets our feet on the path of active discipleship. Remembering the saints this way creates a moral and social force that propels the church out of passivity into active engagement on behalf of all those in agony. It has a transforming power that energizes resistance and active love. In the light of their dangerous memory, we become partners in hope" (29–30). See also Johannes

In her book, Johnson turns to the Scripture and other available documents (archaeological excavations, economic and sociological studies of the Roman Empire, research on the role of women, the study of ancient authors like the Jewish historian Josephus, and other important resources) to retrieve the actual political, economic, religious, and cultural world that Mary of Nazareth inhabited. Miriam of Nazareth—for such was her name in Hebrew—was a young Jewish woman (fifteen or sixteen years old), married to Joseph, the local village carpenter, and a mother, who lived in Galilee in the decades before and after AD 1, "by which the Western calendar now divides the eras."[13] Johnson's further description of Mary is that of a woman subject to social, political, and economic exclusion, yet graced by the Spirit to witness to God's redeeming power in history.

> Miriam of Nazareth lived in a world of social stratification marked by great disparities in wealth and privilege. Her life is typical of that of countless women throughout the ages who experience civic powerlessness, poverty and the suffering that results from low status and lack of formal education. . . . [She] occupied the lower rung of the social and economic ladder, and her life was lived out in an economically poor, politically oppressed, Jewish peasant culture marked by exploitation and publicly violent events. . . . This picture is of interest not simply for historical reasons but also for religious ones. It intrigues us as the locus of Mary's encounter with God. It is precisely in this economic, political, and cultural setting, living out her Jewish faith as a peasant woman of the people, that Mary walked her journey of faith in response to the promptings of the Spirit. It is precisely to such a woman, who counts for nothing on the stage of the world empire, that God has done great things. It is precisely such a woman who sings joyfully that God her savior is coming to overturn oppression in favor of the poor of the earth.[14]

For Johnson, the relevance of Mary's witness lies in being constitutive of the witness of a multigenerational community of saints, graced

---

Baptist Metz, *Faith in History and Society: Toward a Practical Fundamental Theology*, trans. David Smith (New York: Seabury, 1980), esp. "The Dangerous Memory of the Freedom of Jesus Christ" (88–99) and "Categories: Memory, Narrative, Solidarity" (184–237). Johnson's book mentioned above corresponds to chap. 10 of an earlier, broader examination she made of this topic: *Truly Our Sister: A Theology of Mary in the Communion of Saints* (New York: Continuum, 2003).

[13] E. Johnson, *Dangerous Memories*, 12.

[14] Ibid., 20–21.

by the Spirit crossing the boundaries of time and geographical location throughout history. This inclusive community transcending boundaries of language, culture, race, sex, class, sexual orientation, religion, and all other human distinctions, living out its vocation in their own time and place, is linked to all who respond to the gift of the Spirit in their own context. The memory of Mary's company with God releases the power of her life into the world ahead surrounding us with the encouragement of her life to challenge, console, and create liberating energies for our present ministry and mission. This is the type of memory that instead of evoking nostalgic sentimentality inspires the courage, suffering, wisdom, beauty, defeats, and victories of those who preceded us in their witness of faith to provide what according to Augustine are the "lessons of encouragement,"[15] to bolster our commitment and witness in the present.[16] Furthermore, the significance and dangerous nature of this practice lies in its link to the most important act of remembrance that shapes Christian identity: the sacrament of the Eucharist.

> This practice is connected with the central act that shapes Christian identity, the liturgical memorial of the life, passion, death, and resurrection of Jesus Christ. As with every critical memory, remembrance of the crucified and risen Jesus Christ is "dangerous" in a very particular way. Since God sided with this victim of unjust execution rather than with his judges, this memory subverts the expectation that the powerful will always win. Instead, God is in solidarity with those who suffer, galvanizing hope for salvation. This creates a moral and social hope that propels the church out of passivity into active engagement on behalf of all those in agony; in particular, those brought low by human injustice. The effective power of this memory with its hope in the future, promised but unknown, has sustained the church's efforts to live with passion and compassion in the world, and continues to do so even now.[17]

Linda B. Hall has shown in her research the powerful and complex impact that the reverence for the Virgin Mary has in many parts of Latin

---

[15] "Blessed be the saints in whose memory we are celebrating the day they suffered on, they have left us lessons of encouragement" (Augustine, Sermon 273.2, "On the Birthday of the Martyrs, Fructuosus, Bishop, and Augurius and Eulogius, Deacons," in *Sermons*, ed. John Rotelle, trans. Edmund Hill, 11 vols. [Brooklyn, NY: New City Press, 1990–95]).

[16] E. Johnson, *Dangerous Memories*, 26–30.

[17] E. Johnson, *Truly Our Sister*, 320.

America and among Latino/a populations in the United States. One of
the most important findings of her study is the remarkable ambiguity in
the empowerment that reverence for the Virgin provides to her devotees.
While for sixteenth-century Iberian conquistadors their view of the Virgin
tended to support their imperialistic and cultural conquest and justify
their position of dominance, for indigenous people and African slaves
their devotion to the Virgin Mary frequently supported their struggles
for resistance and liberation.

> [The Virgin Mary's] actions can invert or reinforce relations of domi-
> nance; the vision of her is ambiguous and ambivalent among members
> of the same cultural milieu and even within an individual; she can be
> challenging and transforming. Although she may be used in an attempt
> to reinforce gender ideologies of passivity and obedience for women
> and other subordinate people, she may certainly be used to empower
> them as well. I consider, in fact, that in Spain and Latin America and
> among Latino populations in the United States, belief in the Virgin has
> been empowering and that this empowerment has been more impor-
> tant than any sort of gender-related restrictions based on the model of
> Mary as Virgin. Of course, the effects have varied greatly depending on
> time and place.[18]

This profound ambiguity has caused heated debates among Catholic
and Protestant groups regarding the role of this important legacy of our
Christian tradition in the social, political, ideological, and religious arenas.[19]
Recently, however, a new study provided by the Mexican American New
Testament scholar David A. Sánchez[20] has brought important insights to
address this topic. Following a postcolonial approach to social, political,
historical, ideological, religious, and biblical hermeneutics, he argues that

---

[18] Linda B. Hall, *Mary, Mother and Warrior: The Virgin in Spain and the Americas*
(Austin: University of Texas Press, 2004), 16.

[19] See the excellent review provided by Maxwell E. Johnson on this topic from
the origins of the Guadalupan narratives in the sixteenth century to the present
in *The Virgin of Guadalupe*, 35–181.

[20] David A. Sánchez is assistant professor of New Testament at Loyola Mary-
mount University, Los Angeles, California. Along with a new generation of Latino/a
scholars, the quality of his studies and research was impacted by the support of
the Hispanic Theological Initiative that provided both financial assistance and
mentoring from more developed Latino/a scholars whose scholarly works have
already been established and received recognition in the academy.

the story of the Virgin of Guadalupe is a lucid example of an expression from subaltern sectors of society aimed at subverting imperial myths that have subsisted in the Americas over time and cultural transformations to challenge the centers of imperial and colonial power. Using the contributions of political scientist and Yale scholar James C. Scott on the process of social, political, and ideological domination, the arts of resistance, and the weapons of the weak,[21] Sánchez engages in a critical study of what he calls the oversaturation of public images of the Virgin of Guadalupe in the barrios of East Los Angeles as public performances of a unique and socially located form of biblical interpretation.

> To many on the outside, she represents a quirky symbol of a specifically Mexican brand of Roman Catholicism. To some insiders, her role is limited to the feminine representation of the divine that is so firmly embedded in ancient Mexican—and by extension, Chicana/o-religious sensibilities. But to those inclined toward a posture of resistance, the appeal to the iconography of the Virgin of Guadalupe represents a subversive form of countercolonial and counterimperial resistance.[22]

In his analysis Sánchez brings together an intertextual examination of two important sources that have not been given adequate attention in the past as crucial for interpreting the significance of this popular religious expression of resistance.

> The pressing question is, how did she [the Virgin of Guadalupe] become a locus of resistance? Or even more appropriately, how did we come to recognize her as such? To answer these questions, we need to assess two specific moments in history: 1) seventeenth-century Mexico, where the first literary depictions of the apparition of the Virgin of Guadalupe account are attested; and 2) first-century Asia Minor, specifically the island of Patmos, where John the seer received his apocalypse and subsequently wrote the final entry of the New Testament, the book of Revelation. . . .

[21] James C. Scott, *Weapons of the Weak: Everyday Forms of Peasant Resistance* (New Haven, CT: Yale University Press, 1985), and also from the same author, *Domination and the Arts of Resistance: Hidden Transcripts* (New Haven, CT: Yale University Press, 1990).

[22] David A. Sánchez, *From Patmos to the Barrio: Subverting Imperial Myths* (Minneapolis, MN: Fortress Press, 2008), 1–2; see also pp. 3–12.

Therefore, I take the reader back to where it all began. Surprisingly, the beginning is not colonial Mexico, where the apparition of the Virgin presumably took place on a hill just north of Mexico City in 1531. Instead, the beginning can be traced to a most unlikely location and time: a rocky, desolate island in the Aegean Sea, known in the first century C.E. as Patmos. What will emerge is a powerful relationship between an ancient Christian prophet and the subsequent literary and artistic manifestations of the Queen of Heaven in the form of the Virgin of Guadalupe.[23]

Following the contributions of James Scott mentioned above, Sánchez describes the process by which marginalized groups tend to appropriate imperial mythologies as weapons to counter colonial and imperialist power.

Throughout the course of human history, dominating peoples have used imperial myths to justify their claims to power and to subjugate those under their jurisdiction. These myths come in a variety of forms. Some claim a special relationship between a deity or deities and a people, while others draw a direct genealogical line between the gods and a monarch or a prophetic figure of the ruling class. Regardless of the form, these myths serve the ruling class as justification for the construction of a social hierarchy. In contrast, those who have been marginalized by these myths have persistently reconfigured and manipulated them. In moments of resistance, those living on the margins of power claim these imperial myths on their own interpretive terms, creating alternative categories of power in which they construct themselves as the primary beneficiaries of newly reformulated social hierarchies.

Literary and artistic representations of these complex cultural encounters and their subsequent relationships are generally obscured because it is usually those with power who document such encounters, thereby relegating strategies of the marginalized to the fringes of our collective recollections and leaving us a one-sided unbalanced history. As recipients of these unbalanced histories, we must redirect our historical gaze to the shadows of empire, to those interstitial and hybrid spaces where marginalized peoples are actively and continually producing offstage countermythologies.[24]

[23] Ibid., 2–3; see also 13–82.
[24] Ibid., 3; see also 83–113.

The consequence is a compelling and persuasive proposal for interpreting the story of the Virgin of Guadalupe as a religious and cultural representation of a subversive form of countercolonial and counterimperial popular expression of resistance.

To be sure, recent research about the significance of the popular religious story of the Virgin of Guadalupe opens new vistas on the substance and interpretive perspective of this important story. While early Latino/a and non-Latino/a religious scholars focused on the theological significance of this popular story, new generations of scholars broaden the horizon to incorporate additional historical, social, political, ideological, religious, biblical, and theological dimensions of this religious expression. In my estimation, this is such an important expansion in the interpretation of the significance of popular religious symbols that it deserves more attention and intentional investigation by all sectors of society. If this trend continues to expand with new generations of scholars in the various areas of human research laying the ground for important initiatives that may be drawn by our religious leaders, then not only will Protestant circles need to pay more serious attention to popular religious stories like the one about the Virgin of Guadalupe, but the church at large will need to incorporate these "dangerous" subversive religious narratives as important sources informing its ministry and mission. When this view becomes a regular and constitutive element of the public witness of our church bodies, then we may claim it indeed as an important contribution to the ministry and mission of the church drawn from the witness of faith of our Latino/a people.

8

The Development of the Liturgical Feast of the Virgin of Guadalupe and Its Celebration in the Season of Advent

Maxwell E. Johnson

Among Mexican American Roman Catholics and, increasingly, among various Hispanic-Latino Protestant communities as well (especially, but not only, within some communities of Episcopalians and Lutherans[1]), the feast of the Virgin of Guadalupe on December 12 is—or is becoming—an important mid-Advent celebration, important enough in some contexts to challenge even the priority of an Advent Sunday when December 12 itself happens to fall on a Sunday, as it will in 2010.[2] Surely this is due in large part to

---

[1] See the various celebrations noted in chap. 4 of my book, *The Virgin of Guadalupe: Theological Reflections of an Anglo-Lutheran Liturgist*, Celebrating Faith: Explorations in Latino Spirituality and Theology (Lanham, MD: Rowman & Littlefield, 2002), 122–26, and above, p. 2. For an intriguing essay on Guadalupe from a Mexican American Baptist theological perspective see Nora O. Lozano-Díaz, "Ignored Virgin or Unaware Women: A Mexican-American Protestant Reflection on the Virgin of Guadalupe," in *A Reader in Latina Feminist Theology: Religion and Justice*, ed. María Pilar Aquino, Daisy L. Machado, and Jeanette Rodríguez (Austin: University of Texas Press, 2002), 204–16.

[2] See Alex García-Rivera, "Let's Capture the Hispanic Imagination," *U.S. Catholic* (July 1994): 34–35.

the fact that, as John Baldovin has written, "in our own time the Virgin of Guadalupe has served as an effective rallying point for a whole people's hopes for liberation and justice as well as an anchor for their Christian identity."[3] As such, the feast of the Virgin of Guadalupe may well be a rather obvious example of the following primary characteristic of festivity: "[F]easts are extraordinary. They lift people out of ordinary chronological time. . . . Feasts are not merely collective visible events but also 'total social facts.' . . . Pulling all the stops out for a celebration means having it in a larger social context, something that the entire community can celebrate meaningfully."[4] As a "total social fact," a "fiesta" for some communities that goes well beyond the confines of the specific *liturgical* celebration of December 12,[5] the feast of the Virgin of Guadalupe and other similar feasts cannot simply be ignored either by contemporary liturgiologists or pastoral liturgists.

It is thus both with the December 12 feast itself—its origins and development—and with the location of this feast within the Advent season that this essay is concerned. While it is often asserted that feasts such as this point to and underscore an almost irreconcilable tension between official liturgy and popular religion or popular piety,[6] a tension that creates

---

[3] John Baldovin, "The Liturgical Year: Calendar for a Just Community," in *Between Memory and Hope: Readings on the Liturgical Year*, ed. Maxwell E. Johnson (Collegeville, MN: Liturgical Press, Pueblo, 2000), 436–37.

[4] John Baldovin, "On Feasting the Saints," in M. E. Johnson, *Between Memory and Hope*, 382–83.

[5] On the concept of "fiesta" see Virgilio Elizondo, *Galilean Journey: The Mexican-American Promise* (Maryknoll, NY: Orbis, 1983), 120; and the essays in Kenneth G. Davis, ed., *Misa, Mesa y Musa: Liturgy in the U.S. Hispanic Church*, 2nd ed. (Schiller Park, IL: World Library Publications, 1997). For a firsthand experience of this Guadalupan fiesta both in Mexico and Los Angeles see the essay by Rubén Martínez, "The Undocumented Virgin," in *Goddess of the Americas, La Diosa de las Américas: Writings on the Virgin of Guadalupe*, ed. Ana Castillo (New York: Riverhead Books, 1996), 106–9. For a description of events at the plaza and basilica in Mexico City on a Sunday outside of December see Eryk Hanut, *The Road to Guadalupe: A Modern Pilgrimage to the Goddess of the Americas* (New York: Tarcher/Putnam, 2001), 118–26.

[6] On popular religion or popular piety in general see the Congregation for Divine Worship and the Discipline of the Sacraments, *Directory on Popular Piety and the Liturgy: Principles and Guidelines* (Rome: Vatican City, 2001). For discussion of and various approaches to popular religion in a Hispanic-Latino context see Orlando O. Espín, *The Faith of the People: Theological Reflections on Popular*

all kinds of local problems in the celebration of the church's liturgy, I want to question whether this tension is more perceived or imagined than necessarily real in the case of Guadalupe. Might, in fact, the December 12 feast in the middle of Advent represent, at least at some level, a synthesis of what our Advent hopes and expectations are all about? Might the Virgin of Guadalupe herself be an indigenous American "icon" of the Advent stance of the church in the world between the "now" and "not yet" of redemption as well as provide a synthesis of the eschatological and incarnational orientations of this liturgical season? Such questions, I believe, can be answered in the affirmative.

The Development of the Feast of the Virgin of Guadalupe on December 12

The origins and development of the feast of the Virgin of Guadalupe on December 12 are as difficult to discern as are the precise historical origins of the Guadalupan narratives and images themselves.[7] No written record of a feast of Guadalupe celebrated on December 12 at Tepeyac, the location of the alleged apparitions to Juan Diego in 1531, exists before 1662, at which time the cathedral chapter of Mexico City requested approval from Rome for the feast on this date, a request that was delayed until 1667. When finally approved by Rome, the response contained the incorrect date of *September* rather than December 12, an error that served to delay the process even further. Earlier, the feast day at Tepeyac was, apparently, September 8, the feast of both the Nativity of the Blessed Virgin Mary on the general Roman liturgical calendar and of the Extremaduran

---

Catholicism (Maryknoll, NY: Orbis, 1997); Roberto S. Goizueta, *Caminemos con Jesús: Toward a Hispanic/Latino Theology of Accompaniment* (Maryknoll, NY: Orbis, 1995); Alex García-Rivera, *St. Martín de Porres: The "Little Stories" and the Semiotics of Culture* (Maryknoll, NY: Orbis, 1995); and Anita de Luna, *Faith Formation and Popular Religion: Lessons from Tejano Experience*, Celebrating Faith: Explorations in Latino Spirituality and Theology (Lanham, MD: Rowman & Littlefield, 2002). On the resurgence of popular religion in other contexts see Patrick Malloy, "The Re-Emergence of Popular Religion Among Non-Hispanic American Catholics," *Worship* 72, no. 1 (1998): 2–25; and Michael Driscoll, "Liturgy and Devotions: Back to the Future?" in *The Renewal That Awaits Us*, ed. Eleanor Bernstein and Martin Connell (Chicago, IL: Liturgy Training Publications, 1997), 68–90.

[7] On this see chap. 2 of my *The Virgin of Guadalupe*, 35–61.

Guadalupe on the local liturgical calendar of the Extremadura region in Spain.[8] In fact, it was not until May 25, 1754, that Pope Benedict XIV finally confirmed both the patronage of the Virgin Mary under the title of the Mexican advocation of Our Lady of Guadalupe for "New Spain" and approved officially the liturgical Propers (i.e., prayers, readings, and chants) for the Mass and Divine Office for the December 12 feast on the official, local calendar of Mexico.[9] Nevertheless, it is obvious that the feast had been celebrated in Mexico on December 12 for some time prior to this confirmation and approval, *at least* from 1662.

Stafford Poole takes this late acceptance of the December 12 date for the feast as further confirmation of his overall thesis that, directly inspired by the written narratives of Miguel Sánchez (1648)[10] and Luis Laso de la Vega (1649),[11] the origins of Guadalupan devotion itself belong to an overall seventeenth, and not early sixteenth, century context.[12] But the

---

[8] On the relationship between the Extremaduran Guadalupe and the Mexican Guadalupe see Richard Nebel, *Santa María Tonantzin, Virgen de Guadalupe: Religiöse Kontinuität und Transformation in Mexiko* (Immensee, Switzerland: Neue Zeitschrift für Missionswissenschaft, 1992); published in Spanish as *Santa María Tonantzin, Virgen de Guadalupe: Continuidad y transformación religiosa en México* (Mexico City: Fondo de Cultura Económica, 1995), 221–27.

[9] See the detailed doctoral dissertation of J. Jesús Salazar, *"¿No estoy yo aqui, que soy tu Madre?" Investigación teológica-biblica-litúrgica acerca de La Nueva Liturgia de Nuestra Señora de Guadalupe*, vol. 1 (STD dissertation, Pontifical Institute of Liturgy, Rome: Sant' Anselmo, 1981), 141–202.

[10] Miguel Sánchez, *Imagen de la Virgen María, Madre de Dios de Guadalupe: Milagrosamente aparecida en la Ciudad de México, celebrada en su historia, con la profecía del capítulo doze del Apocalipsis* (Mexico City: Imp. Vidua de Bernardo Calderón, 1648; reprinted by Cuernavaca, Morelos, 1952).

[11] Luis Laso de la Vega, *Huei tlamahuiçoltica omonexiti in ilhuicac tlatocacihaupilli Santa Maria totlaçonantzin Guadalupe in nican Huei altepenahuac Mexico itocayocan Tepeyacac* (1649). For the very first time a critical edition of the transliterated Náhuatl text with English translation, notes, and introduction has been published: Lisa Sousa, Stafford Poole, and James Lockhart, eds., *The Story of Guadalupe: Luis Laso de la Vega's Huei tlamahuiçoltica of 1649*, UCLA Latin American Studies, vol. 84 (Stanford, CA: Stanford University Press, 1998).

[12] Stafford Poole, *Our Lady of Guadalupe: The Origins and Sources of a Mexican National Symbol, 1531–1797* (Tucson: University of Arizona Press, 1995), 37–41. Poole's study must be read in conjunction with Richard Nebel, *Santa María Tonantzin, Virgen de Guadalupe* (German, 1992; Spanish, 1995); and D. A. Brading, *Mexican Phoenix: Our Lady of Guadalupe: Image and Tradition across Five Centuries*

lateness of the "official" recognition of the December 12 date for the *feast* only confirms either that the choice of this particular date, the date associated in other narratives with the fourth and final apparition, was inspired possibly by the official written Guadalupan narratives, or, alternatively, that the date in the narratives was possibly inspired by the growing Guadalupan oral tradition itself. Indeed, in the history of especially Marian feasts in Western Christianity, the time it takes from the origins of a particular feast in a local church or religious community to when it becomes recognized officially or incorporated into the general liturgical calendar can take several centuries! This does not mean that the feast is not already being celebrated somewhere by some communities during this period of development but only that official recognition, approval, or incorporation into the official calendar is not the same thing as the origins of its celebration. That is, official confirmation does not mean the beginnings of a feast itself but it is simply the confirmation, permission, and approval for what is already taking place. To give but one obvious example here: The December 8 (now) solemnity of the Immaculate Conception of Mary has its origins in an eighth-century Byzantine Christian December 9 feast called the Conception of St. Anne, a feast still celebrated today in the Christian East.[13] This entered the West via monastic usage in England in the eleventh century, and from England it spread with increasing popularity throughout Western Europe especially within various religious orders and communities, most notably the Franciscans, whose own itinerant lifestyle contributed to its wide dissemination. Together with growing theological speculation about Mary's "immaculate conception" (her preservation, or "redemption by exemption," from original sin), primarily among Franciscan theologians from the thirteenth century on, the feast was accepted for Rome by a Franciscan pope (Sixtus IV) only in 1477, and it became a

---

(Cambridge: Cambridge University Press, 2001). See also Magnus Lundberg, *Unification and Conflict: The Church Politics of Alonso de Montúfar, OP, Archbishop of Mexico, 1554–1572*, Studia Missionalia Svecana 86 (Lund, Sweden: Lund University, 2002), 197–220.

[13] While the date of December 8 for this feast in the West places it exactly nine months before the September 8 feast of Mary's Nativity, the choice of December 9 in the East was made, it appears, for a theological reason. That is, only with regard to Christ can there be a perfect nine-month interval between his conception (the feast of the Annunciation on March 25) and his birth (December 25). In the East, the intervals between the conceptions and births of others, including Mary, are thus symbolically less than a perfect nine months.

universal feast for the entire Roman Catholic Church only in 1708. Even so, the particular title of this feast today, the *Immaculate* Conception of Mary, did not become its official title until after the promulgation of the dogma of Mary's immaculate conception by Pope Pius IX in 1854.[14] From its eighth-century origins in the Christian East, then, it took almost *ten* centuries for it to become a universal feast in the West and *eleven* centuries for it to develop into its current form. Hence, that a local feast like the Virgin of Guadalupe might take from 1531 until 1662 (or 1754) to evolve into its final form is actually a relatively short period of time in the historical development of liturgical feasts.

At the same time, the fact that September 8 may well have been the original date of the feast, corresponding already to both the feast of the Nativity of Mary and the Extremaduran Guadalupe celebrated at Tepeyac, is, again, really no indication whatsoever, pro or con, of the historicity of devotion to the Mexican Guadalupe herself. Indeed, not only do dates of feasts periodically change throughout history, but if the September 8 feast of the Nativity of Mary was already the titular feast of the chapel of Tepeyac, that is, if the feast for the Extremaduran Virgin of Guadalupe at Tepeyac was the Nativity of Mary,[15] there is really no reason to expect an alternate date being sought or established for a separate feast day in honor of the *Mexican* Guadalupe. The Guadalupan narratives themselves nowhere call for the establishment of a new liturgical *feast* in her honor and, in fact, there was really no need for a separate Marian feast. Had there in fact been a call for such an establishment, this would have been undoubtedly resisted by the early Franciscan ecclesiastical authorities as much as they were already highly suspicious and critical of the indigenous Guadalupan devotion itself.[16]

Furthermore, there is early sixteenth-century evidence for the existence of the celebration of the feast of the (Immaculate) Conception of Mary on December 8 in Mexico. If this feast was not yet a universal Roman Catholic

[14] On the development of this feast see Pierre Jounel, "The Veneration of Mary," in *The Liturgy and Time*, vol. 4 of *The Church at Prayer*, ed. A. G. Martimort (Collegeville, MN: Liturgical Press, 1986), 139–40; and Kilian McDonnell, "The Marian Liturgical Tradition," in M. E. Johnson, *Between Memory and Hope*, 390–91.

[15] See Fidel de Jesús Chauvet, "Historia del Culto Guadalupano," in *Album Conmemorative del 450 Aniversario de las Apariciones de Nuestra Señora de Guadalupe* (México, D.F.: Buena Neuva, A.C., 1981), 34. Chauvet refers here to a sixteenth-century journal of a Juan Bautista.

[16] See M. E. Johnson, *The Virgin of Guadalupe*, 57–58.

feast in the early sixteenth century, it was certainly already being celebrated in the region of Tepeyac, as the existence of a poetic homily of Bernardino de Sahagún for the feast (called by him simply "The Conception of the Blessed Virgin Mary") clearly demonstrates.[17] Even if, then, there *had* been some kind of early indigenous push for an additional Marian feast in close association to December 8 one can only imagine that it too would have been met with resistance and rejection for the simple reason that there already *was* a Marian feast in close proximity to the date.

At the same time, the fact that the liturgical Propers (prayers, chants, and Lectionary readings) for the September 8 feast of the Nativity of Mary would have been used to celebrate the Virgin of Guadalupe, whether in her Spanish or Mexican advocation, proves nothing about the existence of the feast itself. It only means that, as in the case of the Extremaduran Guadalupe, the liturgical Propers of the Nativity of Mary came to be used for the Mexican Guadalupe and that both were associated originally with September 8 in Mexico. Indeed, there is some evidence to suggest that in this time period the prayers and readings in what is called the Common of Feasts of the Blessed Virgin Mary, that is, the collection of prayer texts and readings to be used for feasts not having their own assigned Propers, were identical to those also assigned to the September 8 feast of the Nativity of Mary. Further confirmation of this is supplied by the fact that even when Pope Benedict XIV in 1754 finally approved the specific liturgical Propers for the Guadalupe feast on December 12 the Mass for the feast remained, essentially, that of the Nativity of Mary.[18]

As I have argued elsewhere is quite possibly the case with the official Guadalupan narratives of Sánchez and Laso de la Vega in the mid-seventeenth century,[19] I suspect that the *official* establishment of the feast of the Virgin of Guadalupe on December 12 is the response of local (Mexican) ecclesiastical authorities to the increasing popularity of Guadalupan devotion itself. Indeed, as long as that devotion was localized at Tepeyac and associated primarily with the indigenous peoples, there was no perceived need for a "national" feast. But, what Jean-Pierre Ruiz has suggested with regard to how the official narratives appear to reflect the

---

[17] See *Bernardino de Sahagún's Psalmodia Christiana* (Christian Psalmody), trans. Arthur J. O. Anderson (Salt Lake City: University of Utah Press, 1993), 353–59.

[18] On all of this see Salazar, *"¿No estoy yo aqui, que soy tu Madre?,"* vol. 1, 141–202.

[19] See M. E. Johnson, *The Virgin of Guadalupe*, 51–58.

"canonization" of the Guadalupan events might also well be related to the development of the feast itself. That is, if by this time, according to Ruiz, "the Virgin of Guadalupe had reached an important breadth of diffusion throughout the various ethnic and socioeconomic strata of colonial Mexico, ranging from the indigenous Nahuas, to the *criollos*, to the Spanish born,"[20] then the establishment of an official feast in her honor may well have been but another concrete expression and confirmation of this widespread development and acceptance. This kind of development and acceptance, in fact, has continued well until our own day with a revision of the 1754 liturgy by Pope Leo XIII in 1894,[21] and, more important, with new Propers for the solemnity of the Virgin of Guadalupe appearing for Mexico in 1974,[22] and for the "feast" of the Virgin of Guadalupe for the dioceses of the United States appearing in 1987.[23] Prior to this development, the December 12 feast had been permitted for United States dioceses only since 1962 as the equivalent of an optional memorial.

The Feast of the Virgin of Guadalupe and the Season of Advent

However it was that the feast of the Virgin of Guadalupe came to be celebrated ultimately on December 12, this feast, together with the solemnity of the Immaculate Conception of Mary four days before it, tends to provide an overall Marian focus, especially among Mexicans and Mexican Americans, for the liturgical season of Advent. That is, the popular observance of the season of Advent among Mexican and Mexican American Catholics is organized as follows:

[20] Jean-Pierre Ruiz, "The Bible and U.S. Hispanic American Theological Discourse," in *From the Heart of Our People: Latino/a Explorations in Catholic Systematic Theology*, ed. Orlando O. Espín and Miguel H. Díaz (Maryknoll, NY: Orbis, 1999), 112–13.

[21] On this, see Salazar, *"¿No estoy yo aqui, que soy tu Madre?,"* vol. 1, 174ff.

[22] See *Misal Romano*, 2nd ed. (Mexico, D.F.: Obra Nacional de la Buena Prensa, A.C., 2001), 596–97; and *Propio de los Santos y Otras Misas*, vol. 3 of *Leccionario*, 1st ed. (Mexico, D.F.: Obra Nacional de la Buena Prensa, A.C., 2001), 172–74.

[23] Bishops' Committee on the Liturgy, *Newsletter 23: Feast of Our Lady of Guadalupe*, 45; and idem., *Newsletter 24: Feast of Our Lady of Guadalupe and New Liturgical Texts* (Washington, DC: National Conference of Catholic Bishops, 1988), 5–6.

December 3–11: Novena to the Virgin of Guadalupe
> (nine days of special prayer, devotion, and preparation for the December 12 celebration)[24]

December 8: Solemnity of the Immaculate Conception

December 9: (Optional) Memorial of St. Juan Diego Cuauhtlatoatzin

December 12: Solemnity or Feast of the Virgin of Guadalupe

December 16–24: Las Posadas Novena
> (nine days of special prayer, devotion, and preparation, often celebrated in neighborhoods or in parish communities, consisting especially of festive processions, songs, and ceremonies reenacting the search of Mary and Joseph for lodging in Bethlehem, followed by joyful celebrations with food and singing at the final designated home or place in the search)[25]

On the popular religious level, then, the first part of the Advent season is oriented to and concerned with prayerful preparation for the December 12 appearance of the pregnant Virgin of Guadalupe. And after she appears, the rest of the season is devoted to accompanying her and Joseph to Bethlehem for the birth of Christ, an accompaniment often with profound implications for many Hispanic-Latinos, especially immigrants, in the United States. As Virgil Elizondo notes:

> The *posada* is easily a *cultic* reminder and reenactment as well, for Mexican Americans who have walked, often at night and through snake-infested deserts, to the United States in the hope of finding work. What they found instead was rejection after rejection. But, like Joseph and Mary, they did not give up; they followed their star.
> The *posada* is a living symbol of a living faith.[26]

---

[24] For an example of this novena see Celestina Castro, MC-M, *Novena a La Santísima Virgen de Guadalupe, Reina de las Américas* (San Antonio, TX: Mexican American Cultural Center, no date). See also William G. Storey, *Mother of the Americas: A Novena in Honor of Our Lady of Guadalupe/Madre de America: Una Novena en Honor a Nuestra Señora de Guadalupe* (Chicago, IL: Liturgy Training Publications, 2003).

[25] For a brief description see Workshops on Hispanic Liturgy and Popular Piety, *Faith Expressions of Hispanics in the Southwest*, rev. ed. (San Antonio, TX: Mexican American Cultural Center, 1990), 12–13.

[26] Virgilio Elizondo, "Living Faith: Resistance and Survival," in *Mestizo Worship: A Pastoral Approach to Liturgical Ministry*, ed. Virgilio Elizondo and Timothy Matovina (Collegeville, MN: Liturgical Press, 1998), 11–12.

Particularly as the Virgin of Guadalupe, Mary becomes, then, on the popular religious level the image *par excellence* of Advent expectation and preparation and Advent itself becomes a rather Marian season in overall emphasis. Nevertheless, if decidedly Marian in emphasis, even this, of course, is oriented, christologically, to Christmas.

The question, however, is whether such an obvious Marian focus is what the liturgical season of Advent itself is really about. On the official Roman Catholic (and contemporary Protestant) liturgical level the season of Advent is not Marian but primarily eschatological and only secondarily incarnational in focus. That is, within the current three-year Lectionary used by Roman Catholics and adapted by several contemporary Protestant liturgical traditions today, the Lectionary readings assigned to the first three Sundays of this season are all oriented toward the Parousia of Christ in glory and not to his first coming in Bethlehem at Christmas. The Advent call to "prepare the way of the Lord," then, is a call more related to the church's own eschatological stance in the world as oriented in hope toward ultimate fulfillment in Christ when "he will come again to judge the living and the dead" than it is to preparing for Jesus' "birthday." As such, Christmas becomes less a celebration of a past historical event (Christ's birth) and more a kind of anticipated celebration of the Parousia itself, a celebration of the fullness of redemption and *our* new birth by baptism in the One whom the late Raymond Brown referred to as the "adult Christ at Christmas."[27] In fact, it is only on the Fourth Sunday in Advent where the current Lectionary readings themselves shift from a clearly eschatological to an incarnational or Christmas focus, with the gospel pericopes of the annunciation to Joseph (Matt 1:18-24), the annunciation to Mary (Luke 1:26-38), and the visitation of Mary to Elizabeth (Luke 1:39-45), read respectively in Years A, B, and C of the three-year cycle. Such a shift to an incarnational focus is supported also by the use of the famous "O" antiphons connected to the gospel canticle of the *Magnificat* at Evening Prayer beginning on December 17.

It is because of both the strong eschatological character of Advent (assuming its final and current form in the Roman liturgy under Pope Gregory I at the beginning of the seventh century) and its actual location within the classic Roman liturgical books at the *end*—and not at the *beginning*—of the

---

[27] See Raymond Brown's delightful short commentaries on the infancy narratives of Matthew and Luke in *An Adult Christ at Christmas* (Collegeville, MN: Liturgical Press, 1978). These essays are also available in Raymond Brown, *Christ in the Gospels of the Liturgical Year*, ed. Ronald D. Witherup, exp. ed. (Collegeville, MN: Liturgical Press, 2008), 99–142.

liturgical year that some contemporary liturgical scholars are asserting that the eschatological season of Advent has more to do with the *conclusion* of the liturgical year than with its annual beginning. Historically, its proximity to Christmas, therefore, would have been more accidental than deliberate in Rome, although today it is certainly constructed both as the beginning of the year and as a season of preparation for Christmas.[28] But whatever the historical case, the overall eschatological orientation of Advent toward the Parousia in the liturgical books today certainly suggests that there is a tension between the "official" Advent liturgy and the Marian focus of the season in Mexican and Mexican American popular religion. Elizondo himself refers to this tension when he writes that:

> The entire complex of events at Tepeyac was as mysterious as it was ultimately real. The bishop was disconcerted and his household was disturbed, as theologians, liturgists, and catechists usually are with the ways of God's poor. To this day, liturgists do not want to accept the feast of Our Lady of Guadalupe as the *major feast of Advent*. For them, it seems that God made a mistake in placing the feast of Guadalupe during Advent.[29]

Indeed, related to this, it is interesting to note that the liturgical color of royal or Sarum blue, becoming increasingly (and ecumenically) popular as an alternative to the traditional purple or violet Advent color for vestments and paraments during the season, is actually resisted today in several Roman Catholic dioceses precisely *because* blue has traditional Roman Catholic associations with Mary herself (the "lovely Lady dressed in blue").[30] That is, while several contemporary Protestant liturgical tradi-

---

[28] On this see especially J. Neil Alexander, *Waiting for the Coming: The Liturgical Meaning of Advent, Christmas, Epiphany* (Washington, DC: Pastoral Press, 1993), 7–27. See also Bryan D. Spinks, "Revising the Advent-Christmas-Epiphany Cycle in the Church of England," *Studia Liturgica* 17 (1987): 166–75.

[29] Virgilio Elizondo, *Guadalupe: Mother of the New Creation* (Maryknoll, NY: Orbis, 1997), 95; emphasis added.

[30] The use of blue during Advent and the several erroneous assumptions made about its use historically have been surveyed recently by J. Barrington Bates, "Am I Blue? Some Historical Evidence for Liturgical Colors," *Studia Liturgica* 33 (2003): 75–84. Of particular interest is that in the primarily English sources that Bates discusses blue was used in some places during Lent and other times of the year but *not* during Advent, not even at Salisbury (Sarum) Cathedral, the cathedral where the custom is often thought to have been most characteristic.

tions have embraced blue as an alternative color for the season, presumably reflecting Advent "hope," Roman Catholics have tended to resist and, in some cases, not even permit its use because Advent is *not*—and is not to be construed as—a Marian season!

But if there is a tension between the "official" eschatological Advent of modern Western Christianity and the "popular" Marian Advent of Hispanic-Latino piety, a more Marian-focused Advent does appear to have some affinities to the pre-Christmas seasons of preparation in some of the Eastern Christian liturgical rites, to other early non-Roman Western liturgical traditions, and even to some characteristics within the earlier Roman Advent itself. In the Byzantine Rite, for example, beginning with the November 21 feast of the Presentation of Mary in the Temple, multiple Marian images associated with the "Ark of the Covenant," the "Tabernacle," and even as the "heavenly Temple" appear in the various *troparia* and prayers throughout the season.[31] And, two Sundays before Christmas, the Byzantine Rite commemorates the Holy Ancestors of Christ, culminating, of course, in Mary, and on the Sunday before Christmas is celebrated "all the Fathers who down the centuries have been pleasing to God, from Adam to Joseph, husband of the Most Holy Mother of God."[32] Among the Syrian Christian traditions, both West Syrian (i.e., Syrian and/or Antiochene Orthodox and Maronite) and East Syrian (i.e., Church of the East, Chaldean, and Syro-Malabar), the assigned gospel readings on the Sundays for the season of Christmas preparation, called Weeks of Annunciations, include, in order, the annunciation to Zechariah, the annunciation to Mary, the visitation, the nativity of John the Baptist, and, finally, the annunciation to Joseph. Indeed, for these reasons, Eastern Advent is often referred to as a Marian season.

In the ancient liturgies of the non-Roman West there is also some correspondence here. While the precise origins of the March 25 celebration of the Annunciation of Our Lord are obscure,[33] the feast on this date is known to have been celebrated already in the East by the beginning of the sixth century. Before that shift to a calendrical date, the Annunciation

[31] See Mother Mary and Archimandrite Kallistos Ware, *The Festal Menaion* (London/Boston: Faber and Faber, 1969), 164–98.

[32] Pierre Jounel, "The Christmas Season," in Martimort, *The Liturgy and Time*, 93.

[33] In early Christianity, March 25 was one of two calendrical dates assigned to the historical date of Christ's passion as the equivalent to 14 Nisan. In some communities April 6 was recognized as the corresponding date.

appears to have been celebrated on the Sunday before Christmas. Interestingly enough, the location of the feast of the Annunciation actually varied as to date in the calendars of other Western liturgical traditions throughout the Middle Ages. In Spain it was celebrated on December 18 and today, within the recently reformed post-Vatican liturgical books of the Spanish, or Mozarabic, Rite, December 18 has remained a solemnity of Mary called, simply, *Sancta Maria*, where the primary focus is still on the annunciation even though the annunciation itself is celebrated on March 25.[34] And in Milan, Italy, within the Ambrosian Rite, the Annunciation was and still is celebrated on the last of the *six* Sundays of Advent. Even in the liturgical tradition of Rome, a similar correlation between, at least, Annunciation and Christmas was also true of the more eschatologically oriented *Roman* Advent itself, although Rome had clearly accepted the March 25 date of the feast by the time of Pope Sergius I (687–701 CE). Prior to the post–Vatican II liturgical reform of the calendar, in fact, the gospel pericopes of both the annunciation and the visitation were read, respectively, on the Wednesday and Friday of the third week of Advent, formerly known as the Advent Ember Days, one of four annual "seasons" of special prayer and fasting throughout the liturgical year.[35] Hence, even with the acceptance of the March 25 date for the feast in the West, a close proximity between the celebration of the Annunciation (and the Visitation) and Christmas remained a traditional characteristic of Western liturgical history in general.

Because in Mary, according to *Sacrosanctum Concilium*, "the Church admires and exalts the most excellent fruit of redemption, and joyfully contemplates, as in a faultless image, that which she herself desires and hopes wholly to be" (103),[36] some today have begun to call for a reevaluation not only of the current ranking of Marian festivals on the liturgical calendar but also of their particular dates in relationship to the central mysteries of Christ at the obvious core of the liturgical year. Shawn Madigan, for example, writes:

[34] Conferencia Episcopal Española, *Missale Hispano-Mozarabicum* (Barcelona, 1994), 34, 136–42.

[35] On Ember Days, see Thomas J. Talley, "The Origins of the Ember Days: An Inconclusive Postscript," in *Rituels: Mélanges offerts à Pierre-Marie Gy, O.P.*, ed. Paul DeClerck and Eric Palazzo (Paris: Les Éditions du Cerf, 1990), 465–72.

[36] English translation from Austin Flannery, *Vatican Council II: The Conciliar and Post Conciliar Documents*, vol. 1, rev. ed. (Northport, NY: Costello Publishing Co., 1996).

The ranking of present festivals gives non-scriptural imagination as great a place, and occasionally, a greater place, than scriptural imagination. When Mary, Mother of God [Jan. 1], the most traditional scriptural festival is not transferred but dispensed with as a "holy day of obligation" because the clergy are too tired, there is need for liturgical critique. Why not cancel the Immaculate Conception instead? Why are scriptural festivals, such as Visitation and Lady of Sorrows, almost invisible?[37]

And, with particular regard to the appropriateness of Marian festivals and images during Advent, she calls for a kind of rethinking and restructuring of the season itself, asking:

What if the festivals of Annunciation and Visitation were placed early in the Advent season? If the Annunciation were celebrated on the first Sunday of Advent and the Visitation during that week, look at what could be accomplished. Christ the King readings of the end time could stand conclusively as the end of the liturgical year without beginning with another set of end times. The present Annunciation festival (March 25) could be relieved from its non-liturgical presence in the midst of Christ's imaging related to passiontide. This would also lessen the confusion about whether liturgical calendars are planned according to seasons or biological rhythms. Another accomplishment is that the readings for both festivals are appropriate advent reflections about the church (Annunciation: Is. 7:1-14; Heb. 10:4-10; Lk 1:26-38; Visitation: Zeph. 3:14-19; Rom 12:9-16; Lk 1:39-56). If the Visitation were placed on a weekday of the first week of Advent, there is logic to John the Baptist appearing on the second Sunday of Advent. Similar to the Annunciation, the present placement of the Visitation has little relationship to the Christ cycle. If the Annunciation and Visitation festivals occurred in early Advent, fitting gospel readings for the last Sunday of Advent could be found by liturgists and exegetes.[38]

If Madigan's proposal, and others like hers,[39] are certainly consistent with the Advent orientations of both the Christian East and various his-

[37] Shawn Madigan, "Do Marian Festivals Image 'That Which the Church Hopes to Be'?" *Worship* 65, no. 3 (1991): 201.

[38] Ibid., 202.

[39] See also J. Samaha, "Mary in the Liturgical Calendar," *Emmanuel* 100, no. 1 (1994): 45ff. Bryan Spinks also suggests that a couple of Advent Sundays in the West might be devoted to the "Annunciations." See his "Revising the Advent-Christmas-Epiphany Cycle," 172–73.

toric traditions in the West, they also make both liturgical and christological sense by intentionally integrating Marian images and festivals into this
season of incarnational preparation. December as the "month of Mary"
certainly makes a lot more sense than May! But why limit the festival of
the Visitation to a weekday? Indeed, if such a suggestion of restructuring Western Advent is desirable or feasible at all, why not make Advent,
as it is in the Syrian East, the celebration of the various "Annunciations"
from the opening chapters of Matthew and Luke? That is, why not, for
example, celebrate the annunciation to Zechariah and/or the birth of John
the Baptist on the First Sunday of Advent, the annunciation to Mary on
the Second, the visitation on the Third, and the annunciation to Joseph
on the Fourth?

It is amazing how the overall Marian focus of Advent among especially
Mexicans and Mexican Americans already tends to have some affinity to
what has been described above with regard to both the focus of Advent
within various Christian traditions and recent proposals for rethinking
the season of Advent itself. Such a restructuring of Advent itself, as suggested by Madigan, might offer as well the added advantage of bringing
both official and popular religion closer together within an Advent synthesis. For, indeed, I suspect that within most forms of popular religion
and piety, whether Catholic or Protestant, Advent has always been and
will continue to be decidedly incarnational in focus and closely related
to the people and events surrounding the impending birth of Christ, in
spite of what we liturgists and the official liturgy say about eschatology.
But whether such a restructuring of Advent were ever to take place or
not, it is significant that the gospels for the December 8 solemnity of the
Immaculate Conception and now for the solemnity/feast of the Virgin
of Guadalupe are, respectively, the gospel readings of *precisely* both the
annunciation and the visitation in annual proximity to the Second and
Third Sundays of Advent already! If the titles of the solemnity and feast
are different, the biblical contents of both are highly congruent with at
least one traditional Advent characteristic even in the Roman West. In
other words, the Advent liturgy does not really have to change in order
to accommodate the Annunciation and Visitation since it already does
accommodate them. For Roman Catholics, at least, both emphases have
actually remained within the season under different names and, as such,
both already integrate Mary *and* the principal biblical texts associated
with her into Advent itself.

While certainly sympathetic to a rethinking and restructuring of Advent
in this way, I am not yet prepared to give up either the season's overall

eschatological focus or the calls to "prepare the way of the Lord," associated especially with the Second and Third Sundays of the season.[40] But the December 12 festival of the Virgin of Guadalupe, of course, need not be viewed as being inconsistent with even this Advent eschatological focus. Such an eschatological orientation, in fact, certainly appears already in the prayer after communion in the Propers for the feast: "May we who rejoice in the holy Mother of Guadalupe live united and at peace in this world *until the day of the Lord dawns in glory*."[41] Similarly, in spite of the fact that modern biblical scholarship would rightly challenge the late medieval Marian exegesis of Revelation 12,[42] an exegesis certainly presumed in the U.S. suggestion that Revelation 11:19; 12:1-6, 10 be one of the readings for the feast,[43] the obvious visual correlation between the Guadalupan image and this apocalyptic biblical text does make some kind of, at least, symbolic connection possible. That is, even if the woman of Revelation 12 is best understood as personifying both ancient Israel and the New Testament people of God, such personification has certainly come to be embodied symbolically as well in the person of Mary as *the* image *par excellence* of the church itself—the *typus ecclesiae*—an image of "that which [the church] herself desires and hopes wholly to be." If both the pregnant biblical "woman clothed with the sun" and the pregnant Virgin of Guadalupe give birth to the Messiah, both also simultaneously represent the church. At the same time, both the "woman clothed with the sun" in Revelation 12 and the Virgin of Guadalupe are similarly eschatological in orientation, directing attention to the new life and new creation present in the One to whom both give birth. Consequently, if the biblical "woman clothed with the sun" is not really intended to be Mary, she is, nonetheless, like the Virgin of Guadalupe herself, symbolic of the overall Advent stance of

[40] See my essay, "Let's Keep Advent Right Where It Is," in *Worship: Rites, Feasts, and Reflections* (Portland, OR: Pastoral Press, 2004), 237–43.

[41] Bishops' Committee on the Liturgy, *Newsletter 24: Feast of Our Lady of Guadalupe and New Liturgical Texts* (Washington, DC: National Conference of Catholic Bishops, 1988), 6; emphasis added.

[42] On the interpretation of Revelation 12, see Raymond Brown, et al., eds., "The Woman in Revelation 12," in *Mary in the New Testament: A Collaborative Assessment by Protestant and Roman Catholic Scholars* (New York: Paulist Press and Philadelphia: Fortress Press, 1978), 219–39.

[43]This reading does not appear for the solemnity in Mexico where the equivalent New Testament reading is Gal 4:4-7. See *Propio de los Santos y Otras Misas*, vol. 3 of *Leccionario*, 172–74.

the church in the world living in the situation of hope for the ultimate eschatological victory of the fullness of the reign of God over all forms of injustice, oppression, and evil, a victory already revealed in the life, death, and resurrection of her Child.

Conclusion

Whether the liturgical season of Advent is conceived of primarily in incarnational or eschatological ways, it becomes quite easy to understand why for Mexican and Mexican American Catholics, according to Elizondo, "the feast of Our Lady of Guadalupe [is] the *major feast of Advent*." Both traditional orientations associated with the season come to expression in her and, as such, properly understood there is no real need for there to be a tension between the official liturgy of Advent and popular faith expressions. The Virgin of Guadalupe and the liturgical season of Advent, thus, can certainly and properly be viewed as belonging together.

9

Virgin Mary, Mother of God

Kathleen Norris

 During the 1950s, when I was receiving religious formation in Methodist, Congregational, and, in the summer, Presbyterian churches, Mary was more or less invisible to me. Along with the angels of the Nativity, she was one of the decorations my family unpacked every year for Christmas, a strange but welcome seasonal presence who would be relegated to the closet again at the new year. Mary was mysterious, and therefore for Catholics; our religion was more proper, more masculine in ways I had yet to define. As the writer Nancy Mairs has so vividly stated, the Protestantism we both were raised in was one with "all the mystery scrubbed out of it by a vigorous and slightly vinegary reason."[1]

When I first went to a Benedictine abbey fifteen years ago, I wasn't looking for Mary at all. But, over time, as I kept returning to the monks' choir, I found that I was greatly comforted by the presence of Mary in the daily liturgy and also in the church year. I hadn't been to church since high school, and I doubt that I had ever been to a Vespers service. So, at first I had no idea where the lovely *Magnificat* we sang every night was from: "My soul magnifies the Lord, and my spirit rejoices in God my Savior" (Luke 1:46-47). When I eventually found it in the first chapter of Luke's gospel,

---

[1] Nancy Mairs, *A Dynamic God: Living an Unconventional Catholic Faith* (Boston: Beacon Press, 2007), 25.

I was startled but glad to see that it was one pregnant woman's response to a blessing from another. It is the song Mary sings after she has walked to her cousin Elizabeth's village, and on greeting Mary, Elizabeth, who is bearing John the Baptist, recognizes that Mary bears the Messiah.

The song is praise of the God who has blessed two insignificant women in an insignificant region of ancient Judea, and in so doing "has brought down the powerful from their thrones, and lifted up the lowly; [who] has filled the hungry with good things, and sent the rich away empty" (Luke 1:52-53). I later learned that these words echo the song of Hannah in First Samuel, as well as the anguish of the prophets. They are a poetic rendering of a theme that pervades the entire biblical narrative—when God comes into our midst, it is to upset the status quo.

The *Magnificat's* message is so subversive that for a period during the 1980s the government of Guatemala banned its public recitation (a sanction that I'm sure the monasteries of that country violated daily). But when I came to its words knowing so little about them, I found that all too often they were words I could sing with ease at Evening Prayer, with a facile (and sometimes sleepy) acceptance. On other nights, however, they were a mother's words, probing uncomfortably into my life. How rich had I been that day, how full of myself? Too full to recognize need and hunger, my own or anyone else's? So powerfully providing for myself that I couldn't admit my need for the help of others? Too busy to know a blessing when it came to me?

It was many months before I took notice of the Madonna and Child in a niche over my shoulder, thoroughly black except for the gold scepter she held in one hand, an unlikely presence among mostly white-skinned Benedictine monks in North Dakota, their black habits an almost comical echo of her dress. I came to love her face, its calm strength. And I loved the way she held her child, like any mother, on her out-thrust hip. A monk explained that it was the Black Madonna of Einsiedeln, Switzerland, one of many black Madonnas in Europe that has attracted pilgrims for centuries. During the 1980s the Black Madonna of Czestochowa, Poland, became such a potent symbol of resistance to the Communist regime that as many as five million people made an annual pilgrimage to the site. But all of this meant little to me then. I knew only that the statue represented something powerful and that I wanted to be in its presence.

No small part of Mary's emotional weight for many women is the way in which the church has so often used her as an ideal of passive, submissive femininity. But others claim her as a model of strength. I treasure Mary as a biblical interpreter, one who heard and believed what God told her, and who pondered God's promise in her heart, even when, as the Gospel of Luke describes it, it pierced her soul like a sword. This is hardly passivity, but the kind of faith that sustains Christian discipleship. Mary's life is as powerful an evocation of what it can mean to be God's chosen as the life of Moses, or St. Paul. In a recent talk on Mary, Ruth Fox, a Benedictine sister who is president of the Federation of St. Gertrude, a group of women's monasteries, reclaims Mary as a strong peasant woman and asks why, in art and statuary, she is almost always presented "as a teenage beauty queen, forever eighteen years old and . . . perfectly manicured." Depictions of Mary as a wealthy Renaissance woman do far outnumber those that make her look like a woman capable of walking the hill country of Judea and giving birth in a barn, and I believe that Fox has asked a provocative question, perhaps a prophetic one. I wonder if, as Christians, both Protestant and Catholic, seek to reclaim the Mary of Scripture, we may well require more depictions of her as a robust, and even muscular, woman, in both youth and old age.

But I would also caution that if we insist too much on a literal Mary, encasing her too firmly in the dress of a first-century peasant, we risk losing her as a living symbol. Sooner or later a child will inquire, as my ten-year-old niece did recently, after seeing one too many Marys-in-robes, "Why don't people ever show her as a normal person?" The "1996 Virgin Mary" that she drew for herself may be alarmingly perky (shades of Barbie!), but her body is strong. She looks as if she might have come from an aerobics workout, ready for anything. Placed on her torso, where Supergirl's "S" might be, is an equally perky dove, representing the Holy Spirit.

As one Benedictine friend of mine pointed out to me, the youthfulness of Mary in Christian art can have a religious significance that far transcends ideological concerns. When I asked him if he had ever seen a depiction of an aging Mary, one with wrinkles, he referred me to several images of the Italian Renaissance, including a crucifixion by Piero della Francesca, and we ended up discussing the *Pietà* by Michelangelo that is housed in St. Peter's in Rome. That Mary looks much too young to have a thirty-three-year-old son, but in this case the monk believes her depiction to be both aesthetically and theologically right. What he said touched me:

> It's an ageless image of Mary because the effects of salvation are already present. A biblical image of this might be Psalm 103's "your youth is renewed like the eagle's." She's ageless, but she knows the cost of salvation; she sees it in the death of her son. Her serenity is hard-won, and the wonder of the image is that even when she is looking straight at death, holding it, hers is not a grieving face, but one full of divine love and pity.

Mary's love and pity for her children seems to be what people treasure most about her, and what helps her to serve as a bridge between cultures. One great example of this took place in 1531, when the Virgin Mary appeared to an Indian peasant named Juan Diego on the mountain of Tepeyac, in Mexico, leaving behind a cloak, a *tilma*, imprinted with her image. The image has been immortalized as Our Lady of Guadalupe, and Mexican American theologian Virgil Elizondo argues, in *The Future Is Mestizo*,[2] that the significance of this image today is that Mary appeared as a *mestiza*, or person of mixed race, a symbol of the union of the indigenous Aztec and Spanish invader. What was, and still is, the scandal of miscegenation was given a holy face and name. As a Protestant I'll say it all sounds suspiciously biblical to me, recalling the scandal of the incarnation itself, the mixing together of human and divine in a young, unmarried woman.

Over the centuries one of Mary's greatest strengths as a symbol is the considerable tension she exemplifies between the humble peasant woman and the powerful mother of God. In a recent essay the writer Rubén Martínez lovingly articulates the paradoxes that enliven his sense of the officially sanctioned Mary of church doctrine, and, to borrow his phrase, the "Undocumented Virgin" of personal experience and legend, folktale, and myth.[3] I should probably take this opportunity to make an aside and state that by "myth" I mean a story that you know must be true the first time you hear it. Or, in the words of a five-year-old child, as related by Gertrude Mueller Nelson in her recent Jungian interpretation of fairy tales and Marian theology, *Here All Dwell Free*,[4] a myth is a story that isn't true on the outside, only on the inside. Human beings, it seems to me, require myth as one of the basic necessities of life. Once we have our air and water and a bit of food, we turn to metaphor and to myth-making.

Ana Castillo's recent anthology, *Goddess of the Americas: Writings on the Virgin of Guadalupe*,[5] has convinced me that Mary is often a catalyst for boundary-breaking experiences, contradiction, and paradox, which may suit her to postmodernism. The book includes commentary by pagan,

[2] Virgilio Elizondo, *The Future Is Mestizo: Life Where Cultures Meet* (New York: Crossroad, 1992), 57–66.

[3] Rubén Martínez, "The Undocumented Virgin," in *Goddess of the Americas, La Diosa de las Américas: Writings on the Virgin of Guadalupe*, ed. Ana Castillo (New York: Riverhead Books, 1996), 98–112.

[4] Gertrude Mueller Nelson, *Here All Dwell Free: Stories to Heal the Wounded Feminine* (Mahwah, NJ: Paulist Press, 1999).

[5] Castillo, *Goddess of the Americas*.

Jewish, and Christian writers who are bold in revealing and reveling in the implications of the Guadalupe myth. The story of Guadalupe, which has come to provide a deep sense of ethnic pride for Mexican Americans—I once saw a plumber's van in Denver sporting her image on its side—also provides dramatic evidence that it is risky to try to contain a Marian symbol within the confines of either official church doctrine or the narrow mindset of ideological interpretation.

Richard Rodriguez concludes his essay in the anthology by describing his attempts to convey the prophetic power of Guadalupe to a skeptical feminist who can see in this image of a barefoot and pregnant Mary nothing but imperialist oppression and the subjugation of women. You don't understand, Rodriguez says, that the joke is on the living. What joke? the woman responds, and Rodriguez explains:

> The joke is that Spain arrived with missionary zeal at the shores of contemplation. But Spain had no idea of the absorbent strength of Indian spirituality. By the waters of baptism, the active European was entirely absorbed within the contemplation of the Indian. The faith that Europe imposed in the sixteenth century was, by virtue of the Guadalupe, embraced by the Indian. Catholicism has become an Indian religion. By the twenty-first century, the locus of the Catholic church, by virtue of numbers, will be Latin America, by which time Catholicism itself will have assumed the aspect of the Virgin of Guadalupe. Brown skin.[6]

Once Marian imagery has truly been absorbed by a church or a culture, things are never simple. Or they are entirely so. Who is this Mary? For one Benedictine sister the biblical Mary exemplifies an intimate relationship to God, based on listening and responding to God's word, that "calls all Christians to the deep, personal, and daily love of Jesus Christ." As for myself, I have come to think of Mary as the patron saint of "both/and" passion over "either/or" reasoning, and as such, she delights my poetic soul. Ever since I first encountered Mary in that Benedictine abbey I have learned never to discount her ability to confront and disarm the polarities that so often bring human endeavors to impasse: the subjective and objective, the expansive and the parochial, the affective and the intellectual.

I used to feel the dissonance whenever I heard Mary described as both Virgin and Mother; she seemed to set an impossible standard for any woman. But this was narrow-minded on my part. What Mary does is to

---

[6] Richard Rodriguez, "India," in Castillo, *Goddess of the Americas*, 24.

show me how I indeed can be both virgin and mother. Virgin to the extent that I remain "one-in-myself," able to come to things with newness of heart; mother to the extent that I forget myself in the nurture and service of others, embracing the ripeness of maturity that this requires. This Mary is a gender-bender; she could do the same for any man.

I owe my reconciliation of the Virgin and the Mother to the Black Madonna. Late one night at the abbey I sat before her statue, not consciously praying, but simply tired. Suddenly words welled up from deep inside me, words I did not intend to say—I want to know motherhood. Stunned by my boldness and the impossibility of the request—I have known since adolescence that motherhood was beyond my capacities—I began to weep. This remains my only experience of prayer as defined by St. Anthony of the Desert; he called a true prayer one you don't understand. When, a few months later, through an improbable set of circumstances, I found myself caring for a seventeen-month-old niece with a bad case of the chicken pox, I was amazed to realize that my prayer was being answered in a most concrete, exhausting, and rewarding way. I also sensed that the prayer would continue to be answered in many other ways throughout my life.

It is difficult to feel, in the western Dakotas, that one is on the cutting edge of any cultural phenomenon. The stiff breeze of the *Zeitgeist* usually passes us by, barely ruffling the tightly permed and sprayed "bubble cut" hairdos that have been popular with women here since the 1950s. So I was startled to find that so many other Protestants, including many clergy, were drawn to monasteries in the 1980s, and that we became better acquainted with Mary in the process. And I was surprised to find that others had been pondering the Black Madonna. In her book *Longing for Darkness*, China Galland relates that when she found herself alienated from her Catholic faith, it was the loss of the ability to venerate the Virgin Mary that hurt the most. She went far afield in seeking other female images of the holy—to Buddhism (the goddess Tara) and Hinduism (Kali)—and they led her back to Mary. It is in the Benedictine abbey at Einsiedeln, standing before the Black Madonna as the monks sang the *Salve Regina*, that Galland first senses "a way back to what had been lost."[7]

I'm a garden-variety Christian, if an eccentric one; Galland seems a remarkably eclectic Buddhist. We both encountered the Black Madonna, and she changed us. We could do worse than to stick with her, this Mary,

---

[7] China Galland, *Longing for Darkness: Tara and the Black Madonna* (New York: Penguin Books, 1991), 322.

who, as the affable parish priest in my small town has said to me, has her ways of going in, under, around, and through any box we try to put her in. We can sympathize with the Nicaraguan tailor in the village of Cuapa, who, when the Virgin began appearing to him in 1980, prayed that she would choose someone else, as he had problems enough!

There's a lot of room in Mary. A seminary professor, a Presbyterian, employs the language of the early church in telling a student struggling with family problems, "You can always go to *Theotokos* [Greek for 'God-bearer'], because she understands suffering." A grieving Lutheran woman in South Dakota tells me, "I love Mary, because she also knew what it is to lose a child." And an elderly Parsee woman in India proudly shows a visiting Benedictine nun her little shrine to Mary, saying, "I'm not a Christian, but I love *her*."

10

We Sing Mary's Song*

Bonnie Jensen

 Martin Luther sent a letter to Prince John Frederick, Duke of Saxony, introducing his commentary on the *Magnificat*. Luther said that it is a fine custom to sing the *Magnificat* at Vespers each night. He commended the *Magnificat* to Prince John Frederick saying that it "ought to be learned and kept in mind by all who would rule well and be helpful lords."

Each time we sing the *Magnificat*, we proclaim to each other what sort of God we believe in and especially, as Luther says, how God deals with those of low and high degree. Luther says we sing it for three reasons: (1) to strengthen our faith, (2) to comfort the lowly, and (3) to terrify the mighty.[1] We will look at these reasons in reverse order.

To Terrify the Mighty. As a group of Lutheran theologians and church leaders, we fit more properly in the category of the mighty than in that of the lowly. Most of us are white, the color of privilege in our hemisphere. We are mostly middle class, living very comfortable lives and rich by

* A meditation given at the Consultation on Justification and Justice, held December 7–14, 1985, in Mexico City under the auspices of the Division for World Mission and Inter-Church Cooperation of The American Lutheran Church, slightly altered for publication.

[1] See *The Magnificat: Luther's Commentary*, trans. A. T. W. Steinhaeuser (Minneapolis, MN: Augsburg Publishing House, 1967).

most comparisons. Most of us are male, another privileged group in our hemisphere. As church leaders and teachers, we are highly educated. We are the intellectually elite. We are employed in positions of respect and leadership.

Some of us fit all these categories of the mighty. All of us fit in most of them. Luther said, "The mightier you are, the more you must fear" when you sing the *Magnificat*. We fear because we *sing in faith*, believing God does bring down the mighty.

It is risky for the mighty to sing the *Magnificat*. It might mean moving from the center to the fringes. It might mean leaving theologically proper talk to engage in simple, frank discussions. Or it might mean risking tenured positions in our schools of theology, or jobs in the church bureaucracy, as we speak clearly and forthrightly about the implications of our faith. It might mean risking our intellectual credibility as we respect the visions of poor Indians of Guadalupe.

But we take the risk! We sing the *Magnificat* in faith, knowing that fear can lead us to repentance, and repentance prepares us for the coming reign of God.

To Comfort the Lowly. We sing to proclaim comfort to the lowly. Each time we sing Mary's song, we are called to believe once again that God has deep regard for the lowly, the hungry, the poor, the little ones.

I was deeply moved by the story of the poor man's vision of the Lady of Guadalupe.[2] I was struck by how lowly, insignificant people have to beg the church to regard them with the esteem with which God regards them. We are not sure whether Mary appeared in a vision to this poor man. Perhaps we have our Protestant doubts. Yet even if we question the vision, the tragic truth remains: the poor and lowly often have to beg the church to proclaim and live out its message of a merciful, compassionate God! Behind the vision's gilded cactus leaves, miraculous roses, and imprinted cloak is the longing for a God who comes, not in the might of military conquest, nor in the ecclesiastical forms and evangelism plans of a mighty church, but in simple, compassionate respect and regard for the lowly, the hungry, the women, the poor, the children.

---

[2] In the story of the Lady of Guadalupe, Mary encourages a poor peasant to ask the bishop to build a church for the people. The bishop is finally convinced and grants the request when he sees an imprint of Mary's image inside the peasant's cloak.

We sing the *Magnificat* to comfort the lowly. We sing to put ourselves in solidarity with the lowly and those who suffer. We sing in order to bring in the reign and community of our Lord Jesus Christ.

To Strengthen our Faith. Finally, we sing Mary's song to strengthen our own faith. We keep announcing to one another the sort of God in which we believe: a God who has respect for the Marys of Nazareth, for vulnerable, pregnant, unmarried women; a God who rummages through the dump with the hungry;[3] a God who cries when children are killed and women are raped; a God who sees visions with poor farmers and plants roses on their hillsides.

---

[3] The group to whom this address was originally given had traveled to the Mexico City dump, where they observed poor people searching for food.

11

A Space for God

Robert W. Jenson

Doubtless the archetypical Marian devotion, in the Western church, is the *Ave Maria*. The first part is simply biblical and hardly poses any theological task. It is the second part that has the punch: "*Ave Maria, mater dei, ora pro nobis. . . .*" "Hail Mary, Mother of God, pray for us. . . ."

There are two theological questions posed by that address. The one concerns the legitimacy and necessity of invoking Mary's or any other saint's prayer. The other is this question: Why invoke Mary's prayer precisely *as* Mother of God? Is her prayer for us somehow different from the prayer of another saint? In some other way, that is, than that in which each saint is of course a particular person whose intercession will show that? Only the second of these questions is ecumenically interesting or requires any very deep thought and is the question on which I will spend this paper. But the first also continues to divide Christians and must be dealt with in a preliminary way.

It has long seemed plain to this Protestant that the invocation of saints' prayers must be possible and if possible surely desirable. I certainly can ask a living fellow believer to pray for me. If death severed the fellowship of believers, I could not of course ask a *departed* fellow believer to pray for me. But the New Testament hardly permits us to think that death can sever the fellowship of believers—and the eucharistic prayers also of Protestant bodies explicitly deny that it does. Thus there seems to be no reason why I cannot ask also a departed believer to pray for me. And if I *can* do it, there will certainly be contexts where I *should* do it. Thus there should be no problem about asking Mary in her capacity as *sancta*, Saint Mary, to pray for us.

Those of the Reformers who thought otherwise needed to produce more stringent arguments than any I am aware of their adducing. Simply saying with Melanchthon that there is no scriptural mandate to address individual saints, will not do. Magisterial Protestant churches live by all kinds of practices, perhaps most notably infant baptism and the authority of the New Testament canon, for which no scriptural mandate exists and that can be justified only by chains of argument far longer than the one just developed for invoking saints. On infant baptism Luther's final word was simply that this had long been the practice of the church and that he saw no decisive argument against it. One must wonder why the same cannot be said about invocation of the saints.

As for Mary's being θεοτόκος, *mater dei*, Mother of God, that of course is formal dogma for Catholics, Orthodox, and magisterial Protestants alike, laid down among other places in the decrees of Ephesus. If one balks at *that*, one is simply a heretic.

So the interesting theological question lies in the *linking* of these two, of the epithet "Mother of God" with the solicitation of Mary's prayer. Why mention *this* title in asking for her prayer? Why not just "Saint Mary, pray for us"? Is the invocation of the Mother of God different in kind from the invocation of other members of the company of heaven? A difference marked by invoking her explicitly *as* "Mother of God"? What exactly is the difference?

There are doubtless many ways of answering that question, of which I will here pursue only one. Most important, any complete Mariology, Catholic or Protestant, would have to consider in what sense, if any, she can be said to "mediate" salvation; in this essay I am glad to avoid that—mostly, I think, terminological—knot.

For this essay I will start with a type of icon. These are icons, called as a type the Virgin of the Sign, which show a small figure of Christ in a lozenge so located on an image of Mary as to suggest a window into her body. Some such icons carry a Greek inscription, divided to the two sides of the panel and usually in abbreviation. Unabbreviated, the inscription would be: Ἡ χώρη τοῦ ἀχωρίστου.[1] The phrase is virtually untranslatable

---

[1] The notion is otherwise found in the liturgical tradition. So Marian icons at a certain place in an Orthodox church are ἡ πλατύτερα, because Mary is "wider

in English, due to a quirk of English derivatives from the usable roots. "The Container of the Uncontainable" is the closest direct translation, but rings somehow wrong, containment in the sense of restriction not being quite the point; nevertheless in the following I will use it. Perhaps the most *accurate* translation is paraphrastic and just so inelegant: "the space embracing that which can be encompassed by no space."

The inscription—in Greek anyway—is precise. Mary's womb *is* of course a space. And if she is the Mother of God, if what was in her womb was God the Son, then indeed her womb is the container of the uncontainable; then it is indeed her womb that provides space in our space for the gestating God the Son.

The theological question about Mary's unique place among the holy ones can thus, I suggest, be pointed to as a question about God's space in our world. For of no other single person can it be said that he or she contains the uncontainable God.

John of Damascus formulated a maxim for all subsequent theology: God is his own space,[2] in himself he is "in" nothing but himself. If he creates a world, God occupies the space that he himself is, and the world is another space. And these do not overlap; there is no space to accommodate mixtures of God and creature or almost-gods or a-little-more-than-creatures.

But then, if God is to *have to do* with his created world and not just coexist with it, and especially if he is also to allow creatures to have to do with him, he needs space *in* his creation from which to be present to other spaces therein and at which to allow creatures to locate him; he needs, if I may put it so, a "pad" in creation, a pied-à-terre, a created space to be his own, besides the uncreated space he himself is. And of course the Scriptures do in fact speak richly and variously of created space that God takes as his own abode in his creation.

In the first instance, God's own space within the space he creates is heaven. The creation is compendiously the heavens and the earth. And when the creation is in place, it is from its heaven that God "looks down" on his creatures' doings; and when he comes to us it is the division between

---

than the heavens." The Loreto Litany makes her the "Ark of the Covenant," a typology often found. And the Akathistos Hymn makes her, among a plethora of acclamations, the "Space of the Spaceless God." I am indebted to Robin Darling Young for calling my attention to these instances.

[2] *The Orthodox Faith*, 13.11, in *Nicene and Post-Nicene Fathers*, trans. S. D. F. Salmond, vol. 9, Series 2 (Grand Rapids, MI: Eerdmans, 1999).

heaven and earth that he "rends." When Solomon considers the implaus-
ibility of his prayer that the Lord should inhabit the temple he has built,
the miracle is that even heaven cannot properly contain the Lord, much
less this one building on earth, but that nevertheless God truly inhabits
the first and so may perhaps be petitioned to inhabit the second (see 2 Chr
6:18-21). Or consider Jacob's vision at Bethel: at that spot on earth there
is, he sees, a way opened to heaven, a *ladder* reaching upward from earth,
on which creatures, the angels, can go back and forth. "How awesome is
this place!" he says. "This is none other than the house of God, and this is
a gate of heaven" (Gen 28:12-17).

To be sure, Copernicus creates some problems about the location of
heaven. I think I have solved them[3] but have no time here to rehearse
my ideas on that score. Here it must suffice to say that the biblical notion
of heaven is anyway not dispensable: for God to have a history with us,
he must have a place not only in himself but in our world, in our space.
And the Bible first calls this place heaven.

But now, when the God of Israel creates, he does not create a cosmos,
an assemblage of spaces that is in itself and as a whole timeless. What the
God of Israel creates is a history, a reality with a beginning, an end, and a
reconciling course of events from the one to the other. Even the first creation itself, as the fathers of the church noted with some astonishment, is
not accomplished except as the history of six days. If then the God of Israel
is to take space among his creatures, his space cannot be just a geometrical
space beside others, it must be, as we say, a "historical space," a stretch of
time. And so it is not just the heaven generally "up there" that he takes
for his own occupation; his heaven is—at least short of the eschaton—the
heaven *of* a certain nation. The Lord has space in his creation in that he
dwells among a *people*, who as such take temporal space in creation.

Thus there are members of Israel in heaven with God; heaven is a place
for God's people and not just for him. Moses and Elijah accompany Christ
when he appears in his heavenly glory; and when the door is opened to John
the Seer, there is the whole company of saints assembled. And indeed, in
many of the narratives it is not possible to distinguish between heaven as
a sheer space up there and God's presence among the people of Israel. So
the darkness and light from which the Lord thunders at Sinai is at once the
place from which thunder of course comes, the heavens, and the mountain

[3] Robert W. Jenson, *Systematic Theology*, 2 vols. (New York: Oxford University
Press, 1997), 2:120–24.

around which Israel is encamped. When it is said that he "rides upon the wings of the storm" (Ps 104:3), the wings are at once the flying clouds above and the sculptured wings of the cherubim-throne in the temple.

It is the space *taken up, defined, by the people of Israel*, which is, with sheer heaven, God's space in this world, his pied-à-terre. This must and does show itself in actual phenomena of Israel's life, to a few of which we now turn. And be assured, we are working back toward Mary.

The phenomena in which God's taking of this people for his place is most blatant are the tabernacle and its successor the temple. As recent exegesis has made plain,[4] for the writers of the Pentateuch the creation is not complete until the tabernacle is assembled. For the creation—as Barth put it—is but the continuing "outer basis" of the covenant, and the covenant, "I shall be their God and they shall be my people," is not actual until there is the tabernacle, that is, a marked-off space in Israel's midst to which they can come to be coming to him, a "tent of meeting."[5]

According to the Old Testament, the Lord really was *in* there, in the tent of meeting and then in the successor, the Jerusalem temple's most holy place. As sheer architecture, the Jerusalem temple was on the standard pattern of all ancient temples—and indeed Solomon hired foreign architects to build it. An ancient temple was not a hall for assembly, like a church or synagogue; it was a *chamber* enclosing the presence of the god, elsewhere than in Israel mediated by an image. Not to put too fine a point on it, an ancient temple was a God-box; the people assembled for what we would think of as the liturgical functions *outside* the enclosure, in surrounding porticos or courts. Israel's holy place, whether portable or later fixed, was built on just this pattern.

The difference between Israel's holy enclosures and the run of ancient temples was of course that in the tent of meeting and in the most holy room of the Jerusalem temple there was no image of the god, which was the very point of other temples. In the Jerusalem temple's space for God, as in the enclosure of the tabernacle, there was nothing divine to be seen except in vision.

Nevertheless, God was in that space. There was a winged throne there and the Lord did ride on it. And there was in the tabernacle and the temple's inner enclosure another box, another enclosed space, the ark

---

[4] E.g., Gary Anderson, "Biblical Origins and the Problem of the Fall," *Pro Ecclesia* 10, no. 1 (Winter 2001): 18–24.

[5] Karl Barth, *Church Dogmatics* III.I: *The Doctrine of Creation* (New York: Continuum, 2004), 282.

of the covenant. In it again there were no images, as the Philistines who once captured it supposed there must be. But God was *there*: when the Philistines set the ark by Dagon, the impossibility of worshiping both the Lord and another god overthrew Dagon; when David danced before the ark in triumphal procession, it was "before the Lord" that he danced.

In speaking of the Lord's presence in the tabernacle and the temple, in defined spaces in Israel, it is important to keep the order straight: God takes for himself the space enclosed by the tabernacle or the most holy place in order to dwell among the *people*, not vice versa. It is the people as a whole who are thereby the Container of the Uncontainable.

And indeed, since it was a people, a phenomenon of history, that delineated the Lord's created space, such bluntly spatial containers as the most holy place or the ark could not be the only mode of his presence among them. The Lord's presence in Israel was in a "historical space"—the turn of language is odd but telling—and so had more purely historical modes, locations in the *discourse* by which the historical existence of a nation occurs. Two are most noteworthy: prophecy and Scripture.

A prophet was someone to whom "the Word of the Lord" had "come," so that he or she could speak words that were God's words. This is to be very drastically and bluntly understood. As the Lord says in a famous Isaiah passage, the word that the prophet speaks is a word that creates what it speaks to, that will not return empty, but accomplishes events in the world. That is to say, the word that prophets spoke was God's own word, the very word of Genesis 1.

So you could hear the voice of the Lord in Israel, *and* you could tell where that voice was coming from; it had a *location* within Israel. It was coming from the town square or a temple court, where a prophet was standing. In prophecy, God took space amid the people.

A prophet's body, moreover, not only marked the place where God was to be heard, it also marked the place where God might be addressed. For a prophet spoke not only for God to the people, but for the people to God. Indeed, in the case of the archetypal prophet, Moses, this intercessory function dominates the narrative.

Did an Israelite want to approach God? He could visit the temple, or he could go to that "man of God" over there. In a way, a prophet was a sort of historically functioning, mobile temple; the building in Jerusalem could not go with the people into exile, but prophets could. Temples, moreover, could not follow one another as master and disciple, could not through history accumulate and interpret the presence of God; but prophets could.

Which brings us to Scripture. At least in Israel's own self-understanding, written Scripture, the tablets of the Ten Words written by the Lord in person, belonged to Israel's foundation from the first; their existence is identical with the existence of the covenant, and they were the most important content of the ark. It is perhaps not possible to say just when Israel's wider oral tradition of narrative and law began to be written, but also writing did not remove the tradition from being shaped by and shaping Israel's continuing history as the narratives and laws were edited and reedited, each editing both reflecting and shaping a turn in Israel's history with her Lord.

The character of written documents, however, is that, unlike speech per se, they occupy space. Israel's scrolls are portable like prophets, but, unlike prophets, they have no other body than the word they bring. A book of law or prophecy is the very Word of God taking up space. Thus to this day a Torah scroll is sacred space in Judaism; and until yesterday a Bible was sacred space in Christian piety. The fundamentalists have, I fear, a point: what they call the "inscripturation" of God's Word is vital to faith; for God the Word wants to take up space in our churches and houses.

I was supposed to write about Mary, and have instead been writing about heaven and Israel. It is time to get back directly to Mary.

It is of course the heart of Christian faith that God's presence in Israel is gathered up and concentrated in Immanuel, God with us, in this one Israelite's presence in Israel: he is in person the temple's *shekinah*, and the Word spoken by all the prophets, and the Torah. And if that is so, then the space delineated by Israel to accommodate the presence of God is finally reduced and expanded to Mary's womb, the container of Immanuel. We must note the singularity of Mary's dogmatic title: she is not one in a series of God's mothers, she simply is the Mother.

To what did Mary, after all, assent, when she said to Gabriel, "*Fiat mihi*," "Let it happen to me"? Of course it was her womb that with these words she offered, to be God's space in the world. The whole history of Israel had been God's labor to take Israel as his space in the world. And it was indeed a labor, for Israel by her own account was a resistant people: again and again the Lord's angel announced his advent, begged indeed for space, and again and again Israel's answer was, "Let it be, but not yet." Gabriel's mission to Mary was, so to speak, one last try, and this time the response did not temporize.

As the created space for God, Mary is Israel concentrated. Ancient hymns directly apostrophize her as "the ark of the covenant," an analogy so obvious that it is more than an analogy. When God's creating Word came in its own singular identity into the world, Mary brought him forth as though she were all the prophets put together—indeed, "as though" is not a strong enough way to put it. And if Christianity does not quite reverence the Book as Judaism reverences the Torah scroll, it is perhaps because its role has been preempted by Mary's act as Torah's embodiment.

When we ask Mary to pray for us, why should we do this specifically in her capacity as Mother of God? There are two connected answers. First, Mary is Israel in one person, as temple and archprophet and guardian of Torah. To ask her to pray for me is to invoke all God's history with Israel at once, all his place-taking in this people, and all the faithfulness of God to this people, as grounds for his faithfulness to me. It is to have Moses say, "Why should the heathen profane your name, because you leave your people in the lurch? Because you leave Robert Jenson in the lurch?" It is to send Aaron to the tent of meeting on my behalf. It is to quote all Scripture's promises about prayer at once, as summed up by Jesus, "Very truly, I tell you, if you ask anything of the Father in my name, he will give it to you" (John 16:23). "*Fiat mihi*," Mary said, giving her womb as space for God in this world. After all the Lord's struggle with his beloved Israel, he finally found a place in Israel that unbelief would not destroy like the temple, or silence like the prophets, or simply lose like the book of the law before Josiah. This place is a person. To ask Mary to pray for us is to meet him there.

Second, from the beginning of creation, heaven is God's space in his creation. As the created space for God, there must be a mysterious sense in which Mary *is* heaven, the container not only of the uncontainable Son but also of all his sisters and brothers, of what Augustine called the *totus Christus*, the whole Christ, Christ with his body. But Mary is a person, not a sheer container. That she contains the whole company of heaven must mean that she personally is their presence. To ask Mary to pray for us is to ask "the whole company of heaven" to pray for us, not this saint or that, but all of them together. It is to ask the church triumphant to pray for us.

Interestingly, Luther and Melanchthon were happy to say that the saints as a company pray for us, that the church in heaven prays for the church on earth. To invoke Mary's prayer as the prayer of the *mater dei*, the prayer of the Container of the Uncontainable, is to invoke precisely this prayer. Perhaps, indeed, Mary's prayer, as the prayer of the whole company of heaven, is the one saint's prayer that even those should utter who otherwise accept Melanchthon's argument against invoking saints.

12

Concluding Reflection:
Guadalupe as a Precious Gift

Virgil Elizondo

 Recently while presenting a conference on Our Lady of Guada-
lupe at Princeton, a group of evangelical students came to me
praising the conference but asking, "Is it not true that Christ
alone is necessary for salvation? Then why do you need Our
Lady of Guadalupe? Isn't Christ alone sufficient?" I answered,
"Yes, you are correct and that is exactly why Our Lady is so
precious, precisely because she is not necessary." Then I went on to ask
them, "Is it not true that some of the most precious things in your life
are things that were not necessary, like a gift of flowers, jewelry, candies,
or anything else? And sometimes especially at moments of great pain,
people you love will give you a gift to help ease the pain. Our Lady is
such a gift. At a moment of great suffering and pain, out of the love and
graciousness of God came the gift of Our Lady of Guadalupe." Some of
the most precious things in life are those small gifts that are not necessary but powerful gestures of love. Our Lady of Guadalupe is so precious
precisely because she is not necessary.

One of the most amazing aspects of this gift is how more and more
people around the globe are recognizing it as an extraordinary manifestation of God's unlimited love not just for Mexico but for all who are
suffering and in pain. I have been amazed to witness the devotion of the
masses not just in the Mexican parishes across the United States but in

179

St. Patrick's Cathedral in New York City, at a church in Nagasaki, Japan, at Notre Dame Cathedral in Paris, in the church of the Dormition of Mary in Jerusalem, the chapel right next to St. Peter's tomb in St. Peter's basilica in Rome, and many other unsuspected places. And now, in recent times, I have seen her in Baptist, Methodist, Lutheran, Episcopal, Presbyterian, and other Protestant churches. This devotion does not seem to be promoted by anyone, yet it seems to grow and increase through an inner dynamism of its own.

In my own works I have tried to bring out the many beautiful, healing, and liberating aspects of the image on Juan Diego's *tilma* and of the conversations of Our Lady of Guadalupe Tonantzin with Juan Diego Cuauhtlatoatzin during their encounters of December 1531, but the most powerful and visionary ones were her self-identification as "the mother of all the inhabitants who live on this land." Her words were not limited to any one human group but were tenderly addressed to anyone "who would love me, who would speak with me, who would search for me, and who would place their confidence in me. There I will hear their laments and remedy and cure all their miseries, misfortunes, and sorrows." They were truly a motherly invitation to form one human family of love and concern. These words take on a very special relevance when we place them in the context of the very beginning of the so-called new world—a land that would be the gathering place of diverse peoples from all the nations of the world. Would this land become a composite of various ethnic groups competing for the same space or would it be the beginning of something truly new?

She appeared at the geographical center of our Western Hemisphere at a time when none of the present-day national borders had been created and asked for a temple—a sacred space—where all the peoples of this land would be welcomed. It seems to me that what she was asking for is much more than a physical building. In her Náhuatl language, temple indicated the sacred center of a civilization. She is asking for what would truly be a new world—a hemisphere wherein no humanly devised border would keep people apart. Like a true mother, she wants a space where all her children—regardless of anything—might be welcomed, respected, and loved. It is a prophetic vision of who could truly be a real new world—reminiscent of the new heaven and new earth of Isaiah and echoing the prayer of Jesus that all might be one. As Mary of Nazareth announced the coming of the new age in the words of the *Magnificat*, now Mary of Guadalupe announces the beginning of the new world that would learn from the mistakes of the past and usher in a new era of harmony and grace.

The corruption of society and the church in Europe was igniting movements of evangelical reform both within the Catholic Church—such as the renewal movements of Cardinal Francisco Jiménez de Cisneros—and beyond the church by Martin Luther and others. The early missioners to Mexico were convinced that the new era of the Spirit was now beginning and that a true evangelical society was now in the making. In the context of all the upheaval of the conquest in America and a divided church in Europe, Our Lady appears to usher in a new era of unity beyond all the divisive forces of the times. Like Christianity itself, it would take time to comprehend the depth and extent of her message.

There is no doubt that until recently, Mary of Guadalupe has been considered a very Mexican and Catholic devotion. Yet in recent times, the extent of her message has gone far beyond Mexico. The bishops of America unanimously petitioned the Holy Father to name her Mother of America and declare December 12 to be a feast for the entire hemisphere. They realized that the extent of her message went far beyond the boundaries of Mexico. Just like Jesus did not cease being Jewish while being recognized as the savior of the world, so Our Lady of Guadalupe did not cease being Mexican while being recognized as the Mother of all the peoples of this land.

Now, with the publication of this magnificent collection of essays we begin to realize that her message, while being very Catholic, is not limited to Catholicism but is equally inviting and meaningful to many other religious traditions. Like the mother who welcomes all her children in their incredible differences, Our Lady as the mother of all the inhabitants of this land wishes to welcome all her children, all the peoples who come to this land striving for new opportunities.

Reading through this marvelous collection of essays has not only been very inspirational but equally very enlightening—inspirational to see her growing presence among our Protestant brothers and sisters and enlightening to discover many theological aspects of the message and presence of *La Morenita* and Juan Diego that I had never suspected. Like the gospel itself, the Guadalupe narrative is so full of humanizing power and meaning that one can never exhaust discovering new insights of its message. I have always thought of the temple she requested as a way of speaking of the kingdom of God as lived and proclaimed by Jesus, but to read of her as a parable of the reign of God, in Maxwell Johnson's words, deepened my own appreciation of her—especially as the parables of Jesus served as reversals of the structures of society, the Guadalupe parable, if it can be called that, served as the beginning of the reversal, not by a reversal of the conquest but by initiating something new. I wondered, however, if more than Guadalupe being a type of *theologia crucis* it might not be more a *theologia resurrectionis* since the people were undergoing a collective crucifixion and Guadalupe with the beautiful music and flowers arising out of the sacred mountain of Tepeyac signals a resurrection of a crucified people. This would be a good point of conversation.

I was fascinated to read of the *Virgen Mestiza* as a mirror reflection of what the church is called to be—a profound unification in love and justice of the diverse peoples of the world. It was wonderful to read of her *mestiza* face as a contemplative look into the future of the church. These are profound ecclesial interpretations of the challenging and inspiring signification of her image. In Guadalupe we have a profound mutuality between the alphabetic word expressed in the narrative and the visual word revealed in the precious image, a mutuality between what is heard and what is seen, a mirror image of what the church proclaims with her words and lives by her actions. In Guadalupe we see the perfect coherence between word and image, between proclamation and witness. I wonder if one of the great invitational challenges of Guadalupe to Western Christianity is to go beyond the limits of the alphabetic word of dogmas and doctrines to the poetic and artistic word that opens the heart and the imagination to new and unsuspected horizons of God's loving presence among us. The great attractive force of Guadalupe that makes it easily accessible to the intellectual and illiterate alike is that it is a manifestation of God's graciousness and love expressed through beautiful song and flowers. It brings out that the importance of beauty is appreciating the truth and goodness of God.

As these essays bring out, Guadalupe is not about reformation or restoration but about new creation. Tepeyac appears as the paradise where Juan Diego experiences a new birth. He appears as the *homo religiosus*, as the generative man, as the beginning of a new humanity. There are many other fascinating themes throughout these essays that I have no doubt have been real eye-openers to the readers as they have been for me.

I want to thank in a very special way my good friend, Maxwell E. Johnson for his dedication in bringing about this marvelous collection and also all the contributors to this book as we continue to serve the reign of God in our lands of America, ultimately a land without borders wherein there will be no illegals because everyone will be welcomed into the fellowship of the common table, into the temple of God's universal welcome, into the tenderness of Our Mother's homestead.

These essays bring out even more forcefully than ever the incredible coincidence of that special moment of history. At the very moment when

European Christianity was breaking apart, the newborn Christianity of America was offering a new source of unity for all the peoples of this land. In the midst of the most painful and horrible moments of the European conquest of America, God would offer a gift of healing and unification. Truly the ways of God are far beyond our powers to suspect or predict and God's unnecessary and precious gifts at special moments of history are richer than any human treasure could buy or anyone dare to imagine. Such is the gift of Our Lady of Guadalupe and Juan Diego.

Appendix

The Nican Mopohua *in English Translation*

Title

[1] Here we recount in an orderly way how the Ever-Virgin Holy Mary, Mother of God, our Queen, appeared recently in a marvelous way at Tepeyac, which is called Guadalupe.[1]

Summary

[2] First she allowed herself to be seen by a poor and dignified person whose name is Juan Diego; and then her precious image appeared in the presence of the new bishop D. Fray Juan de Zumárraga. The many marvels that she has brought about are also told.

The Situation of the City and Its Inhabitants

[3] Ten years after the conquest of the city of Mexico, arrows and shields were put down; everywhere the inhabitants of the lake and the mountain had surrendered.

---

[1] Tepeyac was the sacred mountain site of the goddess Tonantzin, where she had been venerated from time immemorial. Gradually it came to be known as Guadalupe. Why it came to be known as Guadalupe (from Our Lady of Guadalupe in Extremadura in Spain) is not known, but it was certainly known by that name by 1575. Gradually Our Lady became known by that name. In the redaction of the *Nican Mopohua*, the origins of the designation are attributed to Juan Bernardino.

[4] Thus faith started; it gave its first buds; and it flowered in the knowledge of the One through Whom We live, the true God, Téotl.[2]

[5] Precisely in the year 1531, a few days after the beginning of December, a poor, dignified campesino was in the surroundings [of Tepeyac]. His name was Juan Diego. It was said that his home was in Cuauhtitlán.[3]

[6] And insofar as the things of God, all that region belonged to Tlatelolco.[4]

First Encounter with the Virgin

[7] It was Saturday, when it was still night. He was going in search of the things of God and of God's messages. [8] And when he arrived at the side of the small hill, which was named Tepeyac, it was already beginning to dawn.

[9] He heard singing on the summit of the hill: as if different precious birds were singing and their songs would alternate, as if the hill was answering them. Their song was most pleasing and very enjoyable, better than that of the coyoltotol or of the tzinizcan or of the other precious birds that sing.[5]

[10] Juan Diego stopped and said to himself: "By chance do I deserve this? Am I worthy of what I am hearing? Maybe I am dreaming? Maybe I only see this in my dreams? Where am I? [11] Maybe I am in the land of my ancestors, of the elders, of our grandparents? In the Land of Flower, in the Earth of our flesh? Maybe over there inside of heaven?"

---

[2] "Téotl" was the designation for the God of the Nahuatls while "true God" was the designation for the God of the Christian Spaniards. In using the phrase "true God, Téotl," the text is thus linking the God of the Nahuatls and the God of the Christians.

[3] The use of the word "Cuauhtitlán" indicates that Juan Diego was from the place of the eagles, which was symbolic of the sun; it indicates he was from the land of the people of the sun. By saying he was from there, the text is pointing out that he would be explaining the things of God [Clodomiro L. Siller Acuña, *Para comprender el mensaje de María de Guadalupe* (Buenos Aires: Editorial Guadalupe, 1989), 60].

[4] This was an ancient ceremonial center that had become a center of Spanish evangelization and spiritual domination (see Siller Acuña, *Para comprender el mensaje*, p. 60).

[5] Birds in Nahuatl thought indicate mediation between heaven and earth; the coyoltotol was the symbol of great fecundity.

[12] His gaze was fixed on the summit of the hill, toward the direction from which the sun arises: the beautiful celestial song was coming from there to here. [13] And when the song finally ceased, when everything was calm, he heard that he was being called from the summit of the hill. He heard: "Dignified Juan, dignified Juan Diego."

[14] Then he dared to go to where he was being called. His heart was in no way disturbed, and in no way did he experience any fear; on the contrary, he felt very good, very happy.

[15] He went to the top of the hill, and he saw a lady who was standing and who was calling him to come closer to her side. [16] When he arrived in her presence, he marveled at her perfect beauty. [17] Her clothing appeared like the sun, and it gave forth rays.

[18] And the rock and the cliffs where she was standing, upon receiving the rays like arrows of light, appeared like precious emeralds, appeared like jewels; the earth glowed with the splendors of the rainbow. The mesquites, the cacti, and the weeds that were all around appeared like feathers of the quetzal, and the stems looked like turquoise; the branches, the foliage, and even the thorns sparkled like gold.

[19] He bowed before her, heard her thought and word, which were exceedingly re-creative, very ennobling, alluring, producing love. [20] She said: "Listen, my most abandoned son, dignified Juan: Where are you going?"

[21] And he answered: "My Owner and my Queen: I have to go to your house of Mexico-Tlatelolco, to follow the divine things that our priests, who are the images of our Lord, give to us." [22] Then she conversed with him and unveiled her precious will. She said: "Know and be certain in your heart,[6] my most abandoned son, that I am the Ever-Virgin Holy Mary, Mother of the God of Great Truth, Téotl, of the One through Whom We Live, the Creator of Persons, the Owner of What Is Near and Together, of the Lord of Heaven and Earth."[7]

---

[6] The heart is the active and dynamic center of the person; it is the symbolic place of ultimate understanding and certitude. Truth resides in the heart.

[7] This litany of names is a most important revelation, for they are the same names that were mentioned by the Nahuatl theologians in their dialogues with the Spanish theologians and that were discredited by the Spanish evangelizers. They appeared in the purest preconquest theology of the Nahautls. She reestablishes the authenticity and veracity of these holy names. The names refer to neither demons nor false idols; they are venerable names of God.

[23] "I very much want and ardently desire that my hermitage[8] be erected in this place. In it I will show and give to all people all my love, my compassion, my help, and my protection, [24] because I am your merciful mother and the mother of all the nations that live on this earth who would love me, who would speak with me, who would search for me, and who would place their confidence in me. [25] There I will hear their laments and remedy and cure all their miseries, misfortunes, and sorrows.

[26] "And for this merciful wish of mine to be realized, go there to the palace of the bishop of Mexico, and you will tell him in what way I have sent you as messenger, so that you may make known to him how I very much desire that he build me a home right here, that he may erect my temple[9] on the plain. You will tell him carefully everything you have seen and admired and heard.

[27] "Be absolutely certain that I will be grateful and will repay you; and because of this I will make you joyful; I will give you happiness; and you will earn much that will repay you for your trouble and your work in carrying out what I have entrusted to you. Look, my son the most abandoned one, you have heard my statement and my word; now do everything that relates to you."

[28] Then he bowed before her and said to her: "My Owner and my Queen, I am already on the way to make your statement and your word a reality. And now I depart from you, I your poor servant." Then he went down so as to make her commission a reality; he went straight to the road that leads directly to Mexico [City].

First Interview with the Bishop

[29] Having entered the city, he went directly to the palace of the bishop, who had recently arrived as the lord of the priests; his name was Don Fray Juan de Zumárraga, a priest of Saint Francis.

[30] As soon as he [Juan Diego] arrived, he tried to see him [the bishop]. He begged his servants, his attendants, to go speak to him. After

---

[8] "Hermitage" could refer to a home for the homeless, an orphanage, a hospice—all would have a special meaning for a people who had been totally displaced and left homeless by the conquest.

[9] Notice the progression from hermitage (home for the homeless), to a home (place of affectionate relationships), to a temple (the manifestation of the sacred). Thus, where everyone is welcomed *is* sacred earth.

a long time, they came to call him, telling him that the lord bishop had ordered him to come in. As soon as he entered, he prostrated himself and then knelt. [31] Immediately he presented, he revealed, the thought and the word of the Lady from Heaven and her will. And he also told him everything he had admired, seen, and heard. When he [the bishop] heard all his words, his message, it was as if he didn't give it much credibility. [32] He answered him and told him: "My son, you will have to come another time; I will calmly listen to you at another time. I still have to see, to examine carefully from the very beginning, the reason you have come, and your will and your wish."

[33] He left very saddened because in no way whatsoever had her message been accomplished.

Second Encounter with the Virgin

[34] The same day, he returned [to Tepeyac]. He came to the summit of the hill and found the Lady from Heaven; she was waiting in the very same spot where he had seen her the first time.

[35] When he saw her, he prostrated himself before her, he fell upon the earth and said: "My Owner, my Matron, my Lady, the most abandoned of my Daughters, my Child, I went where you sent me to deliver your thought and your word. [36] With great difficulty I entered the place of the lord of the priests; I saw him; before him I expressed your thought and word, just as you had ordered me. [37] He received me well and listened carefully. But by the way he answered me, as if his heart had not accepted it, [I know] he did not believe it. He told me: 'You will have to come another time; I will calmly listen to you at another time. I still have to see, to examine carefully from the very beginning, the reason you have come, and your will and your wish.' [38] I saw perfectly, in the way he answered me, that he thinks that possibly I am just making it up that you want a temple to be built on this site, and possibly it is not your command.[10]

[39] "Hence, I very much beg of you, My Owner, my Queen, my Child, that you charge one of the more valuable nobles, a well-known person, one who is respected and esteemed, to come by and take your message and your word so that he may be believed. [40] Because in reality I am one

---

[10] In the presence of those in power, the poor understand very well that they are not credible.

of those campesinos, a piece of rope,[11] a small ladder,[12] the excrement of people; I am a leaf;[13] they order me around, lead me by force;[14] and you, my most abandoned Daughter, my Child, my Lady, and my Queen, send me to a place where I do not belong.[15] [41] Forgive me, I will cause pain to your countenance and to your heart; I will displease you and fall under your wrath, my Lady, and My Owner."[16]

[42] The ever-venerated Virgin answered: "Listen, my most abandoned son, know well in your heart that there are not a few of my servants and messengers to whom I could give the mandate of taking my thought and my word so that my will may be accomplished. But it is absolutely necessary that you personally go and speak about this, and that precisely through your mediation and help, my wish and my desire be realized.[17] [43] I beg you very much, my most abandoned son, and with all my energy I command that precisely tomorrow you go again to see the bishop. [44] In my name you will make him know, make him listen well to my wish and desire, so that he may make my wish a reality and build me a temple. And

---

[11] The reference is to the rope that was tied around the Indians' necks as they were chained and pulled around for forced labor.

[12] The Indians were "stepped" on in the process by which others climbed the ladder of social and economic mobility. They were often used as beasts of burden.

[13] Dried leaves were used to wipe oneself after a bowel movement.

[14] The worst part of domination is that the oppressed begin to believe what those in authority say: that they are subhuman, inferior, incapable of dignified tasks, and a burden to society.

[15] The text literally says "a place where I do not walk or put my foot upon." This is the Nahautl expression for a place where one does not belong, that is, a place where one is not wanted or allowed in.

[16] This is a perfect example of the soul-crushing victimization of the victims of society: They are made to feel guilty for their situation of misery and deserving of disgust and punishment.

[17] Consistent with the Gospels and the beginnings of the apostolic movement, it is precisely through mediation of the "nothings of this world" (1 Corinthians 1:28), through the "stone rejected by the builders of this world" (Acts 4:11), that the reign of God will erupt into this world. In the *Nican Mopohua*, the home-temple that the Lady requests is equivalent to the "kingdom" in the Gospel stories. It will begin through the mediation of the poor and the lowly of this world, to whom the kingdom belongs (see *Catechism of the Catholic Church*, no. 544). It is they who will invite all others into the new family home for God's children. The abandoned of this world act under the authority of God.

tell him once again that I personally, the Ever-Virgin Mary, the Mother of God Téotl, am the one who is sending you there."

[45] Juan Diego answered her: "My Owner, my Lady, my Child, I will not cause pain to your countenance and your heart. With a very good disposition of my heart, I will go; there I will go to tell him truthfully your thought and your word. In no way whatsoever will I fail to do it; it will not be painful for me to go. [46] I will go to do your will. But it could well be that I will not be listened to; and if I am listened to, possibly I will not be believed. [47] Tomorrow in the afternoon, when the sun sets,[18] I will return your thought and word to you, what the lord of the priests [has] answer[ed] me.

[48] "Now I take leave of you, my most abandoned Daughter, my Child, my Matron, my Lady, now you rest a bit." Then he went home to rest.

Second Interview with the Bishop

[49] The next day, Sunday, when it was still night, when it was still dark, he left his home and went directly to Tlatelolco to learn about the things divine, and to answer roll call so that afterward he could see the lord of the priests.

[50] Around ten in the morning, when they had gathered together and heard mass and answered roll call and the poor had been dispersed, Juan Diego went immediately to the house of the lord bishop.

[51] And when he arrived there, he made every effort to see him, and with great difficulty he succeeded in seeing him. He knelt at his feet; he cried and became very sad as he was communicating and unveiling before him the thought and the word of the Lady from Heaven, hoping to be accepted as her messenger and believing that it was the will of the Ever Virgin to have him build a dwelling in the place where she wanted it.

[52] But the lord bishop asked him many questions; he interrogated him as to where he saw her and all about her so as to satisfy his heart. And he told the lord bishop everything.

[53] But even though he told him everything, all about her figure, all that he had seen and admired, and how she had shown herself to be the

---

[18] "In the afternoon, when the sun sets," is the Nahuatl expression for coming to an end of a period of life and expectation of something new that is about to begin. It is an expression of hope. Here it could easily mean, "Tomorrow, hoping that something new will take place. . . ."

lovable Ever Virgin and admirable mother of our Lord and our Savior Jesus Christ,[19] yet, he still did not believe him.

[54] He [the bishop] told him that he could not proceed on her wishes just on the basis of his word and message. A sign from her would be necessary for the bishop to believe that he [Juan Diego] was indeed sent by the Lady from Heaven. [55] When Juan Diego heard this, he told the bishop: "My patron and my lord, what is the sign that you want? [When I know, I can] go and ask the Lady from Heaven, she who sent me here." The bishop was impressed that he was so firm in the truth, that he did not doubt anything or hesitate in any way. He dismissed him.

[56] And when he had left, he [the lord bishop] sent some people from his household in whom he trusted, to follow him and observe where he went, what he saw, and with whom he was speaking. And so it was done. [57] And Juan Diego went directly down the road. His followers took the same route. Close to the bridge of Tepeyac, in the hillside, they lost sight of him; they kept looking for him everywhere, but they could not find him anyplace.

[58] Thus they returned infuriated and were angered at him because he frustrated their intentions. [59] In this state of mind, they went to inform the lord bishop, creating in him a bad attitude so that he would not believe him; they told him that he was only deceiving him; that he was only imagining what he was coming to say; that he was only dreaming; or that he had invented what he was coming to tell him. They agreed among themselves that if he were to come again, they would grab him and punish him harshly, so that he would not lie again or deceive the people.

Juan Diego Takes Care of His Uncle

[60] On the next day, Monday, when Juan Diego was supposed to take something to be the sign by which he was to be believed, he did not return, because when he arrived home, one of his uncles, named Juan Bernardino, had caught the smallpox and was in his last moments.

---

[19] Note that it is Juan Diego who recognizes her as the mother of Jesus Christ. She never mentions this in her conversations with him. It is he who makes the connection and thus announces to his people that the mother of their Nahautl God "Téotl" and the mother of the Spanish God "Dios" is likewise the mother of the one and only savior of all, Jesus Christ.

[61] First he went to call a doctor, who helped him, but he could do no more because he [Juan Bernardino] was already gravely ill. [62] Through the night, his uncle begged him that while it was still dark, he should go to Tlatelolco to call a priest to come and hear his confession and prepare him well because he felt deeply in his heart that this was the time and place of his death, that he would not be healed.

Third Encounter with the Virgin

[63] And on Tuesday, when it was still night, Juan Diego left his home to go to Tlatelolco to call a priest.

[64] And when he arrived at the side of Mount Tepeyac at the point where the road leads out, on the side on which the sun sets, the side he was accustomed to take, he said: [65] "If I take this road, it is quite possible that the Lady will come to see me as before and will hold me back so that I may take the sign to the lord of the priests as she had instructed me. [66] But first I must attend to our affliction and quickly call the priest. My uncle is agonizing and is waiting for him."

[67] He then went around the hill; he climbed through the middle; and he went to the other side, to avoid the side of the sunrise, so as to arrive quickly into Mexico, and to avoid the Lady from Heaven delaying him. [68] He thought that having taken this other route, he would not be seen by the one who cares for everyone.

[69] He saw her coming down from the top of the hill; and from there, where he had seen her before, she had been watching him. She came to him at the side of the hill, blocked his passage, and, standing in front of him, said: "My most abandoned son, where are you going? In what direction are you going?"

[70] Did he become embarrassed a bit? Was he ashamed? Did he feel like running away? Was he fearful? He bowed before her, greeted her, and said: "My Child, my most abandoned Daughter, my Lady, I hope you are happy. How did the dawn come upon you? Does your body feel all right, my Owner and my Child? [71] I am going to give great pain to your countenance and heart. You must know, my Child, that my uncle, a poor servant of yours, is in his final agony; a great illness has fallen upon him, and because of it he will die.

[72] "I am in a hurry to get to your house in Mexico; I am going to call one of the beloved of our Lord, one of our priests, so that he may go and hear his confession and prepare him. [73] Because for this have we

been born, to await the moment of our death. [74] But if right now I am going to do this, I will quickly return here; I will come back to take your thought and your word. My matron, and my Child, forgive me, have a little patience with me; I do not want to deceive you, my most abandoned Daughter, my Child. Tomorrow I will come quickly."

[75] After hearing Juan Diego's discourse, the most pious Virgin answered: "Listen and hear well in your heart, my most abandoned son: that which scares you and troubles you is nothing; do not let your countenance and heart be troubled; do not fear that sickness or any other sickness or anxiety. [76] Am I not here, your mother? Are you not under my shadow and my protection? Am I not your source of life? Are you not in the hollow of my mantle where I cross my arms? Who else do you need?[20] [77] Let nothing trouble you or cause you sorrow. Do not worry because of your uncle's sickness. He will not die of his present sickness. Be assured in your heart that he is already healed." (And as he learned later on, at that precise moment, his uncle was healed.)

[78] When Juan Diego heard the thought and word of the Lady from Heaven, he was very much consoled; his heart became peaceful. He begged her to send him immediately to see the lord of the priests to take him his sign, the thing that would bring about the fulfillment of her desire, so that he would be believed.

[79] Then the Lady from Heaven sent him to climb to the top of the hill where he had seen her before. [80] She said to him: "Go up, my most abandoned son, to the top of the hill, and there, where you saw me and I gave you my instructions, there will you see many diverse flowers: cut them, gather them, put them together. Then come down here and bring them before me."

[81] Juan Diego climbed the hill, and when he arrived at the top, he was deeply surprised. All over the place there were all kinds of exquisite

---

[20] Notice the five identifying statements—each one deepening and expanding the meaning of the previous one. Before she had identified herself as the Mother of God; now she introduces herself as the mother of Juan Diego and of the poor; "shadow" is an image-word meaning authority; "hollow of her mantle" refers to tender service as the quality of true authority; the crossing of the arms indicates the cross of sticks that produces fire, out of which new divine life is born; Juan Diego is the firstborn of the new creation; nothing else is needed (see Siller Acuña, *Para comprender el mensaje*, pp. 83–84).

flowers from Castile, open and flowering.[21] It was not a place for flowers, and likewise it was the time when the ice hardens upon the earth. [82] They were very fragrant, as if they were filled with fine pearls, filled with the morning dew. [83] He started to cut them; he gathered them; he placed them in the hollow of his mantle.[22] [84] And the top of the hill was certainly not a place where flowers grew; there were only rocks, thistles, thorns, cacti, mesquites; and if small herbs grew there, during the month of December, they were all eaten up and wilted by the ice.

[85] Immediately he went down; he went to take to the Queen of Heaven the various flowers that he had cut. When she saw them, she took them in her small hands; and then he placed them in the hollow of his mantle.

[86] And she told him: "My most abandoned son, these different flowers are the proof, the sign, that you will take to the bishop. In my name tell him that he is to see in them what I want, and with this he should carry out my wish and my will.

[87] "And you, you are my ambassador; in you I place all my trust.[23] With all my strength [*energía*] I command you that only in the presence of the bishop are you to open your mantle, and let him know and reveal to him what you are carrying. [88] You will recount everything well; you will tell him how I sent you to climb to the top of the hill to go cut the flowers, and all that you saw and admired. With this you will change the heart of the lord of the priests so that he will do his part to build and erect my temple that I have asked him for."

[89] As soon as the Lady from Heaven had given him her command, he immediately took to the road that leads to Mexico. He was in a hurry and

---

[21] Note the insistent reference to "the top of the hill"—a contrast to the top of the pyramid-temple where the old priests ascended to offer human sacrifices. Now Juan Diego (who represents the new priests) ascends to discover beautiful flowers in the place where he had first heard the heavenly music—a true place of divine-human encounter.

[22] He brings the flowers (truth) to her; she touches them (confirms the truth) and places them under his care. Note the contrast to verse 76.

[23] The Indian was considered to be unworthy of any trust, one who imagined things and easily lied and hence one who should be dominated and punished (see vv. 31, 32, 37, 38, 46, 54, 56, 57, 58, 59); the Lady from Heaven reverses this and brings out the ultimate truth about the Indians: they are the most trusted ambassadors of heaven. The Indians, who were declared unworthy of ordination by church regulations, were to be the trusted ambassadors—spokespersons—of God.

very happy; his heart felt very sure and secure; he was carrying with great care what he knew would [bring about] a good end. He was very careful with that which he carried in the hollow of his mantle, lest anything would fall out. He was enjoying the scent of the beautiful flowers.

Third Interview with the Bishop and the Apparition of the Virgin

[90] Upon arriving at the palace of the bishop, he ran into the doorkeepers and the other servants of the king of the priests. He begged them to go tell him [the bishop] that he wanted to see him; but none of them wanted to; they did not want to pay attention to him, both because it was still night and they knew him; he was the one who only bothered them and gave them long faces;[24] [91] and also because their fellow workers had told them how they had lost him from their sight when they had been following him. He waited for a very long time.[25]

[92] When they saw that he had been standing with his head lowered[26] (very sad) for a long time, that he was waiting in vain for them to call him, and that it seemed that he carried something in the hollow of his mantle, they approached him to see what he had and satisfy their hearts.

[93] And when Juan Diego saw that it was impossible to hide from them what he was carrying, that he would be punished for this, that they would throw him out or mistreat him, he showed them just a little of the flowers.

[94] When they saw that they were all different flowers from Castile and that is was not the season for flowers, they were very astonished, especially by the fact that they were in full bloom, so fresh, so fragrant,

---

[24] Note the reappearance of the clause "when it was still night," which refers to the moment at which the new creation is about to begin. However, those whose livelihood and identity depend on the structures of the old creation, that is, the structures of domination, try to prevent the new creation. The rise and liberation of the poor always shake the structures of unjust domination and oppression, and those who rely on those structures try everything within their means to keep that liberation from coming about.

[25] The poor and undignified of the world are always made to wait. Everyone else comes before them. It is as if they do not count.

[26] In preconquest art, prisoners appeared with their heads lowered. This was indicative of their shameful condition, the condition of one who was totally subjected to the will of others.

and very beautiful. [95] Three times they tried to grab some of them and take them from him, [96] but they could not do it because when they were about to grab them, they did not see any more real flowers, but only painted or embroidered ones, or flowers sewn in his mantle.[27]

[97] Immediately they went to tell the lord bishop what they had seen, and that the poor little Indian who had already come many times wanted to see him, and that he had been waiting for a very long time. [98] Upon hearing this, the lord bishop realized this meant the despicable man had the proof to convince him and bring about what he was coming to ask for.

[99] Immediately he ordered that he be brought in to see him. As soon as he [Juan Diego] entered, he knelt before him [the bishop] as he had done before, and once again he told him everything he had seen and admired and also her message.

[100] He said to him: "My owner and my lord, I have accomplished what you asked for; I went to tell my Matron, my Queen, the Lady from Heaven, Holy Mary, the precious Mother of God Téotl, how you had asked me for a sign in order to believe me, so that you might build her temple where she is asking you to erect it. [101] And besides, I told her that I had given you my word that I would bring you a sign and a proof of her will that you want to receive from my hands. When she received your thought and your word, she accepted willingly what you asked for, a sign and a proof so that her desire and will may come about.

[102] "And today when it was still night, she sent me to come and see you once again. But I asked her for the sign and the proof of her will that you asked me for and that she had agreed to give to me. Immediately she complied.

[103] "She sent me to the top of the hill, where I had seen her before, so that there I might cut the flowers from Castile. After I had cut them, I took them to the bottom of the hill. And she, with her precious little hands, took them; she arranged them in the hollow of my mantle, so that I might bring them to you, and deliver them to you personally. [104] Even though I knew well that the top of the hill was not a place where flowers grow, that only stones, thistles, thorns, cacti and mesquites abound there, I still was neither surprised nor doubted. [105] As I was arriving at the top of the hill, my eyes became fixed: It was the Flowering Earth![28] It was covered

[27] In Nahuatl, "sewn in his mantle" meant something had become part of one's innermost being.

[28] "Flowering Earth" was the Nahuatl expression for the place where ultimate truth resides.

with all kinds of flowers from Castile, full of dew and shining brilliantly. Immediately I went to cut them. [106] And she told me why I had to deliver them to you: so that you might see the sign you requested and so that you will believe in her will; and also so that the truth of my word and my message might be manifested. Here they are. Please receive them."

[107] He unfolded his white mantle, the mantle in whose hollow he had gathered the flowers he had cut, and at that instant the different flowers from Castile fell to the ground. In that very moment she painted herself: the precious image of the Ever-Virgin Holy Mary, Mother of the God Téotl, appeared suddenly, just as she is today and is kept in her precious home, in her hermitage of Tepeyac, which is called Guadalupe.[29]

Conversion of the Bishop

[108] When the lord bishop saw her, he and all who accompanied him fell to their knees and were greatly astonished. They stood up to see her; they became saddened; their hearts and their minds became very heavy.

[109] The lord bishop, with tears and sadness, prayed to her and begged her to forgive him for not having believed her will, her heart, and her word.

[110] When he stood up, he untied the mantle from Juan Diego's neck, the mantle in which had appeared and was painted the Lady from Heaven. Then he took her and went to place her in his oratory.

The Construction of the Hermitage

[111] Juan Diego spent one more day in the home of the bishop, who had invited him [to stay]. And on the next day he said: "Let us go to see where it is the will of the Lady from Heaven that the hermitage be built."

[112] Immediately people were invited to construct and build it. And when Juan Diego showed where the Lady from Heaven had indicated that the hermitage should be built, he asked permission to leave. [113] He wanted to go home to see his uncle Juan Bernardino, the one who had been in his final agony, who he had left to go to Tlatelolco to call a priest to come, hear his confession, and prepare him well, the one who, the Lady

---

[29] See footnote 7, p. 187, above.

from Heaven had said, had been healed. But they did not let him go alone; they accompanied him to his home.

The Fourth Apparition and First Miracle

[114] When they arrived, they saw his uncle who was well and with no pains. [115] He [Juan Bernardino] was very much surprised that his nephew was so well accompanied and honored, and he asked him why they were honoring him so much. [116] He told him how when he had left him to go call a priest to come to hear his confession and prepare him well, the Queen of Heaven appeared to him over there, at Tepeyac, and sent him to Mexico to see the lord bishop so that he would build her a home at Tepeyac. [117] And she told him not to be troubled because his uncle was healed, and he was very consoled.

[118] And the uncle said that this was true, that it was precisely then that she had healed him, and he had seen her exactly as she had shown herself to his nephew, and that she had told him that he [Juan Bernardino] had to go to Mexico to see the bishop. [119] And (she told him) also that when he went to see the bishop, he would reveal all that he had seen and would tell him in what a marvelous way she had healed him and that he [the bishop] would call and name that precious image the Ever-Virgin Holy Mary of Guadalupe.

[120] They took Juan Bernardino to the bishop so that he might speak and witness before him. [121] And, together with his nephew Juan Diego, he was hosted by the bishop in his home for several days, until the hermitage of the Queen and Lady from Heaven was built at Tepeyac, where Juan Diego had seen her.

The Entire City before the Virgin

[122] And the lord bishop transferred to the major church the precious image of the Queen and Lady from Heaven; he took her from the oratory of his palace so that all might see and venerate her precious image.

[123] The entire city was deeply moved; they came to see and admire her precious image as something divine; they came to pray to her. [124] The admired very much how she had appeared as a divine marvel, because absolutely no one on earth had painted her precious image.

Contributors

Edgardo A. Colón-Emeric (United Methodist) is director, Hispanic House of Studies, Duke University Divinity School, Durham, NC.

Virgil P. Elizondo (Roman Catholic) is professor of pastoral and Hispanic theology and a fellow of the Institute for Latino Studies and Kellogg Institute, University of Notre Dame, Notre Dame, IN.

Bonnie Jensen (Lutheran) is former executive director of the Evangelical Lutheran Church in America's Division for Global Mission (retired), and currently lives in Apple Valley, MN.

Robert W. Jenson (Lutheran) is senior scholar for research at the Center of Theological Inquiry, Princeton, NJ.

Maxwell E. Johnson (Lutheran) is professor of theology, University of Notre Dame, Notre Dame, IN.

Timothy Matovina (Roman Catholic) is professor of theology and the William and Anna Jean Cushwa Director of the Cushwa Center for the Study of American Catholicism, University of Notre Dame, Notre Dame, IN.

Kathleen Norris (Presbyterian) is a poet, novelist, and author currently living in Honolulu, HI.

Alberto Pereyra (Lutheran) is emeritus professor of theology at Lutheran Seminary Program, Austin, TX, currently living in Chile.

José David Rodriguez Jr. (Lutheran) is professor of systematic theology and holds the Augustana Heritage Chair of Global Mission and World Christianity at the Lutheran School of Theology, Chicago, IL.

Rubén Rosario Rodríguez (Presbyterian) is assistant professor, Department of Theological Studies, Saint Louis University, St. Louis, MO.

Carl C. Trovall (Lutheran) is assistant professor of religion at Concordia University Texas, Austin, TX.

Cody C. Unterseher (Episcopal) is a PhD student in liturgical studies at the University of Notre Dame, Notre Dame, IN.

Acknowledgments

The editor of this volume extends thanks to the following for permission to use previously copyrighted materials.

"Broken Spears," by Miguel Leon-Portilla. Copyright © 1962, 1990 by Miguel Leon-Portilla. Expanded and Updated Edition © 1992 by Miguel Leon-Portilla. Reprinted by permission of Beacon Press, Boston.

Robert W. Jenson, "A Space for God," from *Mary: Mother of God*, ed. Carl E. Braaten and Robert W. Jenson © 2004. Wm. B. Eerdman's Publishing Company, Grand Rapids, Michigan. Reprinted by permission of the publisher; all rights reserved.

Extensive quotations from *Generative Man: Psychoanalytic Perspectives* (Philadelphia, PA: Westminster Press, 1973) by Donald Browning, are used here by permission of the author, to whom the copyright has reverted.

The "Nican Mopohua" from *Guadalupe: Mother of the New Creation* (Maryknoll, NY: Orbis Books, 1997), 1–22; and other lengthy quotations from the writings of Virgil Elizondo from Orbis Books. Used by permission of Orbis Books, Maryknoll, New York.

"Virgin Mary, Mother of God," from *Amazing Grace* by Kathleen Norris, copyright © 1998 by Kathleen Norris. Used by permission of Riverhead Books, an imprint of Penguin Group (USA) Inc.

"The Virgin of Guadalupe: History, Myth, and Spirituality," by Alberto Pereyra, *Currents in Theology and Mission* 24, no. 4 (August 1997): 348–54. Used by permission of the editor of *Currents in Theology and Mission*.

"We Sing Mary's Song," by Bonnie Jensen from *Word and World* 7, no. 1 (1987): 81–82. Used by permission of the editor of *Word and World*.

"The Development of the Liturgical Feast of the Virgin of Guadalupe and Its Celebration in The Season of Advent," by Maxwell E. Johnson, is based on "The Feast of the Virgin of Guadalupe and the Season of Advent," *Worship* 78, no. 6 (2004): 482–99.

An abridged version of "Mary in Contemporary Protestant Theological Discourse," by Cody C. Unterseher appeared in *Worship* 81, no. 3 (2007): 194–211.

Another version of Rubén Rosario Rodríguez, "Beyond Word and Sacrament: A Reformed Protestant Engagement of Guadalupan Devotion," appeared in *Journal of Ecumenical Studies* 42, no. 2 (2007): 173–95.